美国原版经典数学课本

RAY'S INTELLECTUAL ARITHMETIC

美国小学数学 ②

J O S E P H   R A Y

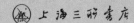

上海三联书店

图书在版编目（CIP）数据

美国小学数学 . 2：英文版 /（美）雷伊（Ray, J.）编 . —上海：上海三联书店，2011.5

ISBN 978-7-5426-3516-7

Ⅰ.①美…　Ⅱ.①雷…　Ⅲ.①小学数学课—教材—英文　Ⅳ.① G624.501

中国版本图书馆 CIP 数据核字（2011）第 043230 号

美国小学数学（第 2 册）

编　　　者/ （美）约瑟夫·雷伊

责 任 编 辑/ 黄　韬
装 帧 设 计/ 子木工作室
监　　　制/ 研　发

出 版 发 行 上海三联书店
　　　　　（200031）中国上海市乌鲁木齐南路 396 弄 10 号
　　　　　http: // www.sanlianc.com
　　　　　E-mail: shsanlian@yahoo.com.cn
印　　刷/ 北京领先印刷有限公司

版　　次/ 2011 年 5 月第 1 版
印　　次/ 2011 年 5 月第 1 次印刷
开　　本/ 640×960 毫米　1/16
字　　数/ 160 千字
印　　张/ 12

ISBN 978-7-5426-3516-7

定价：16.00 元

　　呈现于您面前的这套美国数学课本，是一套在西方流行了近半个世纪、至今仍在使用的经典教材。编者约瑟夫·雷伊教授，1807年出生于美国弗吉尼亚俄亥俄县，从小在当地学校接受教育，成绩优秀。16岁时开始其教师职业生涯。18岁，雷伊来到富兰克林学院跟随乔尔·马丁教授学习医学，此后又进入俄亥俄医学院学习。大学毕业后，他在辛辛那提伍德沃德中学任教，讲授数学。1836年，伍德沃德中学由高中升格为辛辛那提伍德学院，雷伊成为该学院教授。1851年，该校又变为一所公立高中，雷伊一直在此担任校长，直至去世。雷伊一生杰出的成就是他倾心编写的系列数学教材，并以此闻名。这套数学课本与他在伍德学院的同事威廉·麦加菲编写的《美国语文读本》，同时被美国近万所学校作为教材，累计销量均超过 1.22 亿册，对几代美国人的教育产生了很大影响。直至今日，这两套书仍被当作美国家庭教育 (Homeschooling) 的推荐教材，也是美国学生准备 SAT 考试的参考用书。

　　与其他数学书相比，雷伊数学教材至少有以下几个明显特点：

　　第一，强调在"学"中掌握"数"。例如，《小学数学》不完全按难度分册，而是根据其实际应用范围分为四册：初级算术、智力算术、实用算术与高级算术。让学生从对数的认知、运算法则的掌握，延伸到数学在实际生活中的广泛应用，如购物、记账、存款、利息等，并向更高的学术层次过渡。

第二，将数学问题融于文字题（Word Problem）之中。即便最简单的加减运算，它也通过讲故事的方式呈现出来。这样孩子们在学习数学时，不仅可以训练其数学思维，语言能力也可以同步提高。

　　第三，将抽象思维具体化。书中的数学题大都结合现实事物表述出来，让孩子们理解他们所学的数学在现实生活中是如何加以应用的。这对低年级学生来说，尤其帮助很大，他们能更快更清楚地理解那些对其年龄来讲过于抽象的数学概念。

　　第四，将不同学科知识融入数学问题中。这种编写方法能让学生从数学应用的不同领域来掌握数学科学，帮助学生从低年级数学步入更复杂的数学应用领域，如几何学与会计学等。孩子们在学习数学的同时，又能接受其他学科知识。如书中有这样一道题："华盛顿将军出生于公元 1732 年，他活了 67 岁，那么他是于哪一年去世？"这么一道简单的计算题，便将历史知识与数学结合起来，一举多得。

　　对于中国孩子来讲，这套数学课本不仅能教孩子学习数学，更是学习英语的很好途径，让他们换个思维学英语。与阅读文学读本相比，这是另一种不同的感觉，或许更能激发孩子学习英语的兴趣。数学的词汇含义固定，也易于理解记忆，孩子在解题的同时也能提高英语水平，可谓一举多得。对于那些将来准备参加出国英语考试的学生来讲，这套书意义更大，对他们将来的求学之路应该大有帮助。

　　最后，我们需向读者特别说明一点，由于这套书涉及数字与数学符号偏多，考虑到重新录入排版会出现一些难免的错误，给读者学习带来极大不便。于是我们采用了原版影印的办法，以保证内容的高度准确性，但文字清晰度与重新录入相比略有缺陷，敬请读者谅解。

　　衷心祝愿天下孩子们快乐成长，并期待您的宝贵意见与建议。

出版者

2011 年春

CONTENTS

ADDITION

LESSON 1

1. James had 1 apple, and his brother gave him 1 more: how many had he then? *Ans.* 2.

Why? *Ans.* Because 1 and 1 are 2.

2. Henry had 2 cents, and his sister gave him 1 cent more: how many had he in all? *Ans.* 3.

Why? *Ans.* Because 2 and 1 are 3?

3. A boy had 1 marble, and found 3 marbles more: how many did he then have? *Ans.* 4.

Why? *Ans.* Because 1 and 3 are 4.

4. Thomas had 4 cents, and his mother gave him 1 cent more: how much had Thomas altogether?

5. Samuel had 2 cakes, and his father gave him 2 more: how many did he then have?

6. How many are 3 oranges and 2 oranges?

7. James had 3 apples, and his brother gave him 3 more: how many apples had James then?

8. John had 4 plums, and his sister gave him 2 more: how many did he then have?

9. Daniel had 3 cents; his brother gave him 2 cents, and his sister 1 cent: how many did he then have?

10. Mary had 4 pears, and her brother gave her 3 more: how many did she then have?

11. How many fingers have you on one hand? How many on both hands?

12. Ida had 4 cents; her mother gave her 3 cents more at one time, and 1 cent at another: how many cents had she altogether?

13. Three cakes and 3 cakes and 2 cakes are how many cakes?

14. Four cents and 3 cents and 2 cents are how many cents?

15. Five oranges and 2 oranges and 1 orange are how many oranges?

16. Henry had 5 cents, and his mother gave him 2 more at one time, and 3 at another: how many did he then have?

17. Five boys and 4 boys and 1 boy are how many boys?

18. Oliver has 5 dollars; Henry, 3 dollars; and Samuel, 1 dollar: how many dollars have all together?

19. Three peaches and 6 peaches and 1 peach are how many peaches?

20. A lady paid 1 dollar for gloves, 3 dollars for a shawl, and 3 dollars for a dress: how much did she spend?

21. Four cents and 3 cents and 3 cents and 1 cent are how many cents?

22. If a man buy 6 pounds of sugar at one time, 2 at another, and 2 at another, how much does he buy?

23. Seven oranges and 1 orange and 2 oranges are how many?

24. George has 3 cents, his sister 2 cents, and his brother 2 cents: if all the money were given to George, how much would he have?

25. How many are 4 and 4 and 2?

26. James has 4 cents, Joseph 2, and John 2: how many cents have they all?

Addition is the process of uniting two or more numbers. The result is called the *sum*, or *amount*.

The sign of addition (+) is called *plus*. The sign of equality (=) is read *equals*, or *is equal to*.

LESSON 2

1. One and 1 are how many? 1 and 2? 3 and 1? 4 and 1? 1 and 3? 1 and 5? 1 and 6? 6 and 1? 1 and 7? 8 and 1? 9 and 1? 1 and 8?

SOLUTION.—One and one are two.

2. Two and 4 and 1 are how many? 6 and 2 and 3? 4 and 1 and 4?

SOLUTION.—Two and four are six; six and one are seven.

3. Five and 2 are how many? 7 and 3? 2 and 6 and 1? 2 and 1 and 2? 3 and 5? 5 and 4?

4. Nine and 2 are how many? 6 and 1 and 1? 6 and 3? 6 and 4? 7 and 1 and 3? 1 and 2 and 8? 1 and 3 and 8?

5. Eight and 2 are how many? 8 and 3? 10 and 2 and 1? 1 and 4 and 6? 8 and 4? 7 and 4? 6 and 7? 7 and 1 and 4? 1 and 8 and 2 and 2?

6. Ten and 2 are how many? 9 and 3? 9 and 1 and 2? 9 and 1 and 3? 5 and 6? 1 and 4 and 8? 2 and 4 and 6? 3 and 4 and 5? 4 and 7 and 2? 5 and 4 and 8?

7. How many are 1 and 9? 10 and 3? 4 and 9? 7 and 1? 5 and 7? 9 and 4? 2 and 12? 3 and 11? Give two numbers which, added together, make 10?

8. Begin at 4, and add 2 each time up to 16.

9. Begin at 1, and add 3 each time up to 13.

10. Mention two numbers which, added together, will make 12? Three numbers?

11. Seven and 5 and 2 are how many?

12. Seven and 3 and 4 are how many?

13. If 3 be added to 3, and that sum to 5, what will be the result?

14. If you add 3 to the sum of 3 and 1, and then add 7 more, what will be the amount?

15. I have in one basket 8 dozen eggs, in another 4 dozen, in another 3 dozen: how many eggs in all?

SOLUTION.—I have in all 8 dozen and 4 dozen and 3 dozen eggs. 8 dozen and 4 dozen are 12 dozen; 12 dozen and 3 dozen are 15 dozen.

16. A little girl bought two yards of tape for 3 cents, some pins for 5 cents, and received 2 cents in change: how many cents had she at first?

17. Two and 1 more, and 3 and 4 more, are together how many?

18. One and 3 and 4 and 5 are how many? 5 and 1 and 3 and 4?

19. A boy bought 3 cents worth of marbles, and 2 cents worth of candy, and received 5 cents in change: how much money had he?

20. I bought three hams for 8 dollars, and ten bushels of apples for 3 dollars: how much did I spend?

21. Oliver has 4 cents in one hand, 3 in the other, and 4 in his pocket: how many cents has he?

22. A lady made two coats from 8 yards of cloth, two vests from 2 yards, and two pairs of pants from 6 yards: how many yards of cloth did she use in all?

23. A grocer sold a pound of rice for 5 cents, a paper of matches for 3 cents, and a box of mustard for 10 cents: how much did he receive for all?

24. How many are 9 and 3 and 2? 4 and 6 and 8? 10 and 7 and 3?

25. If I have 10 cents in one pocket, 5 cents in another, and 3 cents in each hand, how much have I altogether?

LESSON 3

ADDITION TABLE.

2 + 1 = 3	3 + 1 = 4	4 + 1 = 5
2 + 2 = 4	3 + 2 = 5	4 + 2 = 6
2 + 3 = 5	3 + 3 = 6	4 + 3 = 7
2 + 4 = 6	3 + 4 = 7	4 + 4 = 8
2 + 5 = 7	3 + 5 = 8	4 + 5 = 9
2 + 6 = 8	3 + 6 = 9	4 + 6 = 10
2 + 7 = 9	3 + 7 = 10	4 + 7 = 11
2 + 8 = 10	3 + 8 = 11	4 + 8 = 12
2 + 9 = 11	3 + 9 = 12	4 + 9 = 13
2 + 10 = 12	3 + 10 = 13	4 + 10 = 14
2 + 11 = 13	3 + 11 = 14	4 + 11 = 15
2 + 12 = 14	3 + 12 = 15	4 + 12 = 16
5 + 1 = 6	6 + 1 = 7	7 + 1 = 8
5 + 2 = 7	6 + 2 = 8	7 + 2 = 9
5 + 3 = 8	6 + 3 = 9	7 + 3 = 10
5 + 4 = 9	6 + 4 = 10	7 + 4 = 11
5 + 5 = 10	6 + 5 = 11	7 + 5 = 12
5 + 6 = 11	6 + 6 = 12	7 + 6 = 13
5 + 7 = 12	6 + 7 = 13	7 + 7 = 14
5 + 8 = 13	6 + 8 = 14	7 + 8 = 15
5 + 9 = 14	6 + 9 = 15	7 + 9 = 16
5 + 10 = 15	6 + 10 = 16	7 + 10 = 17
5 + 11 = 16	6 + 11 = 17	7 + 11 = 18
5 + 12 = 17	6 + 12 = 18	7 + 12 = 19

8 + 1 = 9	9 + 1 = 10	10 + 1 = 11
8 + 2 = 10	9 + 2 = 11	10 + 2 = 12
8 + 3 = 11	9 + 3 = 12	10 + 3 = 13
8 + 4 = 12	9 + 4 = 13	10 + 4 = 14
8 + 5 = 13	9 + 5 = 14	10 + 5 = 15
8 + 6 = 14	9 + 6 = 15	10 + 6 = 16
8 + 7 = 15	9 + 7 = 16	10 + 7 = 17
8 + 8 = 16	9 + 8 = 17	10 + 8 = 18
8 + 9 = 17	9 + 9 = 18	10 + 9 = 19
8 + 10 = 18	9 + 10 = 19	10 + 10 = 20
8 + 11 = 19	9 + 11 = 20	10 + 11 = 21
8 + 12 = 20	9 + 12 = 21	10 + 12 = 22

LESSON 4

1. Three and 8 are how many? 6 and 9?

2. Four and 4 are how many? 4 and 11? 4 and 10? 4 and 12?

3. Five and 9 are how many? 5 and 12? 5 and 10? 5 and 8? 5 and 11? 6 and 6? 6 and 8?

4. Seven and 7 are how many? 7 and 10? 7 and 8? 7 and 12? 7 and 9? 7 and 11? 8 and 8?

5. Nine and 11 are how many? 9 and 9? 9 and 12? 9 and 10? 9 and 8?

6. Ten and 6 are how many? 10 and 8? 10 and 10? 10 and 12? 10 and 11?

7. Eleven and 2 are how many? 11 and 4? 11 and 6? 11 and 8? 11 and 3? 11 and 11?

8. Twelve and 3 are how many? 12 and 4? 12 and 6? 12 and 8? 12 and 11? 12 and 12?

9. Thirteen and 4 are how many? 13 and 6? 13 and 5? 13 and 7? 13 and 9? 13 and 10? 13 and 8? 13 and 11? 13 and 12?

10. Fourteen and four are how many? 14 and 6? 14 and 8? 14 and 5? 14 and 7? 14 and 10? 14 and 9? 14 and 11? 14 and 12?

11. Fifteen and 5 are how many? 15 and 7? 15 and 9? 15 and 4? 15 and 8? 15 and 10? 15 and 12? 15 and 11?

12. Sixteen and 4 are how many? 16 and 6? 16 and 8? 16 and 5? 16 and 7? 16 and 9? 16 and 11? 16 and 10? 16 and 12?

13. Seventeen and 6 are how many? 17 and 4? 17 and 7? 17 and 5? 17 and 9? 17 and 8? 17 and 10? 17 and 12? 17 and 11?

14. Eighteen and 10 are how many? 18 and 4? 18 and 7? 18 and 5? 18 and 8? 18 and 6? 18 and 9? 18 and 11? 18 and 12?

15. Nineteen and 5 are how many? 19 and 3? 19 and 2? 19 and 7? 19 and 9? 19 and 8? 19 and 10? 19 and 6? 19 and 12? 19 and 11?

16. How many are 29 and 2? 49 and 2? 69 and 2? 39 and 2? 59 and 2? 79 and 2? 99 and 2?

17. How many are 29 and 3? 3 and 49? 59 and 3? 3 and 39? 69 and 3? 3 and 79? 3 and 89? 99 and 3?

18. How many are 29 and 7? 7 and 49? 39 and 7? 7 and 59? 79 and 7? 7 and 69? 89 and 7? 7 and 99?

19. How many are 29 and 8 ? 49 and 8? 39 and 8? 8 and 69? 59 and 8? 79 and 8?

20. How many are 19 and 9? 9 and 29? 49 and 9? 69 and 9? 59 and 9? 79 and 9? 89 and 9? 9 and 99?

21. How many are 28 and 3? 48 and 3? 68 and 3? 88 and 3? 98 and 3?

22. How many are 28 and 7? 7 and 38? 48 and 7? 68 and 7? 58 and 7? 88 and 7?

23. How many are 17 and 7? 27 and 7? 47 and 7? 57 and 7? 37 and 7? 67 and 7? 87 and 7? 77 and 7? 97 and 7?

24. How many are 27 and 10? 47 and 10? 37 and 10? 57 and 10?

25. How many are 15 and 6? 26 and 5? 25 and 6? 24 and 6? 26 and 4? 36 and 6? 48 and 6? 45 and 6? 57 and 6? 59 and 6? 66 and 6? 75 and 6? 86 and 6?

26. How many are 17 and 3? 23 and 8? 24 and 8? 33 and 8? 3 and 37? 8 and 43? 47 and 3? 7 and 53? 58 and 3? 67 and 3? 3 and 87? 97 and 3? 88 and 3?

27. How many are 9 and 24? 25 and 9? 9 and 34? 36 and 9? 9 and 44? 9 and 47? 54 and 9? 9 and 56? 9 and 64? 74 and 9? 9 and 72? 84 and 9? 86 and 9? 94 and 9?

28. How many are 6 and 21? 10 and 26? 46 and 10? 10 and 35? 10 and 55? 56 and 10? 10 and 66? 10 and 69? 76 and 10? 10 and 86? 96 and 10?

29. How many are 11 and 16? 11 and 27? 25 and 11? 11 and 23? 31 and 11? 11 and 35? 37 and 11? 11 and 59? 46 and 11? 11 and 48? 52 and 11? 11 and 63?

LESSON 5

1. Three and 6 and 4 are how many?

SOLUTION.—Three and six are nine, and four are thirteen.

2. Four and 5 and 7 are how many?
3. Five and 6 and 2 are how many?
4. Six and 4 and 5 are how many?

5. Seven and 3 and 5 and 2 are how many?

6. Eight and 2 and 3 and 4 are how many?

7. Nine and 2 and 4 and 3 are how many?

8. Two and 8 and 5 and 4 are how many?

9. Three and 9 and 5 and 4 are how many?

10. Four and 8 and 3 and 5 and 2 and 6 and 3 and 1 are how many?

11. Five and 7 and 2 and 3 and 4 and 6 and 5 and 2 are how many?

12. Two and 4 and 3 and 5 and 6 and 2 and 7 and 4 are how many?

13. Three and 2 and 4 and 5 and 4 and 6 and 3 and 7 and 5 are how many?

14. Four and 3 and 5 and 7 and 6 and 8 and 2 and 4 are how many?

15. Four and 9 and 3 and 5 and 6 and 7 and 8 and 9 are how many?

16. Five and 8 and 5 and 8 and 5 and 8 and 5 and 8 are how many?

17. Six and 8 and 7 and 3 and 5 and 4 and 7 and 1 and 9 are how many?

18. Seven and 9 and 5 and 4 and 6 and 3 and 8 and 5 and 9 are how many?

19. Eight and 7 and 6 and 5 and 4 and 9 and 3 and 7 and 8 are how many?

20. Nine and 6 and 7 and 4 and 5 and 3 and 8 and 2 and 9 are how many?

21. Seven and 6 and 5 and 8 and 7 and 9 and 8 and 4 and 9 and 8 are how many?

22. Nine and 8 and 7 and 5 and 8 and 9 and 5 and 4 and 7 and 3 and 9 and 8 are how many?

23. Twelve and 11 and 7 and 4 and 9 are how many?

24. Thirteen and 10 and 8 and 6 and 4 and 10 are how many?

25. Fourteen and 16 and 7 and 5 and 9 and 8 and 9 and 6 and 4 are how many?

26. James gave 7 cents for apples, and 8 cents for peaches: how many cents did he spend?

SOLUTION.—He spent 7 cents and 8 cents, which are 15 cents.

27. Seven dollars and 5 dollars and 3 dollars are how many dollars?

28. David had 11 books; he bought 7 more, and his brother gave him 5: how many had he then?

29. A man gave 13 dollars for a cart, 9 dollars for a plow, and 1 dollar for a rake: how much did he spend?

30. James has 8 marbles in one pocket, 5 in another, 6 in another, and 7 in another: how many in all?

31. If a dozen eggs cost 18 cents, and a pound of ham 10 cents, how much will both cost?

32. A man owes to one person 8 dollars, to another 5 dollars, to another 3 dollars, and to another 7 dollars: how much does he owe?

33. A boy gave 19 cents for a spelling-book, 8 cents for a slate, and 6 cents for pencils: how many cents did he spend?

34. A drover bought hogs as follows: of one man 17, of another 9, of another 7, of another 8: how many did he buy?

35. A little girl gave 10 cents for thread, 7 cents for pins, 6 cents for needles, and 9 cents for tape: how many cents did she spend?

36. William has 7 cents, Thomas 10 cents, David 9 cents, and Moses 8 cents: if the other boys give their money to Moses, how many cents will he have?

37. The age of Thomas is 8 years; of Frank, 5 years; and William is as old as both together: what is the sum of all their ages?

38. Joseph has 4 marbles, William has 2, and David has 16: how many have they all?

39. Begin with 2, and count one hundred by adding 2 successively. Thus, 2, 4, 6, 8, 10, and so on.

40. Begin with 3, and count ninety-nine by adding 3 successively. Thus, 3, 6, 9, 12, and so on.

41. Begin with 4, and count one hundred by adding 4 successively.

42. Begin with 5, and count one hundred by adding 5 successively.

43. Begin with 6, and count one hundred and two by adding 6 successively.

44. Begin with 7, and count ninety-eight by adding 7 successively.

45. Begin with 8, and count one hundred and four by adding 4 successively.

46. Begin with 9, and count ninety-nine by adding 9 successively.

47. Begin with 1, and count one hundred by adding 3 successively.

48. Begin with 3, and count one hundred and three by adding 4 successively.

49. Begin with 2, and count one hundred and two by adding 5 successively.

50. Begin with 5, and count one hundred and seven by adding 6 successively.

51. Begin with 6, and count one hundred and four by adding 7 successively.

52. Begin with 7, and count one hundred and three by adding 8 successively.

53. Begin with 8, and count one hundred and seven by adding 9 successively.

SUBTRACTION

LESSON 6

1. James had 2 apples, and gave 1 to his brother: how many had he left? *Ans.* 1.

Why? *Ans.* Because 1 from 2 leaves 1.

2. Joseph had 3 apples and lost 1: how many had he left? *Ans.* 2.

Why? *Ans.* Because 1 from 3 leaves 2.

3. Thomas had 4 cents, and gave 1 of them to Frank: how many had he left?

4. One from 5 leaves how many? From 6? 7? 8? 9? 10?

5. John had 4 cents and gave his sister 2: how many had he left?

6. James had 5 apples, and gave his brother 2: how many had he left?

7. Two from 6 leaves how many? From 7? 8? 9? 10? 11?

8. Thomas had 5 cents and lost 3: how many had he left?

9. Three from 6 leaves how many? From 7? 8? 9? 10? 11? 12?

10. Joseph had 9 marbles and lost 4: how many had he left?

11. Four from 10 leaves how many? From 11? 12? 13? 14? 15?

12. William had 10 apples and gave Joseph 5: how many had he left?

13. Five from 11 leaves how many? From 12? 13? 14? 15? 16?

14. James had 11 marbles and lost 6: how many had he left?

15. Six from 12 leaves how many? From 13? 14? 15? 16? 17?

16. William had 12 cents and lost 7: how many had he left?

17. Seven from 13 leaves how many? From 14? 15? 16? 17? 18? 19?

18. James had 13 apples and gave his sister 8: how many had he left?

19. Eight from 14 leaves how many? From 15? 16? 17? 18? 19? 20?

20. Thomas had 13 apples and gave his sister 9: how many had he left?

21. Nine from 14 leaves how many? From 15? 16? 17? 18? 19? 20?

22. Henry had 17 cents and lost 5: how many had he remaining?

23. Mary is 12 years old, and Anna is 8: how much older is Mary than Anna?

24. Sold a load of corn for 17 dollars; received for it a barrel of flour worth 6 dollars, and the rest in money: how much money did I receive?

25. A boy had 18 marbles and lost 10: how many had he then?

Subtraction is the process of finding the *difference* between two numbers.

The larger number is called the *minuend;* the smaller number, the *subtrahend;* and the result, the *difference* or *remainder.*

The sign of subtraction (—) is called *minus.*

LESSON 7

$2-2=0$	$3-3=0$	$4-4=0$
$3-2=1$	$4-3=1$	$5-4=1$
$4-2=2$	$5-3=2$	$6-4=2$
$5-2=3$	$6-3=3$	$7-4=3$
$6-2=4$	$7-3=4$	$8-4=4$
$7-2=5$	$8-3=5$	$9-4=5$
$8-2=6$	$9-3=6$	$10-4=6$
$9-2=7$	$10-3=7$	$11-4=7$
$10-2=8$	$11-3=8$	$12-4=8$
$11-2=9$	$12-3=9$	$13-4=9$
$12-2=10$	$13-3=10$	$14-4=10$
$13-2=11$	$14-3=11$	$15-4=11$
$14-2=12$	$15-3=12$	$16-4=12$
$5-5=0$	$6-6=0$	$7-7=0$
$6-5=1$	$7-6=1$	$8-7=1$
$7-5=2$	$8-6=2$	$9-7=2$
$8-5=3$	$9-6=3$	$10-7=3$
$9-5=4$	$10-6=4$	$11-7=4$
$10-5=5$	$11-6=5$	$12-7=5$
$11-5=6$	$12-6=6$	$13-7=6$
$12-5=7$	$13-6=7$	$14-7=7$
$13-5=8$	$14-6=8$	$15-7=8$
$14-5=9$	$15-6=9$	$16-7=9$
$15-5=10$	$16-6=10$	$17-7=10$
$16-5=11$	$17-6=11$	$18-7=11$
$17-5=12$	$18-6=12$	$19-7=12$

$8 - 8 = 0$	$9 - 9 = 0$	$10 - 10 = 0$
$9 - 8 = 1$	$10 - 9 = 1$	$11 - 10 = 1$
$10 - 8 = 2$	$11 - 9 = 2$	$12 - 10 = 2$
$11 - 8 = 3$	$12 - 9 = 3$	$13 - 10 = 3$
$12 - 8 = 4$	$13 - 9 = 4$	$14 - 10 = 4$
$13 - 8 = 5$	$14 - 9 = 5$	$15 - 10 = 5$
$14 - 8 = 6$	$15 - 9 = 6$	$16 - 10 = 6$
$15 - 8 = 7$	$16 - 9 = 7$	$17 - 10 = 7$
$16 - 8 = 8$	$17 - 9 = 8$	$18 - 10 = 8$
$17 - 8 = 9$	$18 - 9 = 9$	$19 - 10 = 9$
$18 - 8 = 10$	$19 - 9 = 10$	$20 - 10 = 10$
$19 - 8 = 11$	$20 - 9 = 11$	$21 - 10 = 11$
$20 - 8 = 12$	$21 - 9 = 12$	$22 - 10 = 12$

LESSON 8

1. A boy gave 9 cents for a slate, worth only 7 cents: how much did he pay for it more than it was worth?

SOLUTION.—He paid more than it was worth the difference between 9 cents and 7 cents, which is 2 cents.

2. A man, having 16 dollars, lost 12: how many dollars had he left?

3. Bought a book for 12 cents, and a top for 7 cents: how much did the book cost more than the top?

4. Thomas had 18 cents given him by two boys; one gave 9: how many did the other give?

5. Bought a book for 14 cents, and gave the shop-keeper 20 cents: how much change did he return me?

6. William has 19 hazel-nuts in his two pockets; in one pocket he has 15: how many are in the other?

7. A man has 25 miles to travel: when he has gone 19 miles, how far will he still have to travel?

8. A boy gave 24 cents for a book, and sold it for 16 cents: how much did he lose?

9. James had 24 marbles; he gave 19 to his brother: how many had he left?

10. A man bought a horse for 19 dollars, and sold him for 27 dollars: how much did he gain?

11. A man, owing 26 dollars, paid 18; how many did he still owe?

12. Frank had 26 cents given him by William and Thomas. William gave him 17: how many did Thomas give? How many more did William give than Thomas?

SOLUTION.—Thomas gave him 26 cents less 17 cents, which are 9 cents; William gave more than Thomas 17 cents less 9 cents, which are 8 cents.

13. If you had 10 apples, and should give 2 to John, and 6 to your sister: how many would you have left?

14. Abel had 36 cents, and his mother gave him enough more to make 40 cents: how many did she give him?

15. George had 40 marbles; he lost 20: how many did he then have?

16. A man bought 100 barrels of flour; he sold 50 barrels: how many did he have left?

17. A farmer had 35 bushels of grain; a part having been wasted, he found there were but 22 bushels remaining: how much was wasted?

18. John's father is 36 years old; John is 12: how many years older than John is his father?

19. I had 65 cents; spent 20 cents for a book and 10 for a slate: how much had I left?

20. If you take 10 from the sum of two numbers, there will be 8 left: what is their sum?

21. If you take 16 from the difference of two numbers, there will remain 12: what is their difference?

22. The sum of two numbers is 20: what number must be added to make their sum 30?

23. The sum of two numbers is 16 more than their difference; if their difference is 4, what is their sum?

24. The greater of two numbers is 12, and their difference 5: what is the less?

25. The sum of two numbers is 21; the less number is 8: what is the greater?

LESSON 9

REVIEW.

1. James had 13 marbles; he gave 2 to Henry, and 3 to Thomas: how many had he left?

SOLUTION.—James gave away 2 marbles and 3 marbles, which are 5 marbles; then he had left 13 marbles less 5 marbles, which are 8 marbles.

2. A merchant had 40 barrels of flour; he sold to one man 9, to another 21: how many had he left?

3. On Christmas day, William had 36 cents given him; he spent 6 cents for apples, 9 cents for cakes, and 10 cents for candy: how many had he left?

4. A man paid 30 dollars for a horse, the keeping cost 9 dollars, and he sold him for 29 dollars: how many dollars did he lose?

5. A man, having 34 dollars, bought a barrel of molasses for 15 dollars, and a bag of coffee for 10 dollars: how many dollars had he left?

6. A grocer bought some oranges for 9 dollars, some lemons for 7 dollars, some prunes for 5 dollars, and some figs for 9 dollars; he then sold them for 41 dollars: how much did he gain?

7. A lady bought a comb for 25 cents, some pins for 10 cents, tape for 7 cents, thread for 6 cents, and a toy-book for 5 cents; she gave 60 cents to the shop-keeper: how much change ought she to receive?

8. Two boys commenced playing marbles; each had 18 when they began; when they quit, one had 25: how many had the other?

SOLUTION.—When they began, both had 18 marbles and 18 marbles, which are 36 marbles; then, when they quit, the other had 36 marbles less 25 marbles, which are 11 marbles.

9. Thomas has 7 marbles, David 5, and Moses 11; how many have they all? How many more than Thomas have Moses and David together?

10. Three boys played marbles: Thomas had 20, David 10, and Moses 4; when they quit, David had 6 and Moses 12: how many had Thomas?

11. A farmer had 24 sheep; 9 of them were killed by wolves, 5 of them were stolen, and 6 he sold: how many had he left?

12. A grocer bought sugar for 12 dollars, flour for 6 dollars, and coffee for 5 dollars; he sold the whole for 30 dollars: how much did he make?

13. A lady had 50 cents; she spent 25 cents for butter, and 10 cents for eggs: how much had she left?

14. A man is indebted to A, 5 dollars; to B, 6 dollars; and to C, 10 dollars: he has cash to the amount of 20 dollars, and goods valued at 10 dollars: should he pay his debts, how much would he be worth?

15. How many are 90 less 35, less 25, less 15?

1. $3 - 2 + 1 = ?$

SOLUTION.—3 minus 2 plus 1 equals 2.

2. $4 - 3 + 2 = ?$
3. $6 - 5 + 4 = ?$
4. $8 - 7 + 6 = ?$
5. $7 - 3 + 5 = ?$
6. $9 - 4 + 7 = ?$
7. $4 - 3 + 2 - 1 = ?$
8. $6 - 5 + 4 - 3 = ?$
9. $8 - 4 + 6 - 5 = ?$

10. $9 - 5 + 7 - 2 = ?$
11. $9 - 4 + 3 - 2 + 1 = ?$
12. $8 - 5 + 4 - 3 + 2 = ?$
13. $7 - 3 + 5 - 4 + 3 = ?$
14. $8 - 2 + 6 - 5 + 4 = ?$
15. $9 - 5 + 7 - 6 + 5 = ?$
16. $6 - 2 + 4 - 3 + 2 - 1 = ?$
17. $7 - 4 + 5 - 4 + 3 - 2 = ?$
18. $8 - 5 + 6 - 5 + 4 - 3 = ?$

19. $9 - 6 + 7 - 6 + 5 - 4 = ?$
20. $7 - 6 + 5 - 4 + 3 - 2 + 1 = ?$
21. $8 - 6 + 6 - 5 + 4 - 3 + 2 - 1 = ?$
22. $9 - 5 + 7 - 6 + 5 - 4 + 3 - 2 + 1 = ?$
23. $1 + 2 + 3 - 4 + 5 - 6 + 7 - 5 + 9 = ?$
24. $9 - 1 - 2 - 3 + 4 - 5 + 6 - 4 + 8 = ?$
25. $1 + 9 - 2 - 3 + 3 + 7 - 6 - 4 + 5 = ?$
26. $9 - 7 + 8 - 5 + 6 - 3 + 4 - 2 + 1 - 10 = ?$
27. $1 + 3 - 2 + 4 - 5 + 7 - 6 + 8 - 9 + 10 = ?$

1. Henry had 24 cents, and spent all but 15 : how many did he spend?

2. A man bought a cask of wine containing 27 gallons; after selling 10 gallons, he found there were but 9 gallons remaining, the rest having leaked out: how much did he lose?

3. If from 20 you take 12 less 3, how many will remain?

4. If from the sum of 19 and 10 you take the difference between 17 and 10, what will be left?

SOLUTION.—19 plus 10 equals 29; 17 minus 10 equals 7; 29 minus 7 equals 22.

5. A man owed 60 dollars : he paid at one time 20 dollars, and at another 30 dollars; he afterwards borrowed 5 dollars : how much does he still owe?

6. A man paid 38 dollars for a horse, and 20 for a colt: he afterwards sold the colt for 10 dollars, and the horse for 65 : how much did he make by the transaction?

7. Twenty-four less 8, and 12 less 5, are together how much less than 25?

8. Engaged to do a piece of work for 60 dollars : had an assistant 25 days at a dollar a day, and paid 20 dollars for materials : how much did I earn?

9. If from the sum of 8 and 9 and 10 and 11, you take the sum of 4 and 5 and 6 and 7, what will you have remaining?

10. A jeweler bought a watch for 40 dollars, a chain for 15 dollars, and a key for 3 dollars : he sold them for 63 dollars : what did he gain?

11. A drover bought sheep as follows: of one man, 10; of another, 12; of another, 5; of another, 3: he sold at one time, 15; and at another, 5: how many were left?

12. A gentleman, having 40 dollars, purchased a suit of clothes: his pants cost 7 dollars; vest, 5 dollars; coat, 25 dollars: how much had he left?

13. What number must be added to 25 to make a sum 14 less than 45?

14. What number must be taken from 62 to give a result which shall be 12 more than 45?

15. If from the sum of 25 and 10 and 12, you take the difference between 28 and 19, what will remain?

16. A man bought a horse for 40 dollars: and, after paying 15 dollars for keeping him, sold him for 75 dollars: how much did he make?

17. A gentleman engaged in trade with 75 dollars: after losing at one time 10 dollars, and at another 5, he gained 20 dollars: how much did he then have?

18. The difference between two numbers is 17: the greater number is 85: what is the less?

19. John and James entered into partnership in business, with a joint capital of 100 dollars. John furnished 60 dollars of the money: what was James's share?

20. A barrel contained 30 gallons of syrup. Of this, 14 gallons were sold, 5 gallons leaked out, and 3 gallons were given away: how much syrup remained in the barrel?

21. An orchard contains, in one row, 5 apple trees and 15 peach trees; in another row, 11 apple trees and 9 peach trees; and in another, 10 trees of each kind: how many more peach trees in the orchard than apple trees?

22. How many are 87 less 14, less 21, less 51?

MULTIPLICATION

LESSON 12

1. A boy gave 2 cents for one lemon, and 2 cents for another: how many cents did he give for both? *Ans.* 4 cents.

Why? *Ans.* Because 2 times 2 are 4.

2. A boy gave 3 cents for one peach, and 3 cents for another: how many cents did he give for both?

3. At 4 cents apiece, what will 2 pears cost?

4. At 3 cents apiece, what will 3 peaches cost?

5. At 3 cents apiece, what will 4 apples cost?

6. At 3 cents apiece, what will 5 postage stamps cost?

7. At 4 cents apiece, what will 4 lemons cost?

8. At 5 dollars a yard, what will 4 yards of cloth cost?

9. At 6 dollars a barrel, what will 4 barrels of flour cost?

10. At 5 cents apiece, what will 5 bananas cost?

11. At 6 cents a yard, what will 5 yards of tape cost?

12. At 6 cents apiece, what will 6 oranges cost?

13. At 7 cents a yard, what will 2 yards of calico cost?

14. At 7 cents apiece, what will 3 papers cost?

15. At 7 cents apiece, what will 4 toys cost?

16. If 1 marble is worth 7 apples, how many apples are 5 marbles worth?

17. If 1 peach is worth 8 apples, how many apples are 2 peaches worth?

18. If 1 orange cost 8 cents, how many cents will 3 oranges cost? 4 oranges?

19. If 1 orange is worth 8 apples, how many apples are 5 oranges worth?

20. At 9 cents a yard, what will 2 yards of calico cost? 3 yards?

21. What will 4 quarts of nuts cost, at 10 cents a quart?

22. What will 3 yards of muslin cost, at 11 cents a yard?

Multiplication *is taking one number as many times as there are units in another.*

The *multiplicand* is the number to be taken. The *multiplier* is the number denoting how many times the multiplicand is to be taken. The *product* is the result.

The sign of multiplication (×) is read *multiplied by*.

LESSON 13

MULTIPLICATION TABLE.

$1 \times 1 = 1$	$1 \times 2 = 2$	$1 \times 3 = 3$
$2 \times 1 = 2$	$2 \times 2 = 4$	$2 \times 3 = 6$
$3 \times 1 = 3$	$3 \times 2 = 6$	$3 \times 3 = 9$
$4 \times 1 = 4$	$4 \times 2 = 8$	$4 \times 3 = 12$
$5 \times 1 = 5$	$5 \times 2 = 10$	$5 \times 3 = 15$
$6 \times 1 = 6$	$6 \times 2 = 12$	$6 \times 3 = 18$
$7 \times 1 = 7$	$7 \times 2 = 14$	$7 \times 3 = 21$
$8 \times 1 = 8$	$8 \times 2 = 16$	$8 \times 3 = 24$
$9 \times 1 = 9$	$9 \times 2 = 18$	$9 \times 3 = 27$
$10 \times 1 = 10$	$10 \times 2 = 20$	$10 \times 3 = 30$
$11 \times 1 = 11$	$11 \times 2 = 22$	$11 \times 3 = 33$
$12 \times 1 = 12$	$12 \times 2 = 24$	$12 \times 3 = 36$

$1 \times 4 = 4$	$1 \times 5 = 5$	$1 \times 6 = 6$
$2 \times 4 = 8$	$2 \times 5 = 10$	$2 \times 6 = 12$
$3 \times 4 = 12$	$3 \times 5 = 15$	$3 \times 6 = 18$
$4 \times 4 = 16$	$4 \times 5 = 20$	$4 \times 6 = 24$
$5 \times 4 = 20$	$5 \times 5 = 25$	$5 \times 6 = 30$
$6 \times 4 = 24$	$6 \times 5 = 30$	$6 \times 6 = 36$
$7 \times 4 = 28$	$7 \times 5 = 35$	$7 \times 6 = 42$
$8 \times 4 = 32$	$8 \times 5 = 40$	$8 \times 6 = 48$
$9 \times 4 = 36$	$9 \times 5 = 45$	$9 \times 6 = 54$
$10 \times 4 = 40$	$10 \times 5 = 50$	$10 \times 6 = 60$
$11 \times 4 = 44$	$11 \times 5 = 55$	$11 \times 6 = 66$
$12 \times 4 = 48$	$12 \times 5 = 60$	$12 \times 6 = 72$
$1 \times 7 = 7$	$1 \times 8 = 8$	$1 \times 9 = 9$
$2 \times 7 = 14$	$2 \times 8 = 16$	$2 \times 9 = 18$
$3 \times 7 = 21$	$3 \times 8 = 24$	$3 \times 9 = 27$
$4 \times 7 = 28$	$4 \times 8 = 32$	$4 \times 9 = 36$
$5 \times 7 = 35$	$5 \times 8 = 40$	$5 \times 9 = 45$
$6 \times 7 = 42$	$6 \times 8 = 48$	$6 \times 9 = 54$
$7 \times 7 = 49$	$7 \times 8 = 56$	$7 \times 9 = 63$
$8 \times 7 = 56$	$8 \times 8 = 64$	$8 \times 9 = 72$
$9 \times 7 = 63$	$9 \times 8 = 72$	$9 \times 9 = 81$
$10 \times 7 = 70$	$10 \times 8 = 80$	$10 \times 9 = 90$
$11 \times 7 = 77$	$11 \times 8 = 88$	$11 \times 9 = 99$
$12 \times 7 = 84$	$12 \times 8 = 96$	$12 \times 9 = 108$

$1 \times 10 = 10$	$1 \times 11 = 11$	$1 \times 12 = 12$
$2 \times 10 = 20$	$2 \times 11 = 22$	$2 \times 12 = 24$
$3 \times 10 = 30$	$3 \times 11 = 33$	$3 \times 12 = 36$
$4 \times 10 = 40$	$4 \times 11 = 44$	$4 \times 12 = 48$
$5 \times 10 = 50$	$5 \times 11 = 55$	$5 \times 12 = 60$
$6 \times 10 = 60$	$6 \times 11 = 66$	$6 \times 12 = 72$
$7 \times 10 = 70$	$7 \times 11 = 77$	$7 \times 12 = 84$
$8 \times 10 = 80$	$8 \times 11 = 88$	$8 \times 12 = 96$
$9 \times 10 = 90$	$9 \times 11 = 99$	$9 \times 12 = 108$
$10 \times 10 = 100$	$10 \times 11 = 110$	$10 \times 12 = 120$
$11 \times 10 = 110$	$11 \times 11 = 121$	$11 \times 12 = 132$
$12 \times 10 = 120$	$12 \times 11 = 132$	$12 \times 12 = 144$

EXERCISES ON THE TABLE.

1. 4 times 7 are how many?

   SOLUTION.—4 times 7 are 28.

2. 8 times 2?   7 times 5?   6 times 7?
3. 8 times 6?   6 times 9?   9 times 7?
4. 9 times 8?   7 times 7?   7 times 8?
5. 12 times 2?   2 times 10?   3 times 6?
6. 10 times 5?   4 times 11?   12 times 3?
7. 8 times 8?   6 times 11?   9 times 2?
8. 7 times 10?   12 times 4?   8 times 5?
9. 3 times 2?   4 times 2?   5 times 2?
10. 4 times 3?   7 times 2?   5 times 3?
11. 5 times 4?   6 times 6?   11 times 2?
12. 8 times 3?   5 times 5?   11 times 3?
13. 10 times 6?   6 times 12?   10 times 3?
14. 9 times 12?   9 times 4?   4 times 10?

15. 11 times 10?   10 times 12?   8 times 12?
16. 9 times 5?   9 times 9? 11 times 11?
17. 11 times 12?   11 times 5?   5 times 12?
18. 8 times 10?   7 times 12?   8 times 11?
19. 11 times 9?   10 times 10? 12 times 11?

LESSON 14

1. At 2 cents each, what will 7 oranges cost?

SOLUTION.—7 oranges will cost 7 times 2 cents, which are 14 cents.

2. At 7 cents each, what will 3 melons cost?
3. At 6 cents a dozen, what will 5 dozen apples cost?
4. At 8 cents a pound, what will 7 pounds of beef cost?
5. At $6 a pound, what will 8 pounds of opium cost?

NOTE.—The sign $ means dollars: thus, $6 is read 6 dollars.

6. At $3 a barrel, what will 9 barrels of cider cost?
7. At $4 a pair, what is the cost of 7 pairs of boots?
8. At 8 cents a dozen, what will 10 dozen pens cost?
9. What is the cost of 6 yards of cloth at $7 a yard?
10. What do 8 barrels of flour cost at $5 a barrel?
11. If a man travel 7 miles an hour, how far will he travel in 8 hours?

SOLUTION.—He will travel 8 times 7 miles, which are 56 miles.

12. On a chess-board are 8 rows of squares, and 8 squares in each row: how many squares on the board?
13. An orchard has 11 rows of trees, and 7 trees in each row: how many trees in the orchard?
14. What will 9 yards of cloth cost at $6 a yard?
15. What will 9 oranges cost at 8 cents each?

16. What will 8 quarts of berries cost at 12 cents a quart?

17. Two men start from the same place and travel in opposite directions: one travels 2 miles an hour. the other 4 miles an hour: how far will they be apart at the end of 3 hours?

SOLUTION.—At the end of 1 hour they will be 2 miles plus 4 miles, equal 6 miles, apart; then, at the end of 3 hours they will be 3 times 6 miles, equal 18 miles, apart.

18. If 2 men can do a job of work in 3 days, how many days will it take 1 man to do it?

SOLUTION.—It will take 1 man 2 times 3 days, which are 6 days.

19. If 3 men can do a piece of work in 4 days, in how many days can 1 man do it?

20. If 4 men can do a piece of work in 6 days, in how many days can 1 man do it?

21. If a quantity of bread serve 8 men 4 days, how many days will it serve 1 man?

22. If a man can earn $6 in 1 week, how many dollars can he earn in 8 weeks?

23. A person has a piece of work which 7 men can do in 9 days; but it is necessary to have it done in 1 day: how many men must be employed?

24. If $9 worth of provisions last 8 persons 11 days, how many persons will it last 1 day?

25. I bought 6 barrels of apples at $2 a barrel, and 4 barrels of sugar at $11 a barrel: how much did they both cost?

SOLUTION.—The apples cost 6 times $2, equal $12; the sugar cost 4 times $11, equal $44; then, both cost $12 plus $44, equal $56.

LESSON 15

1. Bought 2 apples at 2 cents each, 2 pears at 3 cents each, and an orange for 5 cents: what did all cost?

2. Two men start from the same place and travel in the same direction; one, 5 miles an hour; the other, 7 miles an hour: how far will they be apart in 10 hours?

3. If, in the above question, the men travel in opposite directions, how far will they be apart in 12 hours?

4. A lady went shopping with $15; she bought 4 yards of cloth at $2 a yard; 2 pairs of gloves at $1 a pair; and a shawl for $2: what did all cost, and how much had she left?

5. A man bought 4 peaches at 5 cents each, 3 pears at 3 cents each, and 2 pints of chestnuts at 5 cents a pint: how much did they cost?

6. What is the sum of 3 and 9 and 7, less the sum of 8 and 6 and 1?

7. If a man earn 5 shillings a day, and a boy 3 shillings, how much will both earn in 7 days?

8. A drover gave $10 and 7 sheep, valued at $4 a head, for a cow and calf: how much did they cost?

9. A merchant sold cloth at $7 a yard: a tailor bought of this cloth, at one time, 5 yards, and, at another, 3 yards: what was the amount of his bill?

10. Two brothers, Henry and Rufus, each received for his work 3 dimes a day: how much did both receive for 6 days' work?

11. If 12 horses can be sustained in a pasture 10 months, how many horses will it feed 1 month?

12. What is 3 times the difference between 15 and the sum of 5 and 2?

13. The sum of two numbers is 23; the smaller is 11: what is 5 times the larger?

14. The difference between two numbers is 7: if the larger be 12, what will 8 times the smaller be?

15. If a boy buy 10 cents worth of apples at 1 cent each, and sell them for 3 cents each, how much will he make?

16. George bought a book for 50 cents and sold it for $1: what would he have made had he bought 2 books, and sold them at the same rate as the first?

17. Albert has 5 times 2 marbles less than 50, and Edward has 5 times 2 more than 50: how many has each? How many more has Edward than Albert?

18. If $3 gain $1 in a year, what will $12 gain in double the time?

19. A man bought a cask of wine containing 20 gallons, at $1 a gallon; 5 gallons having leaked out, he sold the remainder at $2 a gallon: how much did he make?

20. If two men travel in the same direction, one 10 miles and the other 7 miles an hour, how far will they be apart in 7 hours?

21. A stage starts from a certain town, and travels at the rate of 8 miles per hour: at the same time, another starts from the same place, and travels in the same direction, 4 miles per hour: how far will they be apart at the end of 12 hours?

22. A grocer bought 10 pounds of tea at 7 shillings a pound; after using 3 pounds, he sold the remainder at 10 shillings a pound: how much did the 3 pounds which he used cost him in the end?

23. Bought 6 quarts of berries, at 8 cents a quart; sold 4 quarts, at 10 cents a quart, and 2 quarts, at 12 cents a quart: how much did I make?

24. If an orange cost 5 cents, and an apple 2 cents, what will 2 oranges and 4 apples cost?

25. If pork is 8 cents, and beef 10 cents a pound, what will 7 pounds of pork and 6 pounds of beef cost?

26. If an orange cost 5 times as much as an apple, how much more will 6 oranges cost than 25 apples, if an apple is worth 1 cent?

27. Bought, at one time, 5 yards of muslin, at 10 cents a yard; at another, 10 yards, at 5 cents a yard: how much did it all cost?

28. If a man earn $15 per week, and spend $11 a week, how much will he save in 3 weeks? How much can he save in 8 weeks?

29. A miller bought 10 bushels of wheat, at 1 dollar a bushel, from which he made 2 barrels of flour that were sold at 7 dollars each: how much more did he get for the flour than he paid for the wheat?

30. Thomas has 8 books, and his brother has five times as many less 6: how many books have both?

31. What will 9 pounds of figs cost, at 12 cents a pound?

32. A man employed one laborer for 6 weeks, at 7 dollars a week, and another for 5 days, at 2 dollars a day: how much did he have to pay both?

33. A farmer sold 5 dozen eggs, at 11 cents a dozen, and bought 3 pounds of sugar, at 12 cents a pound: how many cents were due him?

34. Seven times 9 are how many?

35. How many are 2 times 3 times 4?

36. How many are 4 times 3 times 12?

37. A man bought a calf for 11 dollars and paid six times as much for a cow: how much did both cost him?

38. Give the product of 8 multiplied by 8?

LESSON 16

1. At 1 cent each, how many cakes can you buy for 4 cents? *Ans.* 4 cakes.

Why? *Ans.* Because 1 is contained in 4, four times.

2. At 2 cents each, how many apples can you buy for 4 cents?

3. Among how many boys can 6 apples be divided, giving to each boy 2 apples?

4. At 2 cents each, how many apples can you buy for 8 cents?

5. At 3 cents each, how many peaches can you buy for 6 cents?

6. At 3 cents each, how many pears can you buy for 9 cents?

7. At 2 cents each, how many cakes can you buy for 10 cents?

8. At 2 cents each, how many balls can you buy for 14 cents?

9. At 5 cents each, how many lemons can you buy for 15 cents?

10. A boy has 16 marbles, and wishes to divide them into piles of 2 each: how many piles must there be?

11. At 3 cents each, how many plums can you buy for 18 cents?

12. At 5 cents each, how many oranges can you buy for 20 cents?

13. At \$3 a yard, how many yards of cloth can you buy for \$21?

14. A lady spent 22 cents for tape at 2 cents a yard: how many yards did she buy?

15. At 6 cents each, how many oranges can you buy for 24 cents? How many at 8 cents each?

16. In an orchard of 25 apple trees there are 5 rows: how many trees in each row?

17. If a man can travel 3 miles in an hour, how many hours will it take him to travel 27 miles?

18. A man gave \$28 for sheep, at \$4 a head: how many did he buy?

19. If you had 30 cents, how many marbles could you buy at 3 cents each?

20. There are 32 dimes on a table in 4 piles: how many in each pile?

21. In an orchard containing 35 apple trees, there are 5 rows: how many trees are there in each row?

22. Six men receive \$36 for a job of work: what is each man's share?

23. Four quarts make 1 gallon: how many gallons in 36 quarts?

24. If a man travel 10 miles in 1 hour, in how many hours will he travel 40 miles?

25. Forty-two cents were divided equally among 6 boys: how many cents did each boy receive?

26. If you divide 45 oranges equally among 9 boys: how many oranges will each boy receive?

Division *is the process of finding how many times one number is contained in another.*

The *divisor* is the number by which to divide. The *dividend* is the number to be divided. The *quotient* is the result. The sign of division (÷) is read *divided by*.

LESSON 17

DIVISION TABLE.

$2 \div 2 = 1$	$3 \div 3 = 1$	$4 \div 4 = 1$
$4 \div 2 = 2$	$6 \div 3 = 2$	$8 \div 4 = 2$
$6 \div 2 = 3$	$9 \div 3 = 3$	$12 \div 4 = 3$
$8 \div 2 = 4$	$12 \div 3 = 4$	$16 \div 4 = 4$
$10 \div 2 = 5$	$15 \div 3 = 5$	$20 \div 4 = 5$
$12 \div 2 = 6$	$18 \div 3 = 6$	$24 \div 4 = 6$
$14 \div 2 = 7$	$21 \div 3 = 7$	$28 \div 4 = 7$
$16 \div 2 = 8$	$24 \div 3 = 8$	$32 \div 4 = 8$
$18 \div 2 = 9$	$27 \div 3 = 9$	$36 \div 4 = 9$
$20 \div 2 = 10$	$30 \div 3 = 10$	$40 \div 4 = 10$
$22 \div 2 = 11$	$33 \div 3 = 11$	$44 \div 4 = 11$
$24 \div 2 = 12$	$36 \div 3 = 12$	$48 \div 4 = 12$
$5 \div 5 = 1$	$6 \div 6 = 1$	$7 \div 7 = 1$
$10 \div 5 = 2$	$12 \div 6 = 2$	$14 \div 7 = 2$
$15 \div 5 = 3$	$18 \div 6 = 3$	$21 \div 7 = 3$
$20 \div 5 = 4$	$24 \div 6 = 4$	$28 \div 7 = 4$
$25 \div 5 = 5$	$30 \div 6 = 5$	$35 \div 7 = 5$
$30 \div 5 = 6$	$36 \div 6 = 6$	$42 \div 7 = 6$
$35 \div 5 = 7$	$42 \div 6 = 7$	$49 \div 7 = 7$
$40 \div 5 = 8$	$48 \div 6 = 8$	$56 \div 7 = 8$
$45 \div 5 = 9$	$54 \div 6 = 9$	$63 \div 7 = 9$
$50 \div 5 = 10$	$60 \div 6 = 10$	$70 \div 7 = 10$
$55 \div 5 = 11$	$66 \div 6 = 11$	$77 \div 7 = 11$
$60 \div 5 = 12$	$72 \div 6 = 12$	$84 \div 7 = 12$

$8 \div 8 = 1$	$9 \div 9 = 1$	$10 \div 10 = 1$
$16 \div 8 = 2$	$18 \div 9 = 2$	$20 \div 10 = 2$
$24 \div 8 = 3$	$27 \div 9 = 3$	$30 \div 10 = 3$
$32 \div 8 = 4$	$36 \div 9 = 4$	$40 \div 10 = 4$
$40 \div 8 = 5$	$45 \div 9 = 5$	$50 \div 10 = 5$
$48 \div 8 = 6$	$54 \div 9 = 6$	$60 \div 10 = 6$
$56 \div 8 = 7$	$63 \div 9 = 7$	$70 \div 10 = 7$
$64 \div 8 = 8$	$72 \div 9 = 8$	$80 \div 10 = 8$
$72 \div 8 = 9$	$81 \div 9 = 9$	$90 \div 10 = 9$
$80 \div 8 = 10$	$90 \div 9 = 10$	$100 \div 10 = 10$
$88 \div 8 = 11$	$99 \div 9 = 11$	$110 \div 10 = 11$
$96 \div 8 = 12$	$108 \div 9 = 12$	$120 \div 10 = 12$

$11 \div 11 = 1$	$12 \div 12 = 1$
$22 \div 11 = 2$	$24 \div 12 = 2$
$33 \div 11 = 3$	$36 \div 12 = 3$
$44 \div 11 = 4$	$48 \div 12 = 4$
$55 \div 11 = 5$	$60 \div 12 = 5$
$66 \div 11 = 6$	$72 \div 12 = 6$
$77 \div 11 = 7$	$84 \div 12 = 7$
$88 \div 11 = 8$	$96 \div 12 = 8$
$99 \div 11 = 9$	$108 \div 12 = 9$
$110 \div 11 = 10$	$120 \div 12 = 10$
$121 \div 11 = 11$	$132 \div 12 = 11$
$132 \div 11 = 12$	$144 \div 12 = 12$

LESSON 18

1. Two is contained in 12 how many times?

SOLUTION.—2 is contained in 12 six times.

2. Two in 16 how many times? 2 in 24? 3 in 9? 3 in 15? 3 in 21? 3 in 27? 4 in 8? 4 in 20? 4 in 28? 4 in 36? 4 in 48?

3. Five is contained in 15 how many times? 5 in 30? 5 in 45? 5 in 60? 6 in 18? 6 in 24? 6 in 36? 6 in 42? 6 in 54? 6 in 66?

4. Seven in 14 how many times? 7 in 28? 7 in 42? 7 in 56? 7 in 63? 7 in 84? 8 in 24? 8 in 40? 8 in 56? 8 in 72? 8 in 96?

5. Nine in 18 how many times? 9 in 27? 9 in 45? 9 in 54? 9 in 63? 9 in 81? 9 in 108? 10 in 20? 10 in 60? 10 in 90? 10 in 100?

6. Eleven in 55 how many times? 11 in 77? 11 in 99? 11 in 110? 11 in 121? 12 in 24? 12 in 48? 12 in 60? 12 in 72? 12 in 96? 12 in 108? 12 in 120? 12 in 144?

7. If 12 peaches be divided equally among 3 children, how many will each child have?

SOLUTION.—Each child will have cne-third of 12 peaches, which is 4 peaches.

8. Four boys gave their sister 24 apples, each an equal number: how many did each give?

9. A mother divided 20 cents equally between her 2 little girls: how many did each receive?

10. Five books cost 35 cents: how much is that apiece?

11. A man has $40: if he spend $5 a week, how long will it last?

SOLUTION.—The money will last as many weeks as $5 are contained times in $40, which are 8.

12. If 5 apples are worth 1 pear, how many pears are 25 apples worth? 35 apples? 45 apples?

13. If 6 pears are worth an orange, how many oranges can you get for 30 pears? For 42 pears? For 54 pears? For 66 pears?

14. If 1 man do a piece of work in 42 days, how many days will it take 7 men to perform it?

15. If 1 man can eat a certain quantity of provisions in 56 days, how many days will it last 7 men?

16. If 1 pipe empty a cistern in 63 hours, in how many hours will 9 pipes of the same size empty it?

17. If hay is worth $9 a ton, how many tons can be bought for $27? For $45? For $54? For $63?

18. Ten men bought a horse for $60: how much did each one pay?

19. If 11 ounces of powder cost 88 cents: what will 1 ounce cost?

20. A man paid $108 for 12 merino sheep: how much was that apiece?

21. In an orchard there are 120 trees in 10 rows: how many trees in each row?

22. A man earns $144 in 12 weeks: how much is that a week? How much a day, allowing 6 working days to the week?

23. If 6 men earn $84 in 7 days, how much does each man earn in 1 day?

SOLUTION.—In one day they earn one-seventh of $84, which is $12; then, each man earns in one day one-sixth of $12, which is $2.

24. If 9 men earn $108 in 3 days, how much does 1 man earn? How much does each man earn in 1 day?

25. One man travels at the rate of 15 miles in 3 days; another at the rate of 20 miles in 2 days: how much further in one day does the latter travel than the former?

LESSON 19

1. Twelve is how many times 2?

SOLUTION.—As many as 2 is contained times in 12, which are 6.

2. Twenty-four is how many times 3? 6? 8? 12?

3. Seventy-two is how many times 12? 8? 6? 9?

4. How many oranges, at 5 cents each, must be given for 10 pears, at 2 cents each?

SOLUTION.—The pears cost 10 times 2 cents, which are 20 cents; for this, as many oranges must be given as 5 cents are contained times in 20 cents, which are 4.

5. A wheel is 10 feet in circumference: how many revolutions will it make in going 120 feet?

6. An orchard contains 10 rows of trees, and 6 trees in a row; if there were but 5 rows, how many trees would there be in a row?

7. I have three times as many marbles as the sum of 1, 2, and 3, is contained times in 60: how many have I?

SOLUTION.—1 and 2 and 3 are 6; 6 is contained in 60, 10 times; 3 times 10 are 30.

8. Bought 6 hats, at $5 apiece, and 4 yards of cloth, at $3 a yard; gave in exchange flour, at $6 a barrel: how many barrels did it take?

SOLUTION.—The hats cost 6 times $5, which are $30; the cloth, 4 times $3, which are $12; both cost $30 plus $12, which are $42. It took as many barrels as $6 are contained times in $42, which are 7.

9. If a man gain 6 miles in 5 hours, how long will it take to gain 24 miles?

SOLUTION.—24 miles are 4 times 6 miles; then, it will take 4 times 5 hours, which are 20 hours.

10. Two times 6 are contained how many times in the sum of 36 and 12?

11. If 60 be divided by some number, the result will be 10: what is that number?

12. I have a number in my mind which, divided by 3, gives 2 times 6: what is the number?

13. If I purchase lemons at the rate of 2 for 6 cents, and sell 7 for 28 cents, how much do I gain?

14. A man has a job of work which 9 men can perform in 2 days; he desires to complete it in 3 days: how many men must he employ?

15. Five times the sum of two numbers is equal to 60; if 7 is one of them, what is the other?

16. Henry has 6 dimes; Thomas, twice as many less 2; and Samuel, 3 times as many as Henry: how many have they together?

17. If to the number of times 4 is contained in 12, you add 3, and subtract the result from 9, what will remain?

18. Five oranges were sold for 25 cents, and 10 cents were gained: what did each cost?

19. What number subtracted from 17, will leave double the remainder that 5 from 9 leaves?

20. A boy said that 10 taken from the number of apples he had, left twice as great a remainder as the difference between 12 and 8: how many had he?

21. If you multiply any number, 10, by any other number, 5, and divide the product by the same number, 5, what will be the result?

22. If 2 oranges are worth 5 apples, how many apples are 12 oranges worth?

SOLUTION.—12 oranges are 6 times 2 oranges; then, they are worth 6 times 5 apples, which are 30 apples.

23. One man goes 10 miles while another goes 7; when the first has gone 90 miles, how far has the second gone?

24. James earns 8 cents while John earns 12; when John has earned 60, how many has James earned?

25. George recites 5 lessons while Charles recites 4; how many lessons have both recited when Charles has recited 20?

26. A man earns $9 while a boy earns $5: how many dollars have both earned when the man has earned $36?

27. A certain number multiplied by 10 is 5 less than 45: what is that number?

28. How many barrels of flour, at $9 a barrel, could you buy for $54?

29. William counts 11 while James counts 7: how many does James count while William is counting 77?

30. How many yards of velvet, at $12 a yard, can be obtained for $108?

31. If 8 sheep cost $56, how much will 3 sheep cost?

32. At 4 cents a pound, how many pounds of salt can you buy with 44 cents?

33. If a man travel at the rate of 10 miles an hour, how long will it take him to go 100 miles?

34. How many men can in 5 days do a piece of work which occupies 3 men 10 days?

35. How many men can in 3 days do the same amount of work that employs 9 men 4 days?

LESSON 20

A *unit* is a single thing; as, one apple.

If a unit is divided into two equal parts, one of the parts is called ONE-HALF.

1. How many halves in 2 apples? In 3? In 4? In 5? In 6? In 7? In 8? In 9? In 10?

SOLUTION.—In 1 apple there are 2 halves, and in 2 apples there are 2 times 2 halves, which are 4 halves.

If a unit is divided into three equal parts, each part is called ONE-THIRD; two parts are called TWO-THIRDS; and three parts, THREE-THIRDS, or the whole.

2. How many thirds in 2 apples? In 3? In 4? In 5? In 6? In 7? In 8? In 9? In 10?

If a unit is divided into four equal parts, each part is called ONE-FOURTH; two parts are called TWO-FOURTHS; three parts, THREE-FOURTHS; and four parts, FOUR-FOURTHS, or the whole.

3. How many fourths in 2 apples? In 3? In 4? In 5? In 6? In 7? In 8? In 9? In 10?

If a unit is divided into 5 equal parts, each part is called ONE-FIFTH; 2 parts are called TWO-FIFTHS; 3 parts, THREE-FIFTHS; 4 parts, FOUR-FIFTHS; and 5 parts, FIVE-FIFTHS, or the whole.

4 How many fifths in 2 apples? In 3? In 4? In 5? In 6? In 7? In 8? In 9? In 10?

If a unit is divided into 6 equal parts, each part is called ONE-SIXTH; 2 parts are called TWO-SIXTHS; 3 parts, THREE-SIXTHS; 4 parts, FOUR-SIXTHS; 5 parts, FIVE-SIXTHS; and 6 parts, SIX-SIXTHS, or the whole.

5. How many sixths in 2 apples? In 3? In 4? In 5? In 6? In 7? In 8? In 9? In 10?

If a unit is divided into 7 equal parts, each part is called ONE-SEVENTH; 2 parts are called TWO-SEVENTHS; 3 parts, THREE-SEVENTHS; 4 parts, FOUR-SEVENTHS; 5 parts, FIVE-SEVENTHS; 6 parts, SIX-SEVENTHS; and 7 parts, SEVEN-SEVENTHS, or the whole.

6. How many sevenths in 2 apples? In 3? In 4? In 5? In 6? In 7? In 8? In 9? In 10?

If a unit is divided into 8 equal parts, each part is called ONE-EIGHTH; 2 parts are called TWO-EIGHTHS; 3 parts, THREE-EIGHTHS; 4 parts, FOUR-EIGHTHS; 5 parts, FIVE-EIGHTHS; 6 parts, SIX-EIGHTHS; 7 parts, SEVEN-EIGHTHS; and 8 parts, EIGHT-EIGHTHS, or the whole.

7. How many eighths in 2 apples? In 3? In 4? In 5? In 6? In 7? In 8? In 9? In 10?

If a unit is divided into 9 equal parts, each part is called ONE-NINTH; 2 parts are called TWO-NINTHS; 3 parts, THREE-NINTHS; 4 parts, FOUR-NINTHS; 5 parts, FIVE-NINTHS; 6 parts, SIX-NINTHS; 7 parts, SEVEN-NINTHS; 8 parts, EIGHT-NINTHS; and 9 parts, NINE-NINTHS, or the whole.

8. How many ninths in 2 apples? In 3? In 4? In 5? In 6? In 7? In 8? In 9? In 10?

9. How many thirds in 3 units? How many fifths? Sevenths? Ninths?

10. How many fourths in 5 oranges? How many eighths? Thirds?

11. In 11 apples, how many sixths? How many halves? Fifths? Ninths?

LESSON 21

A *fraction* is one or more equal parts of a unit.

A fraction is represented by writing two numbers, one above the other, with a line between them. Thus, one-half is written $\frac{1}{2}$; two-fifths are written $\frac{2}{5}$; five-sevenths, $\frac{5}{7}$, etc.

The lower number shows the number of parts into which the unit is divided; it is called the *denominator*.

The upper number shows how many parts of the unit are taken; it is called the *numerator*.

The numerator and denominator are styled the *terms* of the fraction.

Write the following fractions:

Two-thirds, four-fifths, six-sevenths, eight-ninths, one-tenth, three-tenths, nine-tenths, seven-elevenths, five-twelfths, seven-thirteenths, nine-fourteenths, thirteen-fifteenths, one-sixteenth, two-seventeenths, five-eighteenths, six-nineteenths, seventeen-twentieths, twenty-seven thirty-firsts, thirty-four forty-thirds, twenty-nine fifty-sixths, forty-two sixty-sevenths, fifty-seven seventy-firsts, sixty-nine eighty-seconds, seventy-one ninety-eighths, eighty-five one-hundred-and-twenty-thirds.

Read the following fractions:

$$\frac{3}{5}, \quad \frac{4}{7}, \quad \frac{5}{9}, \quad \frac{7}{12}, \quad \frac{8}{17}, \quad \frac{17}{22}, \quad \frac{24}{81}, \quad \frac{35}{42}, \quad \frac{49}{51}.$$

In the fraction $\frac{2}{3}$, the number of parts, *two*, which are taken, is *less* than the number of parts, *three*, into which the unit is divided; hence, the *value* of the fraction is *less than* 1. In the fraction $\frac{3}{3}$, the number of parts taken *equals* the number of parts into which the unit is divided;

42

hence the *value* of the fraction is *equal to* 1. In the fraction $\frac{4}{3}$, the number of parts taken is *greater* than the number of parts into which a single unit is divided, and hence the value of the fraction is *greater than* 1.

A *proper* fraction is one whose value is less than 1.

An *improper* fraction is one whose value is equal to or greater than 1.

Point out the proper and improper fractions in the following examples:

$$\frac{1}{2}, \quad \frac{2}{1}, \quad \frac{3}{4}, \quad \frac{4}{8}, \quad \frac{5}{6}, \quad \frac{6}{5}, \quad \frac{7}{8}, \quad \frac{8}{7}, \quad \frac{9}{10}, \quad \frac{10}{9},$$

$$\frac{11}{12}, \quad \frac{14}{13}, \quad \frac{15}{16}, \quad \frac{17}{18}, \quad \frac{25}{21}, \quad \frac{34}{42}, \quad \frac{54}{45}, \quad \frac{65}{76}.$$

A *mixed number* is composed of a whole number and a fraction. Thus, $2\frac{1}{2}$, $3\frac{1}{3}$, $5\frac{2}{7}$; read, *two and one-half, three and one-third, five and two-sevenths.*

Read the following examples:

$$4\frac{1}{2}, \quad 6\frac{1}{4}, \quad 7\frac{3}{8}, \quad 9\frac{5}{12}, \quad 18\frac{6}{7}, \quad 22\frac{8}{9}, \quad 35\frac{7}{11}, \quad 48\frac{3}{10}, \quad 69\frac{5}{20}, \quad 75\frac{16}{88}.$$

LESSON 22

1. If a yard of tape is worth 2 cents, what is $\frac{1}{2}$ of a yard worth?

SOLUTION.—$\frac{1}{2}$ of a yard is worth $\frac{1}{2}$ of 2 cents, which is 1 cent.

2. If an apple is worth 3 cents, what is $\frac{1}{3}$ of the apple worth?

3. A yard of cloth costs $6, what would $\frac{2}{3}$ of a yard cost?

SOLUTION.—$\frac{1}{3}$ of a yard would cost $\frac{1}{3}$ of $6, which is $2; then, $\frac{2}{3}$ of a yard would cost 2 times $2, which are $4.

43

4. James had 4 apples and gave his brother ½ of them: how many did he give him?

5. If a melon is worth 8 cents, what are ¾ of a melon worth?

6. If a barrel of flour costs $10, what is the cost of $\frac{2}{5}$ of a barrel? Of $\frac{3}{5}$? Of $\frac{4}{5}$?

7. If a dozen eggs are worth 12 cents, what are $\frac{5}{6}$ of a dozen worth?

8. What are $\frac{2}{3}$ of 9?

SOLUTION.—⅓ of 9 is 3; then, $\frac{2}{3}$ of 9 are 2 times 3, which are 6.

9. What are $\frac{3}{4}$ of 20?

10. What are $\frac{2}{5}$ of 15? $\frac{3}{5}$ of 20? $\frac{4}{5}$ of 25?

11. What are $\frac{2}{7}$ of 14? $\frac{3}{7}$ of 21? $\frac{4}{7}$ of 28? $\frac{5}{7}$ of 35? $\frac{6}{7}$ of 42?

12. What are $\frac{3}{8}$ of 16? $\frac{5}{8}$ of 24? $\frac{7}{8}$ of 32?

13. What are $\frac{2}{9}$ of 9? $\frac{4}{9}$ of 18? $\frac{5}{9}$ of 27? $\frac{7}{9}$ of 36? $\frac{8}{9}$ of 45?

14. What are $\frac{3}{10}$ of 10? $\frac{7}{10}$ of 20? $\frac{9}{10}$ of 30?

15. What are $\frac{2}{11}$ of 11? $\frac{3}{11}$ of 22? $\frac{4}{11}$ of 33? $\frac{5}{11}$ of 44? $\frac{6}{11}$ of 55? $\frac{7}{11}$ of 66? $\frac{8}{11}$ of 77?

16. What are $\frac{5}{12}$ of 24? $\frac{7}{12}$ of 36? $\frac{11}{12}$ of 48?

17. If 2 apples cost 4 cents, what will 1 apple cost?

SOLUTION.—1 apple will cost ½ of 4 cents, which is 2 cents.

18. If 3 yards of cloth cost $9, what will 1 yard cost?

19. If 3 oranges are worth 15 cents, what are 2 oranges worth?

SOLUTION.—1 orange is worth ⅓ of 15, or 5, cents; then, 2 oranges are worth 2 times 5 cents, which are 10 cents.

20. If 5 barrels of flour are sold for $30, what would 3 barrels sell for?

21. A grocer sells 7 pounds of sugar for 70 cents: what will he sell 5 pounds for?

22. A lady purchased 8 yards of calico for 72 cents; she afterward found that she needed 5 yards more of the same: how much did it cost?

23. A drover bought 12 calves for $120; he sold 7 of them for what they cost him: what did he get for them?

LESSON 23

1. If an apple costs 2 cents, what part of the apple costs 1 cent?

SOLUTION.—1 cent is the cost of $\frac{1}{2}$ of the apple.

2. A boy bought a pear for 3 cents: what part of the pear cost 1 cent?

3. If the price of a yard of cloth is $3, what part of a yard will cost $2?

SOLUTION.—$1 will be the cost of $\frac{1}{3}$ of a yard; then $2 will be the cost of 2 times $\frac{1}{3}$ of a yard, which are $\frac{2}{3}$ of a yard.

4. If you buy an orange for 4 cents, what part of the orange costs 3 cents?

5. If a melon is worth 5 cents, what part of the melon is worth 2 cents? 3 cents? 4 cents?

6. If a barrel of apples cost $6, what part of a barrel will cost $5?

7. James had 7 marbles and gave his brother 4 of them: what part did he give away?

8. A lady went shopping with $10; she spent $7: what part of her money did she spend?

9. If a bushel of clover seed cost $8, what part of a bushel can be bought for $5?

10. 5 is what part of 7?

SOLUTION.—1 is $\frac{1}{7}$ of 7; then, 5 is 5 times $\frac{1}{7} = \frac{5}{7}$ of 7.

11. 3 is what part of 8? Of 10? Of 11? Of 20?

12. 4 is what part of 9? Of 11? Of 15? Of 25?

13. 5 is what part of 8? Of 9? Of 12? Of 16?

14. What part of 15 is 2? 7? 8? 11? 13?

15. What part of 20 is 3? 7? 11? 13? 17?

16. $\frac{3}{5}$ of 30 is what part of 23?

17. $\frac{5}{7}$ of 28 is what part of 35?

18. $\frac{2}{3}$ of 21 is what part of 19?

19. $\frac{1}{2}$ of 4 is what part of $\frac{1}{3}$ of 9?

20. $\frac{3}{4}$ of 12 is what part of $\frac{5}{6}$ of 24.

21. $\frac{2}{5}$ of 10 is what part of $\frac{3}{7}$ of 21?

22. $\frac{3}{8}$ of 16 is what part of $\frac{5}{7}$ of 35?

23. $\frac{4}{9}$ of 18 is what part of $\frac{3}{11}$ of 77?

24. $\frac{9}{10}$ of 30 is what part of $\frac{5}{7}$ of 49?

LESSON 24

1. If $\frac{1}{2}$ an apple is worth 1 cent, what is the apple worth?

SOLUTION.—The apple is worth 2 times 1 cent $= 2$ cents.

2. If $\frac{1}{3}$ of an orange is worth 2 cents, what is the orange worth?

3. If $\frac{2}{3}$ of a lemon are worth 6 cents, what is the lemon worth?

SOLUTION.—$\frac{1}{3}$ of the lemon is worth $\frac{1}{2}$ of 6 cents $= 3$ cents; then, the lemon is worth 3 times 3 cents $= 9$ cents.

4. If $\frac{3}{4}$ of a barrel of flour cost \$9, what will a barrel cost?

5. If $\frac{2}{5}$ of a pound of coffee cost 10 cents, what is the price of a pound?

6. If $\frac{4}{5}$ of a pound of butter cost 12 cents, what will a pound cost?

7. If $\frac{5}{6}$ of a gallon of wine cost 35 cents, what will a gallon cost?

8. 6 is $\frac{2}{7}$ of what number?

SOLUTION.—$\frac{1}{7}$ of the number is $\frac{1}{2}$ of $6 = 3$; then, the number is 7 times $3 = 21$.

9. 6 is $\frac{2}{9}$ of what number? $\frac{2}{11}$?

10. 12 is $\frac{3}{4}$ of what number? $\frac{3}{5}$? $\frac{3}{7}$? $\frac{3}{8}$? $\frac{3}{10}$? $\frac{3}{11}$?

11. 20 is $\frac{4}{5}$ of what number? $\frac{4}{7}$? $\frac{4}{9}$? $\frac{4}{11}$?

12. 30 is $\frac{5}{6}$ of what number? $\frac{5}{7}$? $\frac{5}{8}$? $\frac{5}{9}$? $\frac{5}{11}$? $\frac{5}{12}$?

13. 42 is $\frac{6}{7}$ of what number? $\frac{6}{11}$?

14. 56 is $\frac{7}{8}$ of what number? $\frac{7}{9}$? $\frac{7}{10}$?

15. 72 is $\frac{8}{9}$ of what number? $\frac{8}{11}$?

16. 90 is $\frac{9}{10}$ of what number?

17. If you have 8 cents, and $\frac{3}{4}$ of your money equals $\frac{2}{3}$ of mine, how many cents have I?

SOLUTION.—$\frac{3}{4}$ of 8 cents $= 6$ cents; then, if $\frac{2}{3}$ of my money $= 6$ cents, $\frac{1}{3}$ of my money is $\frac{1}{2}$ of 6 cents $= 3$ cents, and all my money is 3 times 3 cents $= 9$ cents.

18. William says to Frank: "Your age is 15 years, and $\frac{4}{5}$ of your age is $\frac{3}{4}$ of mine: what is my age?"

19. $\frac{5}{6}$ of 18 are $\frac{3}{5}$ of what number?

SOLUTION.—$\frac{5}{6}$ of $18 = 15$; then, $\frac{3}{5}$ of some number $= 15$. $\frac{1}{5}$ of the number is $\frac{1}{3}$ of $15 = 5$, and the number is 5 times $5 = 25$.

20. $\frac{6}{7}$ of 14 are $\frac{3}{8}$ of what number?

21. $\frac{5}{8}$ of 16 are $\frac{2}{7}$ of what number?

22. $\frac{2}{9}$ of 27 are $\frac{3}{10}$ of what number?

23. $\frac{5}{9}$ of 36 are $\frac{4}{11}$ of what number?

24 $\frac{7}{10}$ of 20 are $\frac{2}{11}$ of what number?

25. $\frac{3}{11}$ of 55 are $\frac{5}{12}$ of what number?

LESSON 25

1. Divide 3 apples between 2 boys, giving to each the same amount.

SOLUTION.—Each boy will receive $\frac{1}{2}$ of 3 apples, which is $\frac{3}{2} = 1\frac{1}{2}$ apples.

2. A grocer gave 4 oranges to 3 boys, provided they would divide them equally: what was the share of each?

3. If 2 pears cost 5 cents, how much is that apiece?

4. If 3 yards of cloth cost $5, what is the price per yard?

5. Henry bought 4 pens for 5 cents: what was the cost of each?

6. $\frac{1}{5}$ of 6 = what?

SOLUTION.—$\frac{1}{5}$ of 6 is $\frac{6}{5} = 1\frac{1}{5}$.

7. $\frac{1}{2}$ of 7 = what? $\frac{1}{3}$ of 7? $\frac{1}{4}$ of 7? $\frac{1}{5}$ of 7? $\frac{1}{6}$ of 7?

8. $\frac{1}{3}$ of 8 = what? $\frac{1}{5}$ of 8? $\frac{1}{7}$ of 8?

9. $\frac{1}{2}$ of 9 = what? $\frac{1}{4}$ of 9? $\frac{1}{5}$ of 9? $\frac{1}{7}$ of 9? $\frac{1}{8}$ of 9?

10. $\frac{1}{3}$ of 10 = what? $\frac{1}{7}$ of 10? $\frac{1}{9}$ of 10?

11. $\frac{1}{2}$ of 11 = what? $\frac{1}{3}$ of 11? $\frac{1}{4}$ of 11? $\frac{1}{5}$ of 11? $\frac{1}{6}$ of 11? $\frac{1}{7}$ of 11? $\frac{1}{8}$ of 11? $\frac{1}{9}$ of 11? $\frac{1}{10}$ of 11?

12. $\frac{1}{5}$ of 12 = what? $\frac{1}{7}$ of 12? $\frac{1}{11}$ of 12?

13. For 5 cents, how many apples can I buy at 2 cents each?

SOLUTION.—I can buy as many apples as 2 cents are contained times in 5 cents, which are $\frac{5}{2} = 2\frac{1}{2}$.

14. At \$3 a yard, how many yards of cloth can be purchased for \$7?

15. Harriet spent 13 cents for braid, at 4 cents a yard, how many yards did she buy?

16. When milk is worth 5 cents a pint, how many pints can you get for 17 cents?

17. For \$23, how much flour can be bought at \$6 a barrel?

18. A lady spent 25 cents for ribbon, at 7 cents a yard, how many yards did she buy?

19. How many times 2 is 13?

SOLUTION.—As many as 2 is contained times in 13, which are $\frac{13}{2}$ = $6\frac{1}{2}$.

20. How many times 2 is 15? 17? 19? 21? 23?
21. How many times 3 is 20? 26? 29? 31? 35?
22. How many times 4 is 27? 33? 39? 41? 47?
23. How many times 6 is 43? 47? 49? 59? 61?
24. How many times 7 is 24? 32? 40? 48? 57?
25. How many times 8 is 45? 55? 67? 71? 81?
26. How many times 9 is 34? 38? 50? 58? 64?
27. How many times 10 is 63? 69? 77? 83? 91?
28. How many times 11 is 42? 46? 54? 60? 70?
29. How many times 12 is 68? 79? 85? 89? 95?

LESSON 26

1. How many halves in $2\frac{1}{2}$?

SOLUTION.—In 1 there are $\frac{2}{2}$; then, in 2 there are 2 times $\frac{2}{2} = \frac{4}{2}$; $\frac{4}{2} + \frac{1}{2} = \frac{5}{2}$.

2. How many halves in $3\frac{1}{2}$? $4\frac{1}{2}$? $5\frac{1}{2}$? $6\frac{1}{2}$?
3. How many thirds in $4\frac{1}{3}$? $5\frac{2}{3}$? $6\frac{1}{3}$? $7\frac{2}{3}$?

4. How many fourths in $3\frac{1}{4}$? $4\frac{3}{4}$? $5\frac{1}{4}$? $6\frac{3}{4}$?

5. How many fifths in $1\frac{1}{5}$? $3\frac{2}{5}$? $6\frac{2}{5}$? $7\frac{1}{5}$?

6. How many sixths in $2\frac{5}{6}$? $4\frac{5}{6}$? $5\frac{1}{6}$? $6\frac{5}{6}$?

7. How many sevenths in $5\frac{3}{7}$? $6\frac{4}{7}$? $7\frac{5}{7}$? $8\frac{6}{7}$?

8. How many eighths in $3\frac{5}{8}$? $4\frac{7}{8}$? $5\frac{1}{8}$? $6\frac{3}{8}$?

9. How many ninths in $6\frac{8}{9}$? $7\frac{1}{9}$? $8\frac{2}{9}$? $9\frac{5}{9}$?

10. How many tenths in $6\frac{3}{10}$? $7\frac{7}{10}$? $8\frac{9}{10}$? $9\frac{1}{10}$?

11. How many elevenths in $6\frac{5}{11}$? $7\frac{6}{11}$? $8\frac{7}{11}$? $9\frac{8}{11}$?

12. How many twelfths in $5\frac{1}{12}$? $6\frac{7}{12}$? $7\frac{5}{12}$? $9\frac{5}{12}$?

LESSON 27

NOTE.—A fraction is in its *lowest terms* when no number greater than 1 will divide both terms.

1. Reduce $\frac{2}{4}$ to its lowest terms.

SOLUTION.—Dividing both terms of $\frac{2}{4}$ by 2, the result is $\frac{1}{2}$.

2. Reduce $\frac{2}{6}$ to its lowest terms.

3. Reduce $\frac{3}{6}$ to its lowest terms.

4. Reduce $\frac{4}{6}$ to its lowest terms.

5. Reduce $\frac{4}{8}$ to its lowest terms.

SOLUTION.—Dividing both terms of $\frac{4}{8}$ by 2, the result is $\frac{2}{4}$; dividing both terms of $\frac{2}{4}$ by 2, the result is $\frac{1}{2}$.

Reduce to their lowest terms:

6. $\frac{5}{10}$, $\frac{3}{9}$, $\frac{6}{8}$, $\frac{4}{10}$, $\frac{8}{10}$, $\frac{10}{12}$.

7. $\frac{6}{12}$, $\frac{5}{15}$, $\frac{6}{9}$, $\frac{9}{12}$, $\frac{12}{15}$, $\frac{15}{18}$.

8. $\frac{8}{12}$, $\frac{12}{16}$, $\frac{10}{25}$, $\frac{12}{20}$, $\frac{20}{24}$, $\frac{21}{49}$.

9. $\frac{9}{24}$, $\frac{10}{35}$, $\frac{15}{20}$, $\frac{18}{30}$, $\frac{25}{30}$, $\frac{32}{56}$.

10. $\frac{12}{27}$, $\frac{14}{21}$, $\frac{18}{24}$, $\frac{21}{35}$, $\frac{30}{36}$, $\frac{36}{63}$.

11. $\frac{12}{30}$, $\frac{16}{24}$, $\frac{21}{28}$, $\frac{24}{40}$, $\frac{30}{42}$, $\frac{35}{56}$.

12. $\frac{18}{27}$, $\frac{20}{25}$, $\frac{24}{32}$, $\frac{25}{40}$, $\frac{25}{45}$, $\frac{35}{42}$.

13. $\frac{27}{36}$, $\frac{36}{45}$, $\frac{45}{54}$, $\frac{48}{56}$, $\frac{49}{63}$, $\frac{56}{64}$.

14. $\frac{28}{35}$, $\frac{40}{48}$, $\frac{42}{49}$, $\frac{42}{54}$, $\frac{63}{72}$, $\frac{72}{81}$.

LESSON 28

1. Reduce $\frac{1}{2}$ to fourths.

SOLUTION.—In 1 there are four-fourths; then, in $\frac{1}{2}$ there is $\frac{1}{2}$ of 4 fourths $= 2$ fourths.

2. Reduce $\frac{1}{3}$ to sixths.   5. Reduce $\frac{1}{6}$ to twelfths.
3. Reduce $\frac{1}{4}$ to eighths.   6. Reduce $\frac{1}{3}$ to ninths.
4. Reduce $\frac{1}{5}$ to tenths.   7. Reduce $\frac{1}{4}$ to twelfths.

8. Reduce $\frac{2}{3}$ to sixths.

SOLUTION.—$1 = \frac{6}{6}$; then, $\frac{1}{3} = \frac{2}{6}$, and $\frac{2}{3} = \frac{4}{6}$.

9. Reduce $\frac{2}{3}$ to ninths.   Reduce $\frac{2}{3}$ to twelfths.
10. Reduce $\frac{3}{4}$ to eighths.   Reduce $\frac{3}{4}$ to twelfths.
11. Reduce $\frac{2}{5}$ to tenths.   Reduce $\frac{2}{5}$ to fifteenths.
12. Reduce $\frac{3}{5}$ to twentieths.   Reduce $\frac{3}{5}$ to twenty-fifths.
13. Reduce $\frac{4}{5}$ to thirtieths.   Reduce $\frac{4}{5}$ to thirty-fifths.
14. Reduce $\frac{5}{6}$ to twelfths.   Reduce $\frac{5}{6}$ to eighteenths.
15. Reduce $\frac{3}{7}$ to fourteenths.   Reduce $\frac{3}{7}$ to twenty-firsts.
16. Reduce $\frac{5}{7}$ to twenty-eighths.   Reduce $\frac{5}{7}$ to thirty-fifths.
17. Reduce $\frac{3}{8}$ to sixteenths.   Reduce $\frac{3}{8}$ to twenty-fourths.
18. Reduce $\frac{5}{8}$ to thirty-seconds.   Reduce $\frac{5}{8}$ to fortieths.
19. Reduce $\frac{2}{9}$ to eighteenths.   Reduce $\frac{2}{9}$ to twenty-sevenths.
20. Reduce $\frac{4}{9}$ to thirty-sixths.   Reduce $\frac{4}{9}$ to forty-fifths.
21. Reduce $\frac{5}{9}$ to fifty-fourths.   Reduce $\frac{5}{9}$ to sixty-thirds.
22. Reduce $\frac{7}{10}$ to 'twentieths.   Reduce $\frac{7}{10}$ to thirtieths.
23. Reduce $\frac{5}{12}$ to twenty-fourths.   Reduce $\frac{5}{12}$ to thirty-sixths.

LESSON 29

NOTE.—When two or more fractions have the same denominators, they are said to have a *common denominator*. The common denominator may be found by multiplying the denominators together, or by finding their least common multiple, that is, the least number that can be divided by them.

1. Reduce $\frac{2}{3}$ and $\frac{3}{4}$ to equivalent fractions having a common denominator.

SOLUTION.—The common denominator is $3 \times 4 = 12$. $1 = \frac{12}{12}$, $\frac{1}{3} = \frac{4}{12}$, $\frac{2}{3} = \frac{8}{12}$: $1 = \frac{12}{12}$, $\frac{1}{4} = \frac{3}{12}$, $\frac{3}{4} = \frac{9}{12}$.

Reduce to equivalent fractions having a common denominator:

2. $\frac{1}{2}$ and $\frac{1}{3}$. $\frac{1}{2}$ and $\frac{1}{5}$. $\frac{1}{3}$ and $\frac{1}{5}$.

3. $\frac{1}{3}$ and $\frac{1}{4}$. $\frac{1}{3}$ and $\frac{1}{5}$. $\frac{1}{4}$ and $\frac{1}{5}$.

4. $\frac{2}{3}$ and $\frac{2}{5}$. $\frac{2}{3}$ and $\frac{3}{5}$. $\frac{2}{3}$ and $\frac{4}{5}$.

5. $\frac{3}{4}$ and $\frac{2}{5}$. $\frac{3}{4}$ and $\frac{3}{5}$. $\frac{3}{4}$ and $\frac{4}{5}$.

6. $\frac{2}{5}$ and $\frac{5}{6}$. $\frac{3}{5}$ and $\frac{5}{6}$. $\frac{4}{5}$ and $\frac{5}{6}$.

7. $\frac{5}{6}$ and $\frac{2}{7}$. $\frac{5}{6}$ and $\frac{3}{7}$. $\frac{5}{6}$ and $\frac{4}{7}$.

8. $\frac{5}{7}$ and $\frac{3}{8}$. $\frac{6}{7}$ and $\frac{5}{8}$. $\frac{7}{8}$ and $\frac{2}{9}$.

9. $\frac{4}{9}$ and $\frac{3}{10}$. $\frac{5}{9}$ and $\frac{7}{10}$. $\frac{7}{9}$ and $\frac{9}{10}$.

10. $\frac{1}{2}$, $\frac{1}{3}$, and $\frac{1}{5}$. $\frac{1}{3}$, $\frac{1}{4}$, and $\frac{1}{5}$.

11. $\frac{2}{3}$, $\frac{3}{4}$, and $\frac{2}{5}$. $\frac{3}{5}$, $\frac{5}{6}$, and $\frac{1}{2}$.

12. $\frac{2}{3}$, $\frac{3}{4}$, $\frac{4}{5}$, and $\frac{1}{2}$.

13. Reduce $\frac{3}{4}$ and $\frac{5}{6}$ to equivalent fractions having the least common denominator.

SOLUTION.—The least common denominator is 12. $\frac{3}{4} = \frac{9}{12}$; $\frac{5}{6} = \frac{10}{12}$.

Reduce to equivalent fractions having the least common denominator:

14. $\frac{1}{2}$ and $\frac{1}{4}$. $\frac{1}{2}$ and $\frac{1}{6}$. $\frac{1}{3}$ and $\frac{1}{6}$.

15. $\frac{2}{3}$ and $\frac{5}{6}$. $\frac{3}{4}$ and $\frac{3}{8}$. $\frac{2}{3}$ and $\frac{2}{9}$.

16. $\frac{5}{6}$ and $\frac{5}{8}$. $\frac{5}{6}$ and $\frac{7}{9}$. $\frac{7}{8}$ and $\frac{5}{12}$.

17. $\frac{1}{2}$, $\frac{1}{3}$, and $\frac{1}{4}$. $\frac{1}{3}$, $\frac{1}{4}$, and $\frac{1}{6}$.

18. $\frac{2}{3}$, $\frac{3}{4}$, and $\frac{5}{6}$. $\frac{2}{3}$, $\frac{3}{4}$, and $\frac{5}{8}$.

19. $\frac{3}{4}$, $\frac{5}{6}$, and $\frac{7}{8}$. $\frac{2}{3}$, $\frac{5}{6}$, and $\frac{2}{9}$.

20. $\frac{3}{4}$, $\frac{4}{9}$, and $\frac{5}{12}$. $\frac{5}{6}$, $\frac{8}{9}$, and $\frac{7}{12}$.

21. $\frac{1}{2}$, $\frac{1}{3}$, $\frac{1}{4}$, and $\frac{1}{6}$. $\frac{1}{3}$, $\frac{1}{5}$, $\frac{1}{6}$, and $\frac{1}{10}$.

22. $\frac{2}{3}$, $\frac{3}{4}$, $\frac{5}{6}$, and $\frac{7}{8}$. $\frac{1}{3}$, $\frac{1}{4}$, $\frac{5}{9}$, and $\frac{7}{12}$.

23. $\frac{3}{4}$, $\frac{5}{6}$, $\frac{7}{8}$, and $\frac{8}{12}$. $\frac{2}{5}$, $\frac{4}{6}$, $\frac{6}{9}$, and $\frac{5}{12}$.

24. $\frac{1}{2}$, $\frac{1}{3}$, $\frac{1}{4}$, $\frac{1}{6}$, and $\frac{1}{8}$. $\frac{2}{3}$, $\frac{3}{4}$, $\frac{5}{6}$, $\frac{7}{8}$, and $\frac{11}{12}$.

25. $\frac{1}{2}$, $\frac{2}{3}$, $\frac{3}{4}$, $\frac{4}{5}$, $\frac{5}{6}$, $\frac{9}{10}$, and $\frac{11}{12}$.

LESSON 30

1. James divided a melon, giving to his sister $\frac{1}{2}$, and to his brother $\frac{1}{4}$: what part did he give away?

SOLUTION.—He gave away $\frac{1}{2} + \frac{1}{4}$. $\frac{1}{2} = \frac{2}{4}$; $\frac{2}{4} + \frac{1}{4} = \frac{3}{4}$ of a melon.

2. Thomas gave $\frac{3}{4}$ of a dollar for a knife, and $\frac{1}{2}$ of a dollar for a ball: how much did he give for both?

3. A yard of flannel costs $\$\frac{1}{2}$, and a yard of cloth, $\$\frac{2}{3}$: how much do both cost?

4. I give Mary $\frac{1}{2}$, Jane $\frac{1}{4}$, and William $\frac{1}{8}$ of an orange: how much do I give to all?

5. What is the sum of $\frac{1}{4}$ and $\frac{1}{3}$?

6. Thomas bought a copy-book for $\$\frac{1}{10}$, and a reader for $\$\frac{1}{2}$: how much did both cost?

7. Bought $1\frac{1}{4}$ yards of muslin at one store, and $2\frac{1}{3}$ yards at another: how many yards did I purchase?

SOLUTION.—$1\frac{1}{4} = \frac{5}{4}$; $2\frac{1}{3} = \frac{7}{3}$. I purchased $\frac{5}{4} + \frac{7}{3} = 3\frac{7}{12}$ yards.

8. I planted $2\frac{1}{2}$ acres of ground in corn, and $8\frac{2}{3}$ acres in oats. how many acres did I plant?

9. John bought a knife for $\$\frac{1}{2}$, a slate for $\$\frac{1}{8}$, and a book for $\$\frac{5}{8}$: how much did all cost?

10. Add $\frac{1}{2}$ and $\frac{3}{5}$. $\frac{1}{2}$ and $\frac{3}{8}$. $\frac{2}{3}$ and $\frac{3}{4}$.
11. Add $\frac{1}{3}$ and $\frac{2}{5}$. $\frac{1}{4}$ and $\frac{1}{6}$. $\frac{1}{4}$ and $\frac{1}{5}$.
12. Add $\frac{1}{2}$ and $\frac{1}{7}$. $\frac{3}{4}$ and $\frac{5}{7}$. $\frac{3}{4}$ and $\frac{5}{8}$.
13. Add $\frac{5}{6}$ and $\frac{4}{5}$. $\frac{5}{9}$ and $\frac{5}{8}$. $\frac{5}{7}$ and $\frac{5}{9}$.
14. Add $1\frac{3}{4}$ and $2\frac{1}{3}$. $\frac{1}{2}$, $\frac{1}{3}$, $\frac{1}{4}$, and $\frac{1}{5}$.
15. Add $3\frac{2}{3}$ and $4\frac{5}{6}$.

SOLUTION.—$3 + 4 = 7$, $\frac{2}{3} + \frac{5}{6} = 1\frac{1}{2}$; $7 + 1\frac{1}{2} = 8\frac{1}{2}$.

16. Add $4\frac{3}{7}$ and $5\frac{1}{3}$. $1\frac{1}{2}$, $2\frac{3}{4}$, $\frac{4}{5}$, and $6\frac{2}{10}$.
17. Add $5\frac{3}{8}$ and $4\frac{4}{9}$, $\frac{5}{6}$, $3\frac{1}{3}$, 4, and $5\frac{5}{8}$.

LESSON 31

1. James received $\frac{1}{2}$ an orange and Charles, $\frac{1}{3}$: how much more did James receive than Charles?

SOLUTION.—James received more than Charles $\frac{1}{2} - \frac{1}{3}$. $\frac{1}{2} = \frac{3}{6}$; $\frac{1}{3} = \frac{2}{6}$. $\frac{3}{6} - \frac{2}{6} = \frac{1}{6}$ of an orange.

2. If I give to Mary $\frac{1}{2}$ of an apple, and to Jane $\frac{1}{4}$, how much more will Mary have than Jane?

3. James bought 2 melons; he gave to Lucy half of the first, and to Jane two-thirds of the second: what part of a melon had Jane more than Lucy?

4. If a bushel of wheat cost $\$1\frac{1}{4}$, and a bushel of corn, $\$\frac{2}{3}$, how much will the wheat cost more than the corn?

5. Joseph bought a quart of chestnuts, and gave $\frac{1}{2}$ to his mother and $\frac{1}{6}$ to his sister: how much more did he give his mother than his sister?

6. Jane gave $1\frac{3}{4}$ oranges to Mary, and $2\frac{1}{3}$ to Lucy: how much more did she give to Lucy than to Mary?

SOLUTION.—$1\frac{3}{4} = \frac{7}{4}$; $2\frac{1}{3} = \frac{7}{3}$. Jane gave Lucy more than Mary $\frac{7}{3} - \frac{7}{4}$, or $\frac{7}{12}$ of an orange.

7. Take $\frac{1}{5}$ from $\frac{1}{2}$. $\frac{1}{4}$ from $\frac{1}{3}$. $\frac{1}{5}$ from $\frac{1}{4}$.

8. Take $\frac{2}{9}$ from $\frac{1}{2}$. $\frac{1}{2}$ from $\frac{3}{5}$. $\frac{1}{3}$ from $\frac{3}{4}$.

9. Take $\frac{1}{3}$ from $\frac{3}{5}$. $\frac{3}{5}$ from $\frac{5}{8}$. $\frac{3}{7}$ from $\frac{2}{3}$.

10. Take $\frac{1}{2}$ from $\frac{7}{9}$. $\frac{1}{3}$ from $\frac{4}{5}$. $\frac{1}{4}$ from $\frac{3}{7}$.

11. Take $\frac{3}{5}$ from $\frac{5}{7}$. $\frac{5}{7}$ from $\frac{3}{4}$. $\frac{3}{5}$ from $\frac{5}{6}$.

12. Take $\frac{1}{3}$ from $\frac{3}{8}$. $\frac{5}{6}$ from $\frac{6}{7}$. $\frac{1}{3}$ from $2\frac{1}{2}$.

13. Take $2\frac{2}{3}$ from $5\frac{1}{6}$.

SOLUTION.—We can not subtract $\frac{2}{3}$ from $\frac{1}{6}$; but we can take 1 from 5, and can subtract $\frac{2}{3}$ from $1\frac{1}{6}$. $1\frac{1}{6} - \frac{2}{3} = \frac{1}{2}$, $4 - 2 = 2$; $2 + \frac{1}{2} = 2\frac{1}{2}$.

14. Take $3\frac{1}{2}$ from $7\frac{3}{5}$. $4\frac{1}{4}$ from $8\frac{5}{6}$.

15. Take $5\frac{2}{7}$ from $7\frac{2}{3}$. $6\frac{4}{9}$ from $8\frac{1}{2}$. $7\frac{4}{5}$ from $9\frac{2}{3}$.

LESSON 32

1. Mary divided a quart of pecans, giving Ann $\frac{1}{3}$, and Jane $\frac{1}{4}$ of them: what had she left?

SOLUTION.—Mary gave away $\frac{1}{3} + \frac{1}{4} = \frac{7}{12}$ of a quart; she had left $\frac{12}{12} - \frac{7}{12} = \frac{5}{12}$ of a quart.

2. After taking away $\frac{1}{2}$ and $\frac{1}{3}$ of an apple, what will be left?

3. Thomas wishes to divide an orange, and give Ann $\frac{1}{2}$, and Lucy $\frac{2}{5}$: how much will he have left?

4. A farmer sows $\frac{1}{2}$ of a field in rye, $\frac{1}{6}$ in barley, and the remainder in oats: how much does he sow in oats?

5. A man having 72 miles to travel, went $\frac{1}{8}$ the dis-

tance the first day, $\frac{2}{9}$ the second, and the remainder the third day: what part did he travel the last day, and how far?

6. David bought a pound of figs: he gave $\frac{1}{3}$ to his mother, $\frac{1}{4}$ to his sister, and $\frac{1}{6}$ to his brother: what part had he left?

7. A farmer had $1\frac{1}{2}$ bushels of wheat: he gave to one poor man $\frac{1}{2}$ of a bushel, and to another $\frac{1}{3}$ of a bushel: how much wheat was left?

8. James had $\frac{7}{8}$ of a pound of raisins: he gave to his brother half of a pound, and to his sister $\frac{1}{4}$ of a pound: how much had he left?

9. A lady bought $3\frac{1}{3}$ yards of muslin at one store, and $2\frac{1}{4}$ yards at another: after using $1\frac{1}{2}$ yards, how much had she left?

10. William's father gave him $\$\frac{5}{8}$: he gave to a poor person $\$\frac{1}{8}$; for apples, $\$\frac{1}{16}$; and for a book, $\$\frac{1}{4}$: what part of a dollar had he left?

11. James' mother gave him a book: he read the first day $\frac{1}{5}$; the second, $\frac{1}{4}$; the third, $\frac{1}{2}$; and the fourth, the remainder: what part did he read the fourth day?

12. A farmer has a flock of 84 sheep in four fields: the first contains $\frac{1}{7}$; the second, $\frac{1}{2}$; and the third, $\frac{1}{4}$ of them: how many does the fourth field contain?

13. Daniel spends $\frac{1}{3}$ of his time in sleep, $\frac{1}{4}$ of it at school, $\frac{1}{12}$ in reading, and $\frac{1}{24}$ in learning music: what part of his time is not employed?

14. A pole is standing in a pond; $\frac{1}{2}$ of it is in the air, and $\frac{1}{3}$ in the water: what part is in the earth?

15. A student devotes $\frac{1}{4}$ of his time to sleep, $\frac{1}{3}$ to study, $\frac{1}{24}$ to reading, $\frac{1}{8}$ to exercise, and $\frac{1}{12}$ to deeds of charity: what part of his time is unemployed?

16. After spending $\frac{1}{2}$ and $\frac{1}{3}$ of my money, and losing $\frac{1}{12}$, I had \$8 remaining: how much had I at first?

LESSON 33

1. A mother gave each of her 3 children $\frac{1}{2}$ an orange: how many oranges did it take?

SOLUTION.—It took 3 times $\frac{1}{2}$ an orange, which are $\frac{3}{2}$. $\frac{3}{2} = 1\frac{1}{2}$ oranges.

2. John fed 5 horses, giving to each $\frac{1}{2}$ a peck of oats: how many pecks did it take?

3. James gave $\frac{1}{3}$ of an orange to each of his 4 sisters: how many did it take?

4. John gave $\frac{2}{3}$ of a pine-apple to each of his 2 brothers: how many did he give to both?

5. What are 4 times $\frac{2}{3}$?

SOLUTION.—4 times $\frac{2}{3}$ are $\frac{8}{3} = 2\frac{2}{3}$.

6. Thomas gave $\frac{1}{4}$ of an apple to each of his 6 playmates: how many apples did it take?

7. Charles gave $\frac{3}{4}$ of a pint of chestnuts to each of his 2 brothers: how many pints did it take?

8. Mary gave $\frac{3}{4}$ of an orange to each of her 3 brothers: how many oranges did it take?

9. What are 6 times $\frac{3}{4}$? 7 times $\frac{3}{4}$? 8 times $\frac{3}{4}$?

10. What are 3 times $\frac{1}{5}$? 5 times $\frac{2}{5}$? 6 times $\frac{3}{5}$?

11. What are 3 times $\frac{1}{7}$? 4 times $\frac{2}{7}$? 5 times $\frac{4}{7}$?

12. What are 5 times $\frac{1}{8}$? 2 times $\frac{3}{8}$? 4 times $\frac{7}{8}$?

13. What are 2 times $\frac{1}{9}$? 4 times $\frac{2}{9}$? 5 times $\frac{4}{9}$?

14. What are 8 times $\frac{3}{9}$? 6 times $\frac{6}{9}$? 7 times $\frac{8}{9}$?

15. What are 5 times $\frac{7}{6}$? 8 times $\frac{3}{5}$? 9 times $\frac{2}{5}$?

16. What are 7 times $\frac{5}{8}$? 6 times $\frac{7}{9}$? 8 times $\frac{3}{7}$?

17. What are 3 times $\frac{5}{4}$? 4 times $\frac{6}{5}$? 6 times $\frac{8}{7}$?

18. What are 7 times $\frac{5}{3}$? 8 times $\frac{5}{2}$? 9 times $\frac{4}{3}$?

LESSON 34

1. If 3 bushels of corn cost $1, what will 2 bushels cost?

SOLUTION.—1 bushel will cost $\$\frac{1}{3}$; then, 2 bushels will cost 2 times $\$\frac{1}{3} = \$\frac{2}{3}$.

2. If 3 bushels of wheat cost $2, what will 2 bushels cost?

3. If 3 barrels of cider cost $8, what will 2 barrels cost?

4. If 4 barrels of apples cost $9, what will 2 barrels cost?

5. If 5 apples cost 2 cents, what will 4 apples cost?

6. James bought 3 lemons for 7 cents, how much would 2 lemons cost?

7. William bought 5 quarts of chestnuts for 18 cents; at that rate, what did 4 quarts cost?

8. If 4 pounds of cheese sell for 30 cents, what should 3 pounds sell for?

9. What are $\frac{3}{4}$ of 9?

SOLUTION.—$\frac{1}{4}$ of 9 is $\frac{9}{4}$; then, $\frac{3}{4}$ of 9 are 3 times $\frac{9}{4}$, which are $\frac{27}{4} = 6\frac{3}{4}$.

10. What are $\frac{4}{5}$ of 6? 7? 8? 9? 11?
11. What are $\frac{5}{6}$ of 5? 7? 10? 11? 12?
12. What are $\frac{6}{7}$ of 8? 9? 10? 11? 12?
13. What are $\frac{7}{8}$ of 5? 7? 9? 11? 12?
14. What are $\frac{8}{9}$ of 6? 7? 8? 10? 12?
15. What are $\frac{9}{10}$ of 6? 8? 9? 11? 12?
16. What are $\frac{10}{11}$ of 3? 5? 8? 9? 12?
17. What are $\frac{11}{12}$ of 7? 8? 9? 10? 11?

18. If 4 men perform a piece of work in 8 days, how long will it take 5 men?

SOLUTION.—It will take 1 man 4 times 8 days = 32 days; then, it will take 5 men $\frac{1}{5}$ of 32 days = $6\frac{2}{5}$ days.

19. If one barrel of flour serve 8 persons 20 days, how long will it last 11 persons?

20. If 7 men can do a piece of work in 5 days, how long will it require 8 men?

21. If 2 men build a wall in 12 days, how long will it take 7 men?

22. If it require 11 days, of 8 hours each, to do a certain work, how many days, of 10 hours each, will be required to accomplish the same?

23. A man paid 37 cents for riding 8 miles: at the same rate, what will it cost to ride 11 miles?

24. If 2 pipes of a certain size empty a cistern in 17 minutes: in what time will 3 pipes empty it?

25. If 18 bushels of oats last 5 horses one week, how many bushels will 7 horses require?

26. If a laborer receive 5 bushels of wheat for 7 days' work, how much should he receive for 11 days?

27. If a carpenter earn $8 in 5 days, how much will he earn in 9 days?

28. A pole, 18 feet long, is two-sevenths in the earth, the rest in the air: what is the length of each part?

29. Three men found a bag containing $15: A got $\frac{2}{9}$, B $\frac{1}{3}$, and C the rest: what was the share of each?

30. If 3 ounces of snuff cost 36 cents, what should be charged for $\frac{2}{3}$ of an ounce?

31. A watchmaker sold a watch for $18, and lost $\frac{2}{5}$ of its value: how much did he lose?

32. A watchmaker sold a watch for $45, and gained $\frac{1}{4}$ of its cost: what was its cost?

1. William gave $1\frac{1}{2}$ oranges to each of his 2 sisters: how many oranges did it take?

SOLUTION.—$1\frac{1}{2} = \frac{3}{2}$. It took 2 times $\frac{3}{2}$ oranges, which are $\frac{6}{2} =$ 3 oranges.

2. How many are 3 times $2\frac{1}{2}$?

SOLUTION.—$2\frac{1}{2} = \frac{5}{2}$. 3 times $\frac{5}{2}$ are $\frac{15}{2} = 7\frac{1}{2}$.

3. If 1 bushel of wheat cost $\$1\frac{1}{3}$, what will 2 bushels cost?

4. How many are 3 times $1\frac{1}{3}$?   2 times $2\frac{2}{3}$?
5. How many are 3 times $3\frac{1}{3}$?   4 times $4\frac{1}{2}$?
6. How many are 5 times $2\frac{2}{3}$?   6 times $3\frac{2}{3}$?
7. How many are 8 times $3\frac{1}{3}$?   9 times $4\frac{2}{3}$?

8. If 1 bushel of barley cost $\$1\frac{1}{4}$, what will 3 bushels cost? 4 bushels?

9. How many are 5 times $1\frac{1}{4}$?   6 times $1\frac{1}{4}$?
10. How many are 2 times $1\frac{3}{4}$?   3 times $2\frac{1}{4}$?
11. How many are 4 times $3\frac{1}{4}$?   5 times $3\frac{3}{4}$?
12. How many are 6 times $3\frac{1}{4}$?   8 times $3\frac{3}{4}$?
13. How many are 7 times $2\frac{1}{4}$?   9 times $2\frac{3}{4}$?
14. How many are 10 times $1\frac{3}{4}$?   10 times $3\frac{1}{4}$?
15. How many are 12 times $3\frac{3}{4}$?

SOLUTION.—12 times $3 = 36$, 12 times $\frac{3}{4}$ are $\frac{36}{4} = 9$; $36 + 9 = 45$.

16. If a family consume $3\frac{1}{5}$ barrels of flour in one month, how much will they require for 3 months?

17. How many are 4 times $3\frac{2}{5}$?   5 times $3\frac{2}{5}$?

18. How many are 2 times $6\frac{3}{5}$?   3 times $2\frac{4}{5}$?

19. How many are 6 times $4\frac{1}{5}$?   6 times $3\frac{4}{5}$?

20. How many are 7 times $4\frac{2}{5}$?   8 times $3\frac{2}{5}$?

21. How many are 9 times $1\frac{4}{5}$?   9 times $3\frac{1}{5}$?

22. Three times $4\frac{1}{2}$ are how many?

23. Four times $4\frac{3}{4}$ are how many?

24. Five times $4\frac{2}{5}$ are how many?

25. Four times $6\frac{1}{3}$ are how many?

26. Five times $6\frac{1}{2}$ are how many?

27. Six times $6\frac{2}{3}$ are how many?

28. Seven times $6\frac{5}{6}$ are how many?

29. Four times $7\frac{3}{7}$ are how many?

30. Five times $7\frac{4}{7}$ are how many?

31. Six times $7\frac{6}{7}$ are how many?

32. Four times $8\frac{3}{8}$ are how many?

33. Five times $8\frac{1}{2}$ are how many?

34. Six times $8\frac{7}{8}$ are how many?

35. Three times $9\frac{5}{9}$ are how many?

36. Five times $9\frac{2}{3}$ are how many?

37. Seven times $9\frac{8}{9}$ are how many?

38. Two times $10\frac{3}{10}$ are how many?

39. Five times $10\frac{3}{5}$ are how many?

40. Six times $10\frac{4}{5}$ are how many?

41. Nine times $10\frac{7}{10}$ are how many?

42. Ten times $9\frac{8}{9}$ are how many?

43. Twelve times $11\frac{9}{11}$ are how many?

44. How many are $9\frac{5}{8}$ multiplied by 6?

45. How many are $7\frac{3}{5}$ multiplied by 7?

46. How many are $4\frac{10}{11}$ multiplied by 11?

47. How many are $10\frac{5}{6}$ multiplied by 11?

48. How many are $12\frac{8}{9}$ multiplied by 10?

LESSON 36

1. Bought 5 boxes of raisins, at $4\frac{4}{5}$ a box; paid for them with flour, at $6 a barrel: how many barrels did it take?

SOLUTION.—The raisins cost 5 times $4\frac{4}{5}$ = $24; then, it took as many barrels of flour to pay for them as $6 are contained times in $24, which are 4.

2. Bought 6 gallons of wine, for $4\frac{2}{3}$ a gallon, and paid for it with raisins, at $5 a box: how many boxes did it take?

3. Bought 7 kegs of tobacco, for $5\frac{4}{7}$ a keg, and paid for it with paper, at $6 a ream: how many reams did it take?

4. Five times $5\frac{2}{5}$ are how many times 6?

SOLUTION.—5 times $5\frac{3}{5}$ = 28. 28 ÷ 6 = $4\frac{2}{3}$.

5. Four times $4\frac{3}{4}$ are how many times 3? 5? 6? 8? 9? 10?

6. Six times $6\frac{5}{6}$ are how many times 4? 5? 7? 8? 9? 10?

7. Five times $5\frac{2}{5}$ are how many times 4? 6? 8? 9? 10?

8. Eight times $8\frac{1}{8}$ are how many times 5? 6? 7? 9? 10?

9. Seven times $6\frac{2}{7}$ are how many times 5? 8? 9? 10?

10. Ten times $5\frac{2}{5}$ are how many times 6? 7? 8? 9? 10?

11. Eight times $8\frac{3}{8}$ are how many times 6? 7? 9? 10? 11?

12. Seven times $7\frac{4}{7}$ are how many times 5? 6? 8? 9? 10?

13. Five times $5\frac{4}{5}$ are how many times 6? 7? 8? 9? 10?

14. Nine times $6\frac{1}{3}$ are how many times 5? 7? 8? 10? 11?

15. Seven times $7\frac{3}{7}$ are how many times 5? 6? 9? 10? 12?

16. Bought $4\frac{2}{3}$ yards of cloth, at $3 a yard, and paid for it with cheese, at $7 a hundred-weight: how many hundred-weights did it take?

SOLUTION.—The cloth cost $3 $\times$ $4\frac{2}{3}$ = $14; it took as many hundred-weights as $7 are contained times in $14, which are 2.

17. Bought $4\frac{4}{5}$ pounds of nails, at 5 cents a pound, and paid for them with eggs, at 12 cents a dozen: how many dozen did it take?

18. Bought $7\frac{5}{7}$ pounds of sugar, at 7 cents a pound, and paid for it with chickens, at 27 cents each: how many did it take?

19. Bought $9\frac{2}{7}$ pounds of sugar, at 7 cents a pound, and paid for it with eggs, at 13 cents a dozen: how many dozen did it take?

20. How many pounds of rice, at 7 cents a pound, can I get for $8\frac{2}{9}$ yards of calico, at 9 cents a yard?

21. How many barrels of flour, at $6 a barrel, must be given in exchange for $4\frac{5}{7}$ yards of cloth, at $7 a yard?

22. Bought $5\frac{3}{7}$ pounds of sugar, at 7 cents a pound, and paid for it with raisins, at 6 cents a pound: how many pounds did it take?

23. How many dozen eggs, at 12 cents a dozen, will pay for $10\frac{10}{11}$ pounds of sugar, at 11 cents a pound?

LESSON 37

1. Mary, having $\frac{1}{2}$ an orange, gave her brother $\frac{1}{2}$ of what she had: what part of an orange did she give him?

SOLUTION.—She gave to her brother $\frac{1}{2}$ of $\frac{1}{2}$ an orange, which is $\frac{1}{4}$ of an orange.

2. James divided $\frac{1}{3}$ of an apple equally between his two brothers: what part did each receive?

3. If $\frac{1}{4}$ of an orange is divided into 2 equal parts, what is 1 of the parts called?

4. If $\frac{1}{3}$ of an apple be cut into 3 equal parts, what part of the apple will each piece be?

5. If $\frac{1}{2}$ of an apple be divided into 5 equal parts, what is each part called?

6. If you divide an orange into 4 equal parts, and cut each part into 3 equal pieces, what will 1 piece be called?

What single fraction equals:

7. $\frac{1}{2}$ of $\frac{1}{7}$?

SOLUTION.—$\frac{1}{2}$ of $\frac{1}{7} = \frac{1}{14}$.

8. $\frac{1}{3}$ of $\frac{1}{5}$? $\frac{1}{4}$ of $\frac{1}{4}$? $\frac{1}{3}$ of $\frac{1}{6}$? $\frac{1}{4}$ of $\frac{1}{5}$? $\frac{1}{3}$ of $\frac{1}{7}$?

9. $\frac{1}{4}$ of $\frac{1}{6}$? $\frac{1}{3}$ of $\frac{1}{8}$? $\frac{1}{5}$ of $\frac{1}{5}$? $\frac{1}{3}$ of $\frac{1}{9}$? $\frac{1}{4}$ of $\frac{1}{7}$? $\frac{1}{5}$ of $\frac{1}{6}$?

10. $\frac{1}{4}$ of $\frac{1}{8}$? $\frac{1}{5}$ of $\frac{1}{7}$? $\frac{1}{6}$ of $\frac{1}{6}$? $\frac{1}{7}$ of $\frac{1}{7}$? $\frac{1}{8}$ of $\frac{1}{8}$? $\frac{1}{9}$ of $\frac{1}{9}$?

11. Thomas has $\frac{3}{4}$ of an apple, and wishes to give his brother $\frac{1}{2}$ of what he has: what part of the whole apple must he give him?

SOLUTION.—He must give him $\frac{1}{2}$ of $\frac{3}{4}$ of an apple; $\frac{1}{2}$ of $\frac{1}{4} = \frac{1}{8}$; then $\frac{1}{2}$ of $\frac{3}{4}$ is 3 times $\frac{1}{8} = \frac{3}{8}$.

12. Daniel has $\frac{3}{5}$ of a melon to divide equally between his brother and sister: how must he divide it, and what part of the whole will each receive?

13. What is $\frac{1}{3}$ of $\frac{2}{5}$?

SOLUTION.—$\frac{1}{3}$ of $\frac{1}{5} = \frac{1}{15}$; then, $\frac{1}{3}$ of $\frac{2}{5} = \frac{2}{15}$.

14. What is $\frac{1}{3}$ of $\frac{5}{6}$? $\frac{1}{4}$ of $\frac{3}{4}$? $\frac{1}{5}$ of $\frac{5}{6}$? $\frac{1}{6}$ of $\frac{3}{4}$?

15. What is $\frac{1}{6}$ of $\frac{4}{7}$? $\frac{1}{7}$ of $\frac{5}{8}$? $\frac{1}{9}$ of $\frac{5}{7}$? $\frac{1}{7}$ of $\frac{4}{5}$?

16. What is $\frac{1}{8}$ of $\frac{4}{9}$? $\frac{1}{9}$ of $\frac{5}{9}$? $\frac{1}{10}$ of $\frac{7}{9}$? $\frac{1}{11}$ of $\frac{8}{9}$?

17. Edward has $\frac{4}{5}$ of a melon, and gives his sister $\frac{2}{3}$ of what he has: what part of the melon does she receive?

SOLUTION.—She receives $\frac{2}{3}$ of $\frac{4}{5}$ of a melon. $\frac{1}{3}$ of $\frac{4}{5}$ is $\frac{4}{15}$; then, $\frac{2}{3}$ of $\frac{4}{5}$ are 2 times $\frac{4}{15} = \frac{8}{15}$.

18. What are $\frac{2}{3}$ of $\frac{3}{4}$?

SOLUTION.—$\frac{1}{3}$ of $\frac{3}{4}$ is $\frac{1}{4}$; then, $\frac{2}{3}$ of $\frac{3}{4}$ are $\frac{2}{4} = \frac{1}{2}$.

19. What are $\frac{2}{3}$ of $\frac{3}{5}$? $\frac{3}{4}$ of $\frac{6}{5}$? $\frac{2}{3}$ of $\frac{5}{6}$? $\frac{3}{4}$ of $\frac{2}{7}$?

20. What are $\frac{3}{5}$ of $\frac{3}{8}$? $\frac{2}{5}$ of $\frac{3}{7}$? $\frac{5}{6}$ of $\frac{4}{7}$? $\frac{2}{3}$ of $\frac{7}{10}$?

21. What are $\frac{3}{5}$ of $\frac{8}{9}$? $\frac{2}{7}$ of $\frac{5}{11}$? $\frac{3}{8}$ of $\frac{5}{7}$? $\frac{5}{7}$ of $\frac{4}{9}$?

22. What are $\frac{3}{2}$ of $\frac{5}{6}$? $\frac{6}{5}$ of $\frac{2}{9}$? $\frac{9}{10}$ of $\frac{7}{6}$? $\frac{7}{8}$ of $\frac{4}{3}$?

23. What are $\frac{9}{8}$ of $\frac{7}{5}$? $\frac{8}{3}$ of $\frac{11}{7}$? $\frac{11}{12}$ of $\frac{5}{6}$? $\frac{6}{5}$ of $\frac{12}{11}$?

24. A person, owning $\frac{3}{4}$ of a ship, sold $\frac{5}{6}$ of his share: what part of the ship did he sell?

25. A banker, owning $\frac{4}{5}$ of the entire stock of a bank, disposed of $\frac{3}{7}$ of his share: what part of the stock did he sell?

26. If a man sell $\frac{2}{9}$ of $\frac{7}{10}$ of his stock of merchandise, what amount does he sell?

27. I buy $\frac{8}{11}$ of $\frac{2}{3}$ of the shares in a corporation, how much do I buy?

28. $\frac{4}{3}$ of $\frac{6}{7}$ of $\frac{5}{12}$ are how many?

LESSON 38

1. If 1 yard of cloth is worth $2\frac{1}{2}$ bushels of wheat, what is $\frac{1}{2}$ a yard worth?

SOLUTION.—$2\frac{1}{2} = \frac{5}{2}$; $\frac{1}{2}$ of $\frac{5}{2} = \frac{5}{4}$, or $1\frac{1}{4}$ bushels.

What single fraction will represent:

2. $\frac{1}{3}$ of $2\frac{1}{2}$? $\frac{1}{2}$ of $1\frac{1}{4}$? $\frac{1}{3}$ of $1\frac{3}{4}$? $\frac{1}{4}$ of $2\frac{1}{5}$? $\frac{1}{5}$ of $3\frac{1}{4}$?

3. $\frac{1}{6}$ of $4\frac{2}{3}$? $\frac{1}{7}$ of $5\frac{1}{6}$? $\frac{2}{3}$ of $1\frac{1}{2}$? $\frac{3}{4}$ of $1\frac{2}{3}$? $\frac{2}{7}$ of $1\frac{1}{3}$?

4. $\frac{2}{5}$ of $4\frac{1}{3}$? $\frac{3}{5}$ of $2\frac{2}{7}$? $\frac{5}{8}$ of $3\frac{1}{2}$? $\frac{3}{8}$ of $2\frac{1}{8}$? $\frac{3}{7}$ of $4\frac{5}{9}$?

5. If 2 yards of cloth cost $1\frac{1}{3}$, what will 3 yards cost?

6. If 3 yards of cloth cost $5\frac{1}{2}$, what will 2 yards cost?

7. If 4 gallons of molasses cost $3\frac{2}{3}$, what will 3 gallons cost?

8. If 7 pounds of sugar cost $1\frac{1}{7}$, what will 4 pounds cost?

9. If 4 pounds of butter cost $1\frac{1}{4}$, what will 7 pounds cost?

10. If 7 yards of cloth cost $5\frac{3}{5}$, what will be the cost of 3 yards? Of 4 yards?

11. If 2 barrels of cider cost $4\frac{2}{3}$, what part of that sum will 5 barrels cost?

12. If 5 gallons of oil cost $2\frac{2}{5}$, what part of that sum will 7 gallons cost?

13. If 3 bottles of wine cost $2\frac{1}{3}$, what will be the cost of 8 bottles? Of 10 bottles?

14. A man can perform a piece of work in $3\frac{2}{3}$ days, of 10 hours each: how many days, of 7 hours each, will it take?

15. If a man can do a piece of work in $14\frac{2}{5}$ days, working 5 hours a day, how many days will it take, working 8 hours a day?

LESSON 39

1. A jockey, by selling a horse for $45, gained $\frac{1}{8}$ of the cost: what was the cost?

SOLUTION.—$45 are $\frac{8}{8} + \frac{1}{8} = \frac{9}{8}$ of the cost; then, $\frac{1}{8}$ of the cost is $\frac{1}{9}$ of $45 = 5, and the cost is 8 times $5 = $40.

2. James gave his brother 4 marbles, which were $\frac{2}{3}$ of all he had: how many had he?

3. Thomas sold a knife for 15 cents, which was $\frac{3}{5}$ of its cost: how much did it cost?

4. William lost 6 marbles, which were $\frac{3}{8}$ of all he had: how many had he?

5. I sold a horse for $42, which was $\frac{6}{5}$ of its cost: what was its cost?

6. A grocer sold a lot of flour for $40, which was $\frac{5}{4}$ of the cost: what was the cost?

7. Sold a horse for $56, which was $\frac{8}{5}$ of the cost: what was the cost?

8. A man sold a watch for $28, which was $\frac{4}{3}$ of its cost: what was its cost?

9. A man sold a pony for $45, which was $\frac{5}{3}$ of its cost: what was the cost?

10. A man purchased a horse: after paying $\frac{3}{5}$ of the price, he owed $20: what was the price of the horse? How much money did he pay?

11. Alexander sold a book for 25 cents, and lost $\frac{2}{7}$ of the cost: what was the cost?

12. In an orchard there are 12 cherry-trees: the remaining $\frac{5}{7}$ of the orchard are apple-trees: how many trees are there in the orchard?

13. Four-fifths of a stick are under water, and 6 feet are out of water: how long is the stick?

14. There is a pole, $\frac{2}{3}$ of which are in the earth, and 12 feet are in the air: how long is the pole?

15. A piece of timber stands $\frac{5}{7}$ in the air, and 5 feet in the ground: how long is the entire piece?

16. $\frac{1}{5}$ of a pole is in the mud, $\frac{2}{5}$ are in the water, and 14 feet in the air: how long is the pole?

17. A man gave to some poor persons $4, which was $\frac{2}{5}$ of his money: how much had he left?

18. At $8 a yard, $\frac{1}{5}$ of the cost of a piece of cloth was lost: what was the cost?

19. If $\frac{2}{5}$ of the cost of a horse were $64, and it was bought with flour, at $4 a barrel: how many barrels did it take?

20. If $\frac{7}{9}$ of a cask of wine cost $42, how much flour, at $8 a barrel, will pay for a whole cask?

21. If $\frac{4}{5}$ of a yard of muslin cost 8 cents, how many yards can be purchased for 25 cents?

22. If $\frac{6}{7}$ of a yard of cloth cost $4, how many yards can be purchased for $12.

23. By selling 5 yards of cloth for $12, I gained $\frac{1}{3}$ of the cost: what did I pay per yard?

24. If $\frac{3}{4}$ of a pound of raisins cost 9 cents, how many lemons, at 2 cents each, will pay for a pound?

25. If $\frac{2}{3}$ of a pound of coffee cost 16 cents, how many oranges, at 4 cents each, will pay for one pound?

26. If $\frac{7}{8}$ of a barrel of wine cost $42, how many barrels of cider, at $6 each, will pay for a barrel of wine?

27. If $\frac{3}{5}$ of a barrel of sugar cost $12, how many barrels of flour, at $10 a barrel, will pay for a barrel of sugar?

2° Sold a horse for $50, which was $\frac{5}{8}$ of his cost: paid for him with cloth, at $4 a yard: how many yards did I give?

LESSON 40

1. 12 is $\frac{4}{7}$ of how many times 5?

SOLUTION.—12 is $\frac{4}{7}$ of 21; $21 \div 5 = 4\frac{1}{5}$.

2. 18 is $\frac{3}{8}$ of how many times 9?
3. 16 is $\frac{2}{7}$ of how many times 9?
4. 36 is $\frac{4}{7}$ of how many times 8?
5. 45 is $\frac{5}{9}$ of how many times 7?
6. 24 is $\frac{4}{3}$ of how many times 5?
7. 72 is $\frac{8}{5}$ of how many times 7?
8. 81 is $\frac{9}{4}$ of how many times 3?
9. 50 is $\frac{10}{7}$ of how many times 4?
10. 63 is $\frac{7}{6}$ of how many times 5?
11. 56 is $\frac{8}{3}$ of how many times 7?

12. A man, having 12 bushels of grain, divided $\frac{5}{6}$ of it among 3 poor persons equally: how many bushels did each receive?

SOLUTION.—$\frac{5}{6}$ of 12 bushels are 10 bushels. Each person received $\frac{1}{3}$ of 10 bushels $= 3\frac{1}{3}$ bushels.

13. A boy, having 25 apples, kept $\frac{1}{5}$ himself, and divided the other $\frac{4}{5}$ equally among 6 companions: how many did each receive?

14. $\frac{3}{4}$ of 24 are how many times 9?

SOLUTION.—$\frac{3}{4}$ of $24 = 18$; $18 \div 9 = 2$.

15. $\frac{7}{4}$ of 24 are how many times 8?
16. $\frac{8}{3}$ of 18 are how many times 6?
17. $\frac{7}{3}$ of 27 are how many times 10?
18. $\frac{3}{5}$ of 60 are how many times 7?
19. $\frac{5}{6}$ of 66 are how many times 8?
20. $\frac{5}{8}$ of 48 are how many times 9?

21. $\frac{3}{7}$ of 56 are how many times 9?

22. $\frac{9}{7}$ of 63 are how many times 10?

23. $\frac{5}{8}$ of 64 are how many times 6?

24. $\frac{5}{6}$ of 40 are how many times 7?

25. $\frac{11}{7}$ of 49 are how many times 8?

26. $\frac{5}{6}$ of 54 are how many times 7?

27. $\frac{10}{9}$ of 63 are how many times 8?

28. $\frac{8}{9}$ of 54 are how many times 5?

29. $\frac{9}{7}$ of 42 are how many times 8?

30. $\frac{7}{11}$ of 55 are how many times 6?

31. $\frac{3}{4}$ of 72 are how many times 10?

32. $\frac{2}{3}$ of 96 are how many times 11?

LESSON 41

1. At $\$\frac{1}{2}$ a yard, how much cloth can be bought for $\$\frac{1}{3}$?

SOLUTION.—For $1, 2 times 1 yard = 2 yards can be bought; then, for $\$\frac{1}{3}$, $\frac{1}{3}$ of 2 yards $= \frac{2}{3}$ of a yard can be bought.

2. At $\$\frac{1}{3}$ a yard, how much gingham can be purchased for $\$\frac{1}{4}$?

3. At $\$\frac{1}{2}$ a yard, how much alpaca can be purchased for $\$\frac{1}{5}$?

4. At $\$\frac{1}{3}$ a bushel, how much corn can be bought for $\$\frac{1}{5}$?

5. At $\$\frac{2}{3}$ a yard, how much cloth can be purchased for $\$\frac{3}{4}$?

SOLUTION.—For $\$\frac{1}{3}$, $\frac{1}{2}$ a yard can be purchased, and for $1, \frac{3}{2}$ of a yard; then, for $\$\frac{1}{4}$, $\frac{1}{4}$ of $\frac{3}{2}$, or $\frac{3}{8}$ of a yard can be purchased, and for $\$\frac{3}{4}$, $\frac{9}{8} = 1\frac{1}{8}$ yards.

6. If a pound of coffee is worth $\$\frac{2}{5}$, how much can John buy for $\$\frac{2}{3}$?

7. If a pound of tea cost $\$\frac{4}{5}$, how much tea can you purchase for $\$\frac{2}{3}$?

8. At $\$\frac{2}{5}$ for one yard, how much cloth can be bought for $\$\frac{3}{4}$? How much for $\$\frac{5}{6}$? For one dollar?

9. One bushel of rye is worth $\frac{3}{4}$ of a bushel of wheat: how much rye is worth $\frac{4}{5}$ of a bushel of wheat? How much is worth 1 bushel?

10. Divide $\frac{1}{5}$ by $\frac{1}{4}$.

SOLUTION.—$\frac{1}{5}$ divided by $\frac{1}{4}$ is 4 times $\frac{1}{5} = \frac{4}{5}$.

11. Divide $\frac{1}{6}$ by $\frac{1}{5}$. By $\frac{1}{4}$. By $\frac{1}{3}$.
12 Divide $\frac{1}{7}$ by $\frac{1}{6}$. By $\frac{1}{5}$. By $\frac{1}{4}$.
13. Divide $\frac{1}{8}$ by $\frac{1}{7}$. By $\frac{1}{6}$. By $\frac{1}{5}$.
14. Divide $\frac{4}{5}$ by $\frac{2}{3}$.

SOLUTION.—$\frac{4}{5} \div \frac{1}{3} = \frac{12}{5}$; then, $\frac{4}{5} \div \frac{2}{3} = \frac{1}{2}$ of $\frac{12}{5}$, which is $\frac{6}{5} = 1\frac{1}{5}$.

15. Divide $\frac{4}{5}$ by $\frac{3}{4}$.
16. Divide $\frac{5}{6}$ by $\frac{4}{5}$. By $\frac{3}{4}$. By $\frac{2}{3}$.
17. Divide $\frac{6}{7}$ by $\frac{5}{6}$. By $\frac{4}{5}$. By $\frac{3}{4}$.
18. Divide $\frac{7}{8}$ by $\frac{6}{7}$. By $\frac{5}{6}$. By $\frac{4}{5}$.
19. Divide $\frac{7}{8}$ by $\frac{3}{4}$.

SOLUTION.—$\frac{7}{8} \div \frac{3}{4}$ is the same as $\frac{7}{8} \times \frac{4}{3} = \frac{28}{24}$, or $1\frac{1}{6}$.

20. Divide $\frac{8}{9}$ by $\frac{7}{8}$. By $\frac{6}{7}$. By $\frac{5}{6}$.
21. Divide $\frac{9}{10}$ by $\frac{8}{9}$. By $\frac{7}{8}$. By $\frac{6}{7}$.
22. Divide $\frac{10}{11}$ by $\frac{9}{10}$. By $\frac{8}{9}$. By $\frac{7}{8}$.
23. Divide $\frac{11}{12}$ by $\frac{10}{11}$. By $\frac{9}{10}$. By $\frac{8}{9}$.
24. Divide $\frac{6}{5}$ by $\frac{2}{3}$. $\frac{7}{6}$ by $\frac{3}{4}$. $\frac{8}{7}$ by $\frac{4}{5}$.
25. Divide $\frac{4}{3}$ by $\frac{5}{8}$. $\frac{9}{8}$ by $\frac{4}{7}$. $\frac{9}{6}$ by $\frac{6}{9}$.
26. Divide $\frac{10}{9}$ by $\frac{10}{11}$. $\frac{11}{10}$ by $\frac{10}{12}$. $\frac{12}{11}$ by $\frac{7}{4}$.
27. Divide $\frac{8}{3}$ by $\frac{8}{5}$. $\frac{7}{4}$ by $\frac{7}{8}$. $\frac{6}{5}$ by $\frac{5}{6}$.
28. Divide $\frac{12}{7}$ by $\frac{11}{7}$. $\frac{10}{9}$ by $\frac{2}{5}$. $\frac{11}{3}$ by $\frac{6}{5}$.

LESSON 42

1. A man, having $10\frac{2}{7}$ acres of land, divided it equally among his 6 children: how much did each receive?

SOLUTION.—$10\frac{2}{7} = \frac{72}{7}$. Each received $\frac{1}{6}$ of $\frac{72}{7}$ acres, which is $\frac{12}{7}$, or $1\frac{5}{7}$ acres.

2. If $2\frac{4}{5}$ be divided by 7, what will be the result?

3. How many times is 6 contained in $3\frac{3}{5}$?

4. How many times is 9 contained in $6\frac{3}{4}$?

5. Divide $8\frac{3}{4}$ by 5. $7\frac{2}{4}$ by 10.

6. Divide $4\frac{5}{7}$ by 11. $8\frac{4}{7}$ by 12.

7. If $1\frac{1}{2}$ yards of ribbon cost 6 cents, what will 1 yard cost?

SOLUTION.—$1\frac{1}{2} = \frac{3}{2}$. $\frac{1}{2}$ a yard cost $\frac{1}{3}$ of 6 cents $= 2$ cents; then, 1 yard cost 2 times 2 cents $= 4$ cents.

8. If $1\frac{1}{3}$ yards of cloth cost \$4, what will 1 yard cost?

9. If a man travel 9 miles in $1\frac{2}{7}$ hours, how far will he travel in 1 hour?

10. A watch was sold for \$18, which equaled $1\frac{1}{5}$ of what it cost me: how much did it cost?

11. A grocer sold a lot of flour for \$25, which was $1\frac{1}{4}$ times the cost: what did it cost? How much did he gain?

12. If a man pays \$6 for $1\frac{1}{3}$ yards of cloth, what is the cost of 1 yard?

13. If a man receives \$10 for $2\frac{2}{3}$ days work, how much is that a day?

14. If a man receives \$12 for $6\frac{2}{5}$ days work, how much is that a day?

15. How many are 9 divided by $3\frac{3}{4}$?

16. How many are 10 divided by $2\frac{1}{7}$?

17. How many are 11 divided by $4\frac{8}{9}$?

72

LESSON 43

1. If a yard of cloth cost $\frac{2}{3}$, how many yards will cost $4\frac{6}{7}$?

SOLUTION.—$4\frac{6}{7} = \frac{34}{7}$. As many yards as $\frac{2}{3}$ are contained times in $\frac{34}{7}$, which are $\frac{51}{7} = 7\frac{2}{7}$.

2. When a bushel of corn costs $\frac{1}{2}$, how many bushels can you buy for $1\frac{1}{2}$?

3. I distributed $2\frac{2}{3}$ bushels of wheat among a number of poor persons, giving to each $\frac{2}{3}$ of a bushel: how many persons were there?

4. At $\frac{1}{4}$ a yard, how many yards of alpaca can be purchased for $3\frac{3}{4}$?

5. At $\frac{3}{4}$ a yard, how many yards of cloth can be purchased for $3\frac{1}{4}$?

6. If an apple cost $\frac{3}{4}$ of a cent, how many apples can be purchased for $3\frac{3}{4}$ cents? For $5\frac{1}{4}$ cents?

7. If a yard of cloth cost $\frac{2}{3}$, how many yards can you purchase for $4\frac{1}{3}$?

8. How often is $1\frac{1}{2}$ contained in $\frac{3}{4}$? In $\frac{4}{5}$? In $2\frac{3}{4}$?

9. How often is $2\frac{1}{4}$ contained in $\frac{5}{6}$? In $\frac{5}{7}$? In $3\frac{7}{8}$?

10. How often is $3\frac{1}{5}$ contained in $\frac{3}{8}$? In $\frac{3}{7}$? In $5\frac{3}{5}$?

11. $5\frac{1}{3}$ is $\frac{1}{2}$ of what number? $\frac{1}{5}$ of what number?

12. $7\frac{3}{4}$ is $\frac{1}{3}$ of what number? $\frac{1}{7}$ of what number?

13. $9\frac{2}{8}$ are $\frac{5}{8}$ of what number? $\frac{5}{6}$ of what number?

14. $4\frac{2}{3}$ are $\frac{2}{5}$ of what number? $\frac{5}{6}$ of what number?

15. $3\frac{2}{3}$ are $\frac{3}{4}$ of what number? $\frac{3}{5}$ of what number?

16. How often is $\frac{1}{6}$ contained in $3\frac{5}{6}$? In $5\frac{1}{6}$? In $4\frac{4}{6}$?

17. How often are $\frac{3}{5}$ contained in $2\frac{2}{5}$? In $4\frac{3}{5}$? In $6\frac{1}{5}$?

18. How often are $\frac{3}{7}$ contained in $3\frac{2}{7}$? In $4\frac{2}{3}$? In $7\frac{3}{4}$?

19. How often are $\frac{5}{8}$ contained in $4\frac{3}{4}$? In $5\frac{3}{5}$? In $8\frac{4}{7}$?

20. How often are $\frac{2}{3}$ contained in $2\frac{3}{10}$? In $6\frac{9}{11}$? In $9\frac{5}{12}$? In $10\frac{2}{3}$?

21. At $\$\frac{2}{5}$ a gallon, how many gallons of vinegar can you buy for $\$2\frac{2}{5}$? For $\$4\frac{1}{5}$?

22. One bushel of rye is worth $\frac{3}{4}$ of a bushel of wheat: how many bushels of rye can be bought with $4\frac{1}{2}$ bushels of wheat? With $8\frac{1}{4}$ bushels?

LESSON 44

The examples in this lesson are to be solved by using the following tables, where applicable:

I.—FRACTIONAL PARTS OF 12.

$$2 = \tfrac{1}{6} \qquad 6 = \tfrac{1}{2}.$$
$$3 = \tfrac{1}{4} \qquad 8 = \tfrac{2}{3}.$$
$$4 = \tfrac{1}{3} \qquad 9 = \tfrac{3}{4}.$$
$$10 = \tfrac{5}{6}.$$

II.—FRACTIONAL PARTS OF 100.

$$12\tfrac{1}{2} = \tfrac{1}{8} \qquad 37\tfrac{1}{2} = \tfrac{3}{8}.$$
$$16\tfrac{2}{3} = \tfrac{1}{6} \qquad 50 = \tfrac{1}{2}.$$
$$20 = \tfrac{1}{5} \qquad 62\tfrac{1}{2} = \tfrac{5}{8}.$$
$$25 = \tfrac{1}{4} \qquad 66\tfrac{2}{3} = \tfrac{2}{3}.$$
$$33\tfrac{1}{3} = \tfrac{1}{3} \qquad 75 = \tfrac{3}{4}.$$
$$87\tfrac{1}{2} = \tfrac{7}{8}.$$

1. Bought $\frac{3}{4}$ of a dozen shirts, at $\$24$ a dozen: what did they cost?

SOLUTION.—They cost $\frac{3}{4}$ of $\$24 = \$18$.

2. Bought $\frac{2}{3}$ of a dozen linen collars, at $\$3$ a dozen: what did they cost?

3. Bought $\frac{5}{6}$ of a dozen handkerchiefs, at $\$4$ a dozen: how much did they cost?

4. A grocer bought $6\frac{1}{2}$ dozen eggs, for 16 cents a dozen: how much did they cost?

5. Bought $1\frac{2}{3}$ dozen pairs of hose, for $2\frac{2}{5}$ a dozen: how much did they cost? What did each pair cost?

SOLUTION.—$1\frac{2}{3} = \frac{5}{3}$; $2\frac{2}{5} = \frac{12}{5}$. They cost $\frac{5}{3}$ of $\$\frac{12}{5} = \$4$. Each pair cost $\frac{1}{12}$ of $\$\frac{12}{5} = \$\frac{1}{5}$.

6. Bought $2\frac{1}{4}$ dozen copy-books, for $\$1\frac{1}{5}$ a dozen: how much did they cost? What was the cost of each book?

7. A merchant bought $6\frac{1}{2}$ dozen knives, for $\$1\frac{4}{5}$ a dozen: what did they cost? What did 1 knife cost?

8. Paid $5 a set, or $\frac{1}{2}$ dozen, for $2\frac{1}{2}$ dozen spoons: what did they cost?

9. Bought $4\frac{1}{6}$ dozen spelling-books, at $\$2\frac{1}{4}$ a dozen: how much did they cost? What did 1 book cost?

10. A man bought $2\frac{1}{4}$ dozen handkerchiefs, for $\$6\frac{3}{4}$: how much was that apiece?

SOLUTION.—$2\frac{1}{4} = \frac{9}{4}$; $6\frac{3}{4} = \frac{27}{4}$. He bought $\frac{1}{9}$ of a dozen, or 3, handkerchiefs, for $\frac{1}{9}$ of $\$\frac{27}{4} = \$\frac{3}{4}$; then, 1 handkerchief cost $\frac{1}{3}$ of $\$\frac{3}{4} = \$\frac{1}{4}$.

11. A merchant paid $3\frac{1}{10}$ for $7\frac{3}{4}$ dozen pairs of damaged hose, and sold them for $\$\frac{1}{10}$ a pair: how much did he gain on each pair?

12. A merchant paid $15 for $2\frac{1}{2}$ dozen silk handkerchiefs, and sold them for $\$\frac{3}{5}$ apiece: how much did he gain on each handkerchief? How much on the whole lot?

13. Paid $\$18\frac{3}{4}$ for $6\frac{1}{4}$ dozen knives, and sold them for $\$2\frac{1}{10}$ a set, or $\frac{1}{2}$ doz.: how much did I gain?

14. What will 16 pounds of soap cost, at $12\frac{1}{2}$ cents a pound?

SOLUTION.—$12\frac{1}{2}$ cents $= \$\frac{1}{8}$; then, 16 pounds will cost 16 times $\$\frac{1}{8} = \frac{16}{8}$, or $2.

15. What will 12 pounds of prunes cost, at $16\frac{2}{3}$ cents a pound?

16. What will 24 yards of alpaca cost, at $37\frac{1}{2}$ cents a yard?

17. What will 16 yards of flannel cost, at $62\frac{1}{2}$ cents a yard?

18. What will 15 pounds of coffee cost, at $33\frac{1}{3}$ cents a pound?

19. What will 27 yards of flannel cost, at $66\frac{2}{3}$ cents a yard?

20. What will 15 yards of cloth cost, at 1.66\frac{2}{3}$ a yard?

21. Paid $12 for coffee, at $33\frac{1}{3}$ cents a pound: how many pounds did I buy?

SOLUTION.—$33\frac{1}{3}$ cents $=\$\frac{1}{3}$. I bought as many pounds as $\frac{1}{3}$ is contained times in 12, which are 36.

22. Paid $1\frac{1}{4}$ for eggs, at $12\frac{1}{2}$ cents a dozen: how many dozen did I buy?

23. Paid $7\frac{1}{2}$ for flannel, at $62\frac{1}{2}$ cents a yard: how many yards did I buy?

24. Paid $8 for flannel, at $66\frac{2}{3}$ cents a yard: how many yards did I buy?

25. Multiply 32 by $12\frac{1}{2}$.

SOLUTION.—$12\frac{1}{2} = \frac{1}{8}$ of 100; then, $32 \times 12\frac{1}{2} = 32 \div 8 \times 100 = 400$.

26. Multiply 18 by 50.   40 by $62\frac{1}{2}$.   68 by 75.
27. Multiply 48 by 75.   24 by $37\frac{1}{2}$.   51 by $33\frac{1}{3}$.
28. Multiply 39 by $66\frac{2}{3}$.   64 by $87\frac{1}{2}$.   96 by $62\frac{1}{2}$.
29. Divide 150 by $12\frac{1}{2}$.

SOLUTION.—$150 \div 12\frac{1}{2} = 150 \times 8 \div 100 = 12$.

30. Divide 200 by $16\frac{2}{3}$.   560 by 20.   250 by 25.
31. Divide 350 by $37\frac{1}{2}$.   600 by 50.   750 by $62\frac{1}{2}$.

REVIEW.

LESSON 45

1. William had 23 cents: Thomas gave him 8 cents more, George 6, James 5, and David 7; he gave 15 cents for a book: how many cents had he left?

2. A grocer paid $12 for sugar, $9 for coffee, $5 for tea, $7 for flour, and had $10 left: how many dollars had he at first?

3. A boy has 11 cents: his father gives him 9 cents, his mother 6, and his sister enough more to make 34: how many cents does his sister give him?

4. Five men bought a horse for $42: the first gave $13; the second, $7; the third, $5; and the fourth, $9: how many dollars did the fifth give?

5. A man purchased 8 sheep, at $4 a head; 5 barrels of flour, at $3 a barrel; 4 yards of cloth, at $3 a yard; and 5 ounces of opium, at $1 an ounce: how much did he spend?

6. A boy lost 25 cents: after finding 15 cents, he had 25: how many cents had he at first?

7. A man owed a debt of $28, and paid all but $9: how much did he pay?

8. Borrowed $56: at one time I paid $23; at another, all but $7: how much did I pay the last time?

9. James borrowed 37 cents: at one time he paid 5 cents, at another 8, and the third time, all but 15: how many cents did he pay the third time?

10. A farmer sold 1 cow, at $18, and 5 pigs, at $3 each, receiving in payment 3 sheep, at $3 each, and the rest in money: how much money did he receive?

11. A farmer sold 12 barrels of cider, at $3 a barrel: he then purchased 5 barrels of salt, at $3 a barrel, and some sugar, for $8: how many dollars had he left?

12. A merchant purchased 13 hats, at $4 each; 5 pairs of shoes, at $2 a pair; and an umbrella, for $7: what must he sell the whole for to gain $9?

13. If 2 barrels of flour cost $12, what will 7 barrels cost? 5 barrels?

14. If 3 barrels of cider cost $12, what will 4 barrels cost? 9 barrels?

15. If 4 yards of cloth cost $28, what will 7 yards cost?

16. If 5 tons of hay cost $35, what will 8 tons cost?

17. If 7 apples cost 28 cents, what will 3 apples cost?

18. If 8 oranges are worth 24 apples, how many apples are 3 oranges worth?

19. If 2 pounds of cheese cost 36 cents, what will 3 pounds cost?

20. If 8 yards of cloth cost $56, what will 7 yards cost?

21. If 9 yards of calico cost 72 cents, what will 6 yards cost? 8 yards? 10 yards?

22. A walks 5 miles, while B walks 3: when A has gone 35 miles, how far has B gone?

23. Joseph and his father are husking corn: the father can husk 7 rows while Joseph husks 3: how many rows will Joseph husk while his father husks 42?

24. Charles can earn $9 while Mary earns $4: how many dollars will Charles earn while Mary earns $28.

25. If 6 horses eat 12 bushels of oats in a week, how many bushels will 10 horses eat in the same time?

26. If five horses eat 16 bushels in 2 weeks, how long would it take them to eat 56 bushels?

27. If 6 apples are worth 18 cents, how many apples must be given for 5 oranges, worth 6 cents each?

28. How many horses can eat in 9 days the same amount of hay that 12 horses eat in 6 days?

LESSON 46

1. If 4 yards of cloth cost $16, what will 5 yards cost? 9 yards?

2. What are $\frac{8}{9}$ of 72? $\frac{2}{8}$ of 72?

3. If you had 64 cents, how many oranges could you buy, at 8 cents each?

4. Ninety-six is how many times 6?

5. James had 48 chestnuts: he gave $\frac{1}{2}$ of them to his brother, and $\frac{1}{3}$ to his sister: how many had he left?

6. Nine times 9 are how many times 12?

7. In $8\frac{5}{9}$ how many ninths? In $9\frac{1}{5}$?

8. Reduce $\frac{48}{120}$, $\frac{54}{189}$, $\frac{240}{288}$, to their lowest terms.

9. Reduce $\frac{3}{9}$, $\frac{4}{16}$, $\frac{17}{72}$, to a least common denominator.

10. A farmer planted $4\frac{1}{2}$ acres in potatoes, $20\frac{3}{4}$ acres in wheat, and $24\frac{7}{8}$ acres in oats: how many acres did he plant?

11. From $9\frac{3}{8}$ take $5\frac{2}{3}$.

12. A man having 84 miles to travel, went $\frac{1}{4}$ of the distance the first day, $\frac{1}{3}$ the second, and the rest the third day: what part did he travel the last day, and how far?

13. What are 9 times $\frac{7}{18}$?

14. What are $\frac{7}{11}$ of 12?

15. If 4 yards of cloth cost $15, what will 7 yards cost?

16. How many are 7 times $7\frac{5}{7}$?

17. Four times $6\frac{3}{7}$ are how many times 7?

18. Bought $8\frac{3}{4}$ pounds of sugar, at 8 cents a pound, and paid for it with milk, at 5 cents a quart: how many quarts did it take?

19. What are $\frac{5}{6}$ of $\frac{3}{4}$ of $\frac{2}{3}$ of 6?

20. If 6 kegs of tar cost $\$1\frac{3}{10}$, what will 9 kegs cost?

21. A farmer sold a horse for $99, and gained $\frac{2}{8}$ of its cost: what did it cost?

22. If $\frac{4}{5}$ of the cost of a horse was $96, and it was paid with flour, at $6 a barrel, how many barrels did it take?

23. 84 is $\frac{7}{6}$ of how many times 9?

24. $\frac{9}{25}$ of 125 are how many times 5?

25. $\frac{8}{9}$ of 81 are $\frac{9}{8}$ of what number?

26. $\frac{4}{7}$ of 35 are $\frac{5}{6}$ of how many times $\frac{3}{8}$ of 16?

27. If a man pays $\$17\frac{1}{2}$ for $4\frac{3}{8}$ yards of cloth, what is the cost of 1 yard?

28. If an apple is worth $\frac{3}{4}$ of a cent, how many apples can be purchased for 18 cents?

29. $7\frac{2}{3}$ are $\frac{5}{7}$ of what number?

30. Bought $3\frac{1}{2}$ dozen hinges, at $\$1\frac{1}{3}$ a dozen: how much did they cost?

31. Bought 30 yards of percale, at $12\frac{1}{2}$ cents a yard: how many dollars did it cost?

32. Paid $\$7\frac{3}{4}$ for alpaca, at $33\frac{1}{3}$ cents a yard: how many yards did I buy?

33. How much a day must a man earn to receive $72 for 8 weeks, 6 days to the week?

34. If $\$2\frac{2}{3}$ are divided equally among 4 boys, what is each boy's share?

35. At 5 lemons for 3 cents, how many lemons can be bought for 12 cents?

36. If $1\frac{1}{3}$ yards of cloth cost $8, how much can be purchased for $12?

37. The age of Joseph is 20 years, which is $\frac{2}{5}$ of the

age of his father: the father's age is 10 times that of his youngest son: what is the age of the father? what the age of the youngest son?

38. By selling a quantity of cloth for $21, I made $\frac{2}{5}$ of the cost: I paid for it with corn, at $\$\frac{1}{3}$ per bushel: how many bushels did I give?

39. If $\frac{3}{5}$ of a yard of cloth cost $\$\frac{2}{3}$, what will 3 yards cost?

40. What will be the cost of 11 yards of cloth, if $5\frac{1}{2}$ yards cost $\$4\frac{2}{5}$?

41. $\frac{1}{3}$ of a certain number is 2 more than $\frac{1}{2}$ of 12: what is the number?

42. $\frac{1}{4}$ of a certain number is 3 less than $\frac{1}{5}$ of 30: what is the number?

43. $\frac{2}{5}$ of 20 are 6 less than how many thirds of 21?

44. $\frac{3}{4}$ of 24 are 6 more than $\frac{2}{3}$ of what number?

45. $\frac{5}{6}$ of 30, increased by 4, are 1 less than $\frac{3}{4}$ of some number: what is the number?

46. $\frac{3}{5}$ of 40 are 3 less than $\frac{9}{10}$ of how many times 6?

47. A boy having 40 cents gave $\frac{3}{5}$ of them for 2 melons: what was the price of 1 melon?

48. James had 14 cents, and gave $\frac{4}{7}$ of them to his sister: how many cents had he left?

49. John had 15 pears: he gave $\frac{1}{3}$ to Frank, and $\frac{2}{5}$ to Harry: how many had he left?

50. A man had 30 yards of cloth, and sold $\frac{2}{5}$ of it for $48: how much was that a yard?

51. John had 25 cents, and gave $\frac{4}{5}$ of them for peaches, at 2 cents each: how many did he buy?

52. A boy having 54 chestnuts, divided $\frac{5}{9}$ of them among 3 girls: how many did each receive?

53. A man had 28 barrels of flour, and sold $\frac{2}{7}$ of them for $48: what was that a barrel?

54. James had 48 cents: he gave $\frac{3}{8}$ to his brother, and

spent the rest in chestnuts, at 9 cents a quart: how many quarts of chestnuts did he buy?

55. Thomas had 28 cents: he gave $\frac{1}{4}$ to his sister, and $\frac{3}{7}$ to his brother, and with the remainder he bought 3 newspapers: what did each cost?

56. If 5 men earn $30 in 3 days, how much will 2 men earn in the same time? How much will 2 men earn in 1 day?

57. 6 is what part of $\frac{3}{5}$ of 40?

58. $\frac{3}{7}$ of 14 is what part of 54?

59. $\frac{5}{6}$ of 12 is what part of $\frac{4}{9}$ of 72?

60. $\frac{3}{5}$ of 20 is what part of twice that number of which 14 is $\frac{7}{9}$?

61. If $\frac{3}{8}$ of a ton of hay cost $9, what will $\frac{5}{6}$ of a ton cost?

62. If $7 will buy 56 yards of muslin, how many yards will $4 buy?

63. If 3 men can do a job of work in 16 days, in how many days can 4 men do it?

64. If 3 men spend $12 in 1 week, at the same rate, how many dollars would 2 men spend in 6 weeks?

65. If 6 men do a piece of work in 7 days, in how many days can 3 men do it?

66. If 5 men do a piece of work in 8 days, in how many days can 4 men do a piece twice as large?

67. If 6 men perform a certain amount of labor in 5 days, in how many days can 2 men do $\frac{1}{2}$ that amount?

68. James had 16 apples: he kept $\frac{1}{4}$ of them himself and divided the remainder equally among 3 of his companions: how many did each receive?

69. Three-fourths of 24, increased by $\frac{2}{3}$ of 12, are equal to how many?

70. Five-sixths of 24, diminished by $\frac{3}{4}$ of 20, equal how many?

71. Two-thirds of 12, less $\frac{1}{2}$ of 12, are $\frac{2}{5}$ of what number?

72. Add together $\frac{1}{2}$, $\frac{2}{3}$, and $\frac{3}{4}$ of 12.

73. From 10 take $\frac{3}{5}$ of itself; add to the remainder its $\frac{1}{2}$: what is the result?

74. Thomas had 28 cents: he gave $\frac{2}{7}$ of the amount to his sister, and $\frac{2}{5}$ of the remainder to his brother: how much more did he give away than he had left?

75. James had 35 marbles: he gave to Thomas $\frac{3}{7}$ of them, to Charles $\frac{2}{5}$: to which did he give the most, and how many? What number had he left?

76. Thomas had $28: he kept $\frac{2}{7}$ of the whole, and divided the remainder equally among his 4 brothers: how many dollars did each receive?

77. A grocer had 14 barrels of flour: he sold $\frac{4}{7}$ of it at $3 a barrel, and the remainder at $5 a barrel: what amount did he receive?

78. Bought 15 yards of cloth, at $2 a yard: I sold $\frac{1}{3}$ of it at $4 a yard, $\frac{2}{5}$ at $3 a yard, and the remainder at $5 a yard: how much did I gain?

79. Bought 10 yards of cloth for $90, and sold $\frac{2}{5}$ of it for $40: how much a yard did I gain on the quantity sold?

80. Two men travel the same direction: A is 40 miles ahead of B; but B travels 23 miles a day, and A 18: in how many days will B overtake A?

81. A hare is 90 yards in advance of a hound: the hound goes 10 feet in a second, and the hare 7 feet in a second: in how many seconds will the hound overtake the hare? How far will each run?

82. If a hound run 7 rods while a hare runs 4, how far will the hare run while the hound runs 35 rods?

83. C and D travel in the same direction: C is 15 miles ahead of D; but D travels 5 miles an hour, and C only 2: in how many hours will D overtake C? How far will D have traveled?

84. A cistern containing 24 gallons, is filled by a pipe at the rate of 8 gallons an hour, and emptied by a pipe at the rate of 5 gallons an hour: if both pipes are open, how long will the cistern be in filling?

85. A cistern containing 36 gallons has 2 pipes; by the first it receives 6 gallons an hour, and by the second it discharges 9 gallons an hour: if both pipes are left open, how long will it take to empty the cistern?

86. A pair of pants cost $8, which was $\frac{2}{5}$ of the cost of a coat; a vest cost $\frac{1}{2}$ as much as the pants: what was the cost of the whole suit?

87. Joseph had $1: he spent $\frac{2}{5}$ of the amount for oranges; $\frac{2}{3}$ of the remainder for lemons; and $\frac{1}{2}$ of the last remainder for an illustrated paper: how much had he left?

88. When hay was $20 a ton, I gave $\frac{3}{4}$ of a ton for 4 tons of coal: what was the coal worth per ton?

89. A man can perform a journey in $3\frac{3}{8}$ days: what part of the journey can he perform in $2\frac{1}{4}$ days?

90. A can do a piece of work in 2 days; B, in 4 days; and C, in 6 days: in what time will they all do it when working together?

91. Bought 20 yards of cloth, at $4 a yard, and 15 yards, at $3 a yard: sold $\frac{6}{7}$ of the whole, at $3 a yard, and the remainder, at $4 a yard: what was the entire loss? What the average loss per yard?

92. William had $96. He spent $\frac{1}{12}$ for books, $\frac{5}{11}$ of the remainder for clothing, $\frac{5}{6}$ of what then remained for furniture, and, with what was left, bought wheat, at $1 a bushel: how many bushels did he buy?

93. A and B are traveling in the same direction, A being 36 miles ahead of B; A travels $\frac{3}{4}$ of the distance per hour that B travels, and B travels 6 miles an hour: in how many hours will B overtake A?

LESSON 47

UNITED STATES MONEY.

10 mills, marked m.,   are 1 cent,   marked ct.

10 cents,   are 1 dime,   marked d.

10 dimes or 100 cents   are 1 dollar,   marked $.

10 dollars   are 1 eagle,   marked E.

1. How many mills in 2 cents?

SOLUTION.—In 1 cent there are 10 mills; then, in 2 cents there are 2 times 10 mills = 20 mills.

2. How many mills in 3 cents? In 4 cents? 5 cents? 6 cents? 7 cents? 8 cents? 9 cents?

3. How many cents in 2 dimes? In 3 dimes? 4 dimes 5? 6? 7? 8? 9?

4. How many dimes in 2 dollars? In 3 dollars? 4 dollars? 5? 6? 7? 8? 9?

5. How many dollars in 2 eagles? In 3 eagles? 4 eagles? 5? 6? 7? 8? 9?

6. How many cents in 2 dollars?

SOLUTION.—In 1 dollar there are 10 dimes; then, in 2 dollars there are 2 times 10 dimes = 20 dimes. In 1 dime there are 10 cents; then, in 20 dimes there are 20 times 10 cents = 200 cents.

7. How many cents in 3 dollars? In 4 dollars? 5 dollars? 6? 7? 8? 9?

8. Twenty cents are how many dimes?

SOLUTION.—10 cents are 1 dime; then, 20 cents are as many dimes as 10 is contained times in 20, which are 2.

9. Thirty cents are how many dimes? 40 cents? 50? 60? 70? 80? 90?

10. Twenty dimes are how many dollars? 30 dimes? 40? 50? 60? 70? 80? 90?

11. Two hundred cents are how many dollars?

SOLUTION.—10 cents are 1 dime; then, 200 cents are as many dimes as 10 is contained times in 200, which are 20. 10 dimes are 1 dollar; then, 20 dimes are as many dollars as 10 is contained times in 20, which are 2.

12. Three hundred cents are how many dollars? 400 cents? 500? 600? 700? 800? 900?

LESSON 48

DRY MEASURE.

2 pints (pt.)	are 1 quart,	marked qt.
8 quarts	are 1 peck,	marked pk.
4 pecks	are 1 bushel,	marked bu.

1. How many pints in 2 quarts? In 3 quarts? 4 quarts? 5? 6? 7?

2. How many quarts in 2 pecks? In 3 pecks?

3. How many pecks in 2 bushels? In 3 bushels? 4 bushels? 5? 6? 7? 8? 9? 10? 11? 12?

4. Four pints are how many quarts? 6 pints? 8? 10? 12? 14?

5. Sixteen quarts are how many pecks? 24 quarts?

6. Eight pecks are how many bushels? 12 pecks? 16? 20? 24? 28?

7. Reduce 3 qt. 1 pt. to pints.

SOLUTION.—In 1 qt. there are 2 pt.; then, in 3 qt. there are 3 times 2 pt. = 6 pt.; 6 pt + 1 pt. = 7 pt.

8. Reduce 3 pk. 5 qt. to quarts.
9. Reduce 3 bu. 2 pk. to pecks.
10. Reduce 2 pk. 3 qt. 1 pt. to pints.
11. Reduce 2 bu. 3 pk. 7 qt. to quarts.
12. Reduce 1 bu. 2 pk. 2 qt. 1 pt. to pints.
13. Reduce 7 pt. to quarts.

SOLUTION.—2 pt. are 1 qt.; then, 7 pints are as many quarts as 2 is contained times in 7, which are 3 and 1 rem. = 3 qt. 1 pt.

14. Reduce 9 pt. to quarts. 11 pt. 13. 15.
15. Reduce 10 qt. to pecks. 11 qt. 12. 13. 17. 19. 23. 27.
16. Reduce 7 pk. to bushels. 10 pk. 13. 15. 17. 23.
17. Reduce 27 pt. to pecks.

SOLUTION.—27 pt. = 13 qt. 1 pt.; 13 qt. = 1 pk. 5 qt.: therefore, 27 pt. = 1 pk. 5 qt. 1 pt.

18. Reduce 35 pt. to pecks. 39 pt. 43. 45.
19. Reduce 53 qt. to bushels. 55 qt. 57. 59.
20. Reduce 83 qt. to bushels. 86 qt. 89. 92.
21. Reduce 223 pt. to bushels. 224 pt. 226. 228.
22. Reduce 345 pt. to bushels. 346 pt. 347. 348.
23. Reduce 6 bu. 2 qt. to quarts.
24. Reduce 2 bu. 1 pt. to pints.
25. Reduce 4 bu. 2 pk. to pints.
26. Reduce 3 bu. 7 qt. 1 pt. to pints.
27. Reduce 5 bu. 3 pk. 1 pt. to pints.
28. Reduce 7 bu. 3 pk. 7 qt. to pints.

LESSON 49

4 gills (gi.)   are 1 pint,   marked   pt.
2 pints   are 1 quart, marked   qt.
4 quarts   are 1 gallon, marked   gal.

1. How many pints in 2 qt.? In 3 qt.?

2. How many quarts in 2 gal.? In 3 gal.? 4 gal.?
5? 6? 7? 8? 9? 10? 11? 12?

3. 5 gi. are how many pints? 6 gi.? 7?

4. 3 pt. are how many quarts? 4 pt.? 5? 6? 7?

5. 5 qt. are how many gallons? 6 qt.? 7? 8? 9?
10? 11? 12?

6. How many gills in 1 qt.? In 2 qt.? 3 qt.?

7. How many pints in 1 gal.? In 2 gal.? 3 gal.?
4? 5?

8. How many gills in 1 gal.? In 2 gal.? 3 gal.?
4? 5?

9. Reduce 1 pt. 3 gi. to gills.

10. Reduce 3 qt. 1 pt. to pints.

11. Reduce 5 gal. 2 qt. to quarts.

12. Reduce 2 qt. 1 pt. 1 gi. to gills.

13. Reduce 4 gal. 3 qt. 1 pt. to pints.

14. Reduce 1 gal. 1 qt. 1 pt. 3 gi. to gills.

15. Reduce 13 gi. to quarts.

16. Reduce 23 pt. to gallons.

17. Reduce 79 gi. to gallons.

18. Reduce 97 gi. to gallons. 98. 100. 102.

19. Reduce 187 gi. to gallons. 188. 190. 192.

20. Reduce 6 gal. 2 pt. to gills.

21. Reduce 8 gal. 3 gi. to gills.

22. Reduce 10 gal. 10 qt. 10 pt. to gills.

LESSON 50

AVOIRDUPOIS WEIGHT.

16 drams (dr.)   are 1 ounce,   marked oz.
16 ounces   are 1 pound,   marked lb.
100 pounds   are 1 hundred-weight, marked cwt.
20 hundred-weights are 1 ton,   marked T.

1. How many drams in 2 oz.? In 3 oz.? 4 oz.? 5? 6?

2. How many ounces in 2 lb.? In 3 lb.? 4 lb.? 5? 6? 10?

3. How many pounds in 2 cwt.? In 3 cwt.? 4 cwt.? 5? 6? 7? 8? 9?

4. How many hundred-weights in 2 tons? In 3 tons? 4 tons? 5? 6?

5. Twenty dr. are how many ounces? 27 dr.? 35?

6. Forty-two oz. are how many pounds? 53 oz.? 75? 90?

7. Three hundred lb. are how many hundred-weights? 450 lb.? 575? 1200?

8. Forty cwt. are how many tons? 50 cwt.? 75? 80? 96?

9. How many ounces in $\frac{1}{2}$ lb.?

Solution.—In 1 lb. there are 16 oz.; then, in $\frac{1}{2}$ lb. there are $\frac{1}{2}$ of 16 = 8 oz.

10. How many ounces in $\frac{1}{4}$ lb.? $\frac{3}{4}$ lb.?

11. How many pounds in $\frac{1}{2}$ cwt.? In $\frac{1}{4}$ cwt.? In $\frac{3}{4}$ cwt.? $\frac{1}{5}$? $\frac{2}{5}$? $\frac{3}{5}$? $\frac{4}{5}$?

12. Reduce 4 oz. 11 dr. to drams.

13. Reduce 10 lb. 10 oz. 11 dr. to drams.

14. Reduce 15 cwt. 45 lb. to pounds.

15. Reduce 4 T. 10 cwt. 75 lb. to pounds.

16. Twelve ounces are what part of a pound?

SOLUTION.—In 1 lb. there are 16 oz.; then, 12 oz. are $\frac{12}{16} = \frac{3}{4}$ lb.

17. Eight oz. are what part of a pound? 10 oz.? 14?

18. Ten lb. are what part of a hundred-weight? 20 lb.? 25? 40? 50? 60? 75? 80?

19. Four cwt. are what part of a ton? 5 cwt.? 6? 8? 10? 12? 15? 16? 18?

LESSON 51

LONG MEASURE.

12	inches (in.)	are 1 foot,	marked	ft.
3	feet	are 1 yard,	marked	yd.
$5\frac{1}{2}$	yards	are 1 rod,	marked	rd.
40	rods	are 1 furlong,	marked	fur.
8	furlongs	are 1 mile,	marked	mi.

1. How many inches in 2 ft.?

2. How many feet in 2 yd.? In 3 yd.? 4 yd.? 5?

3. How many yards in 2 rd.? In 4 rd.? 5 rd.? 7? 10?

4. How many rods in 3 fur.? In 4 fur.? 5 fur.? 6? 7? 9?

5. How many furlongs in 9 miles?

6. Thirty-six in. are how many feet? 48 in.?

7. Fifteen ft. are how many yards? 21 ft.?

8. Twenty-two yd. are how many rods? 33 yd.?

9. Six hundred and forty rd. are how many miles?

10. What is the value of $\frac{5}{6}$ yd.?

SOLUTION.—In 1 yd. there are 3 ft.; then, in $\frac{5}{6}$ yd. there are $\frac{5}{6}$ of 3 ft. = $\frac{15}{6}$, or $2\frac{1}{2}$ ft. In 1 ft. there are 12 in.; then, in $\frac{1}{2}$ ft. there are $\frac{1}{2}$ of 12 in. = 6 in.; therefore, $\frac{5}{6}$ yd. = 2 ft. 6 in.

11. What is the value of $\frac{2}{3}$ ft.? $\frac{3}{4}$ ft.?

12. What is the value of $\frac{2}{3}$ yd.? $\frac{3}{4}$ yd.?

13. What is the value of $\frac{6}{11}$ rd.? $\frac{1}{2}$ rd.? $\frac{2}{3}$? $\frac{2}{5}$?

14. What is the value of $\frac{1}{4}$ mi.? $\frac{1}{3}$ mi.? $\frac{2}{3}$? $\frac{3}{4}$? $\frac{2}{5}$?

15. Sixteen rd. are what part of a mile?

Solution.—In 1 mi. there are 8 fur.; in 8 fur. there are 320 rd.; then, 16 rd. are $\frac{16}{320} = \frac{1}{20}$ of a mile.

16. Twenty-four rd. are what part of a mile?

17. Three yd. are what part of a rod?

18. Two ft. are what part of a yard? Of a rod?

19. Six in. are what part of a foot? Of a yard? Of a rod?

LESSON 52

TIME TABLE.

60 seconds (sec.)	are 1 minute,	marked min.
60 minutes	are 1 hour,	marked hr.
24 hours	are 1 day,	marked da.
365 days	are 1 common year,	marked c. yr.
366 days	are 1 leap-year,	marked l. yr.
100 years	are 1 century,	marked cen.
7 days	are 1 week,	marked wk.
4 weeks	are 1 month,	marked mon.
12 calendar months	are 1 year,	marked yr.

One solar year contains 365 days, 5 hours, 48 minutes, and 46 seconds, or $365\frac{1}{4}$ days, *nearly*.

The following table shows the names of the different months of the year, and the number of days embraced in each:

January,	1st	month,		31 days.
February,	2d	month,	28 or	29 days.
March,	3d	month,		31 days.
April,	4th	month,		30 days.
May,	5th	month,		31 days.
June,	6th	month,		30 days.
July,	7th	month,		31 days.
August,	8th	month,		31 days.
September,	9th	month,		30 days.
October,	10th	month,		31 days.
November,	11th	month,		30 days.
December,	12th	month,		31 days.

The names of the months which have 30 days each may be remembered by the following couplet:

Thirty days have September,
April, June, and November.

1. What is the value of $\frac{1}{2}$ min.? $\frac{1}{3}$ min.? $\frac{2}{3}$? $\frac{3}{4}$?

2. What is the value of $\frac{1}{5}$ hr.? $\frac{2}{5}$ hr.? $\frac{3}{5}$? $\frac{4}{5}$? $\frac{1}{6}$? $\frac{5}{6}$? $\frac{1}{7}$?

3. What is the value of $\frac{1}{2}$ da.? $\frac{2}{3}$ da.? $\frac{5}{6}$? $\frac{2}{7}$? $\frac{3}{8}$? $\frac{7}{10}$?

4. What is the value of $\frac{3}{7}$ wk.? $\frac{5}{7}$ wk.?

5. What is the value of $\frac{1}{2}$ mon.? $\frac{3}{4}$ mon.? $\frac{2}{7}$? $\frac{6}{7}$? $\frac{9}{14}$? $\frac{13}{14}$?

6. Twenty sec. are what part of a minute?

7. Fifty min. are what part of an hour?

8. Twelve hr. are what part of a day? Of a week?

9. Five days are what part of a week?

10. Eight calendar months are what part of a year?

11. Three hr. 30 min. are what part of a day?

12. Three da. 12 hr. are what part of a week?

13. One wk. 3 da. are what part of a month?

14. One wk. 3 da. 16 hr. are what part of a month?

15. How many days in April and May taken together?

16. How many days in June, July, and August taken together?

17. How many days in September, October, and November taken together?

18. How many days from July 12 to July 28?

19. How many days from October 27 to December 25?

20. How many days from the Vernal Equinox, March 20, to the Autumnal Equinox, September 22?

21. How many days from the Summer Solstice, June 21, to the Winter Solstice, December 21?

LESSON 53

1. What is the cost of 5 bu. 3 pk. of corn, at 60 cents a bushel?

2. When milk is 5 cents a pint, what does a milkman get for 4 gal. 2 qt. 1 pt.?

3. At 10 cents a pound, what will be the cost of 7 lb. 12 oz. sugar?

4. What will it cost to build a fence 5 rd. 2 yd. 2 ft. 3 in. long, at $12 a rod?

5. A steamer from Milwaukee to Grand Haven, at the average rate of 9 miles an hour, was 9 hr. 26 min. 40 sec. in making the trip: what is the distance?

6. How much wine, at $8 a gallon, can be purchased for $23?

7. How much coffee, at 30 cts. per lb., can be bought for $5?

8. Add $\frac{3}{10}$ da. and $\frac{2}{5}$ hr.

9. Add $\frac{1}{3}$ rd., $\frac{1}{2}$ yd., and $\frac{3}{4}$ ft.

10. From $\frac{3}{8}$ bu., take $\frac{3}{4}$ pk.

11. If 1 bu. 3 pk. of oats are worth 70 ct., what are 2 bu. 1 pk. 4 qt. worth.

12. If a wagon-wheel go 3 yd. 1 ft. in making 1 revolution: how far will it go in making 7 revolutions?

13. If $\frac{2}{3}$ T. of hay cost $8, what will 3 cwt. 75 lb. cost?

14. The time by rail from Cincinnati to Dayton, a distance of 60 miles, is 2 hr. 24 min., what is the rate of travel per hour of the train?

15. If a cart-wheel make 1 revolution in going 3 yd. 1 ft. 6 in., how many revolutions will it make in going 1 rd. 5 yd.?

16. How many weeks in April, May, and June taken together?

17. I bought some roasted Java coffee for $2 and 35 ct., paying 40 ct. a lb.: how many lb. and oz. did I buy?

18. If there are 3 gal. in a dozen bottles of wine, how much will 3 dozen bottles cost, at 50 ct. a quart?

19. If 2 bu. 3 pk. of corn cost $1 and 65 ct.: how much is that a bushel?

20. If there are 25 bu. in a ton of coal, how much will 150 bu. cost, at $3 and 75 ct. a ton? How much a bushel?

21. A lot is 50 ft. wide, and 100 ft. long: how much will it cost to put a fence around it, at $5 a rod?

LESSON 54

1. A merchant bought at one time 33 gallons of oil; at another, 20 gallons; at another, 50; and at another, 62: how many gallons did he buy in all?

2. A lady paid $23 for a dress, $18 for a shawl, and $9 for a bonnet: what did she pay for all?

3. I owe A $50, B $75, C $40, and D $20: how much money do I owe altogether?

4. Having $92, I purchased a watch for $73: how much money had I left?

5. A man bought a horse for $110, and sold him for $145: how much did he make?

6. George bought candles for 25 ct., soap for 10 ct., sugar for 35 ct., and starch for 3 ct.; he gave the grocer $1, and received 30 ct. change: how much was this incorrect?

7. A boy had $5, from which he took at one time $1 and 50 ct.; at another, 40 ct.; at another, $1 and 10 ct.: how much money had he left?

8. What will be the cost of 5 yd. of cloth, at $2 and 50 ct. a yard?

9. A man traveling at the rate of 5 miles an hour, meets a stage going at the rate of 9 miles an hour: how far apart will they be in 10 hours?

10. Bought 15 lb. of sugar, at 11 ct. a pound, and 13 lb., at 9 ct. a pound, what did the whole cost?

11. Henry has 19 ct., George 3 times as many, lacking 10 ct.: how many have both?

12. How many yards in 3 bales of cloth, each containing 5 pieces, of 40 yd. each?

13. If a boat sail 48 miles in 12 hours, how far will it sail in 7 hours?

14. At 15 ct. a pound, how many pounds of beef can be purchased for $6?

15. Three men bought a horse for $90; after keeping him 6 weeks, at $3 a week, and the use of him being worth $42, they sold him for $99: what did each man make?

16. A farmer sold 12 bu. of corn, at 45 ct., and 8 bu. of wheat, at 95 ct. a bushel; he then bought 7 yd. of cloth, at 80 ct. a yard, and spent the balance for coffee, at $33\frac{1}{3}$ ct. a pound: how much coffee did he buy?

17. If I buy 9 bbl. of flour, at $6.50 a barrel, and 12 lb. of sugar, at $12\frac{1}{2}$ ct. a pound: how many apples, at 60 ct. a bushel, will I have to sell to pay for them?

LESSON 55

1. If $\frac{1}{3}$ of a yd. of cloth cost $2, what will $\frac{1}{4}$ of a yd. cost?

2. If $\frac{2}{3}$ of a yd. of cloth cost $5, what will $\frac{3}{4}$ of a yd. cost?

SOLUTION.—The cost of $\frac{1}{3}$ of a yard will be $\frac{1}{2}$ of $5 = \$\frac{5}{2}$; and a yard will cost 3 times $\$\frac{5}{2} = \$\frac{15}{2}$: then, $\frac{1}{4}$ of a yard will cost $\frac{1}{4}$ of $\$\frac{15}{2}$ $= \$\frac{15}{8}$; and $\frac{3}{4}$ of a yard will cost 3 times $\$\frac{15}{8} = \$5\frac{5}{8}$.

3. If $\frac{2}{5}$ of a bbl. of flour cost $3, what will $\frac{2}{3}$ of a bbl. cost?

4. If $\frac{4}{7}$ of a yd. of flannel cost 24 cts., what will $\frac{5}{14}$ of a yd. cost?

5. If $\frac{5}{9}$ of a ton of hay cost $15, what will one-half a ton cost?

6. If $\frac{3}{8}$ of an orchard contain 30 fruit trees, how many trees are there in $\frac{7}{16}$ of it?

7. If $1\frac{2}{5}$ yd. of cloth cost $14, what will $2\frac{1}{2}$ yd. cost?

8. If $1\frac{1}{2}$ bbl. of flour cost $5\frac{1}{4}$, what will $2\frac{1}{2}$ bbl. cost?

9. If $3\frac{1}{3}$ lb. of cheese cost 60 ct., what will $2\frac{5}{6}$ lb. cost?

10. A traveled 30 mi. in $3\frac{3}{4}$ hr.: at that rate, how far could he travel in $7\frac{1}{4}$ hr.?

11. If a man earn $1\frac{1}{4}$ in 10 hr., how much can he earn in 11 hr.?

12. A can earn $9\frac{3}{5}$ in 6 da., of 8 hr. each: how much can he earn in 7 da., of 9 hr. each?

13. If $5\frac{3}{4}$ bu. of wheat cost $9\frac{1}{5}$, what will $3\frac{1}{3}$ bu. cost?

14. If $8\frac{1}{3}$ is $\frac{5}{7}$ of a number, what is $\frac{4}{5}$ of it?

15. If $3\frac{1}{2}$ is $2\frac{1}{3}$ times some number, what is $2\frac{1}{2}$ times that number?

16. If $\frac{3}{4}$ of a barrel of flour cost $4\frac{1}{2}$, what will $\frac{3}{5}$ of a barrel cost?

17. If $\frac{2}{3}$ of a yard of lace cost $\frac{3}{5}$, what will $\frac{5}{6}$ of a yard cost?

18. Two-thirds of $1\frac{1}{5}$ are $\frac{2}{7}$ of what number?

19. Five-ninths of $5\frac{2}{5}$ are $\frac{8}{9}$ of what number?

20. Four-sevenths of $4\frac{3}{8}$ are $\frac{5}{11}$ of what number?

21. Five-sevenths of $5\frac{4}{9}$ are $\frac{7}{10}$ of what number?

22. Two-thirds of $2\frac{2}{5}$ are $\frac{1}{2}$ of how many times 2?

23. Three-fifths of $1\frac{1}{9}$ are $\frac{2}{7}$ of how many times 4?

24. Three-fourths of $3\frac{1}{5}$ are $\frac{3}{8}$ of how many times 3?

25. John has 10 marbles, and $\frac{4}{5}$ of what John has are $\frac{8}{11}$ of what James has: how many has James?

26. Jane received $\frac{3}{5}$ of 60 plums; she gave away $\frac{4}{9}$ of $\frac{3}{4}$ of them: how many were left?

27. James has a given distance to travel; after going 35 mi., there remain $\frac{2}{7}$ of the distance: when he has gone $\frac{3}{7}$ of the remainder, how far must he then go?

28. A horse cost $40; $\frac{3}{4}$ of the price of the horse $= \frac{6}{5}$ of the price of a cart: what did the cart cost?

29. B's coat cost $27, and his hat $8; $\frac{4}{9}$ of the cost of the coat $+\frac{3}{4}$ that of the hat $= \frac{3}{5}$ of the cost of his watch: what did the watch cost?

30. Mary lost $\frac{2}{7}$ of her plums; she gave $\frac{2}{5}$ of the re-

mainder to Sarah, and had 6 plums left: how many had she at first?

31. John has 12 cents; $\frac{2}{3}$ of his money $= \frac{1}{2}$ of $\frac{4}{5}$ of William's money: how much has William?

32. On counting their money, it was found that A had 12 cents more than B; and that $\frac{1}{2}$ of B's money $= \frac{2}{7}$ of A's: how much had each?

33. In an orchard, $\frac{1}{3}$ are apple-trees, $\frac{1}{4}$ are pear-trees, $\frac{1}{12}$ are plum-trees, and the remainder, which is 32, cherry-trees: how many trees are there of each kind?

34. In an orchard of apple and pear-trees, the latter are $\frac{2}{9}$ of the whole; the apple-trees are 25 more than the pear-trees: how many are there of each?

LESSON 56

1. What number added to itself will give a sum equal to 14?

Solution.—A number added to itself is twice the number; then, twice the number is 14; and the number is $\frac{1}{2}$ of $14 = 7$.

2. What number added to itself 3 times will make 32?

3. Divide 16 in two parts, so that the second part shall be 3 times the first.

4. Divide 48 into two such parts, that the second shall be 7 times the first.

5. Divide 24 into three parts, so that the second shall be 2 times and the third 3 times the first.

6. Divide 45 into three parts, so that the second shall be three times and the third 5 times the first?

7. When 10 was taken from a number, $\frac{2}{3}$ of it remained: what was the number?

8. The sum of two numbers is 25; if 10 is the less number, what is their difference?

9. The sum of two numbers is 12; if 6 be added to the sum, the result will be twice the greater number; what are the numbers?

10. If 6 be taken from the difference of two numbers, the remainder will be 2; if 4 is one of the numbers, what is the other?

11. If 10 be added to the difference of two numbers, the sum will be 6 more than the greater number, which is 19: what is the less number?

12. If 10 be taken from the sum of two numbers, 8 will be left; if 5 is one of the numbers, what is the other?

13. The sum of two numbers is 16, and their difference 4: what are the numbers?

SOLUTION.—Twice the greater number is $16 + 4 = 20$; then, the greater number is $\frac{1}{2}$ of $20 = 10$, and the less number is $10 - 4 = 6$.

14. The sum of two numbers is 25, and their difference 5: what are the numbers?

15. The sum of two numbers is 31, and the greater exceeds the less by 7: what are the numbers?

16. Divide 15 cents between A and B, so that B may have 3 cents more than A.

17. Thomas has 5 apples more than James, and both together have 19: how many has each?

18. Thomas and James each had the same number of cents, when Thomas found 8 more; they then had together 32 cents: how many had each?

19. Thomas and William each bought the same number of peaches; after Thomas ate 4, and William 6, they both together had 20 left: how many peaches had each remaining?

20. Mary bought twice as many cherries as Sarah; and, after Mary ate 7, and Sarah 5, they had only 24 left: how many had each left?

21. If 5 be added to three times a certain number, the sum will be 50: what is the number?

22. If $\frac{3}{4}$ of a certain number be increased by 10, the sum will be 31: what is the number?

23. If $\frac{4}{5}$ of a number be diminished by 7, the remainder will be 21: what is the number?

24. James is 4 years older than Henry, and Henry is 3 years younger than Oliver; the sum of all their ages is 37 years: what is the age of each?

SOLUTION.—3 times Henry's age is 37 yr. — 4 yr. — 3 yr. = 30 yr.; then, Henry's age is $\frac{1}{3}$ of 30 yr. = 10 yr., James' age is 10 yr. + 4 yr. = 14 yr., and Oliver's age 10 yr. + 3 yr. = 13 yr.

25. Mary has 8 cts. more than Jane, and Sarah 3 less than Mary; they all have 43 ct.: how many has each?

26. The sum of the ages of Mary and Frank is 42 years; Mary is twice as old as Frank, less 3 years: what is the age of each?

27. I bought a watch, a chain, and a ring, for $62; the chain cost $5 less than the ring, and the watch $12 more than the chain: what did I pay for each?

28. Thirty cents are 6 cents less than $\frac{1}{2}$ of $\frac{4}{7}$ of my money: how much have I?

29. John has twice as much money as James, + $3; Frank has as much as John and James, + $7; together they have $55: how much has each?

30. Joseph has 3 times as much money as Thomas—$2; Paul has twice as much as Joseph and Thomas together —$20; together they have $22: how much has each?

31. A horse, buggy, and harness cost $225; the horse cost $50 more than the harness, and the buggy $25 more than the horse and harness together: what was the cost of each?

LESSON 57

1. Divide 15 into two parts, so that the less part may be $\frac{2}{3}$ of the greater.

SOLUTION.—$\frac{3}{3} + \frac{2}{3} = \frac{5}{3}$; $\frac{5}{3}$ of the greater part = 15: then, $\frac{1}{3}$ of the greater part is $\frac{1}{5}$ of 15 = 3, and the greater part is 3 times 3 = 9; the less part is 15 — 9 = 6.

2. Thomas and John have $60 to pay; John has $\frac{3}{7}$ as much to pay as Thomas: what must each pay?

3. I had 56 mi. to travel in 2 da.; the second da. I went $\frac{3}{4}$ as far as the first: how far did I travel each da.?

4. Divide 100 into two such parts, that $\frac{5}{7}$ of the first less 8 will equal the second.

5. Divide the number 45 into three such parts, that the second shall be $\frac{1}{2}$, and the third $\frac{3}{4}$ of the first part.

6. A, B, and C, together have 40 ct.; B has $\frac{3}{5}$ as many as A, and C $\frac{2}{3}$ as many as B: how many cents has each?

SOLUTION.—C has $\frac{2}{3}$ of $\frac{3}{5} = \frac{2}{5}$ as many as A; then, $\frac{5}{5} + \frac{3}{5} + \frac{2}{5} = \frac{10}{5}$; and $\frac{10}{5}$, or twice as many as A, = 40 ct. Then, A has $\frac{1}{2}$ of 40 ct. = 20 ct., B has $\frac{3}{5}$ of 20 ct. = 12 ct., and C has $\frac{2}{5}$ of 20 ct. = 8 ct.

7. A tree 70 ft. long was broken into 3 pieces; the middle part was $\frac{5}{6}$ of the top part; the lower part was $\frac{3}{5}$ of the middle part: what was the length of each?

8. I bought a hat, coat, and vest, for $34; the hat cost $\frac{2}{5}$ of the price of the coat, and the vest $\frac{3}{4}$ the price of the hat: what was the cost of each?

9. Divide 38 ct. between A and B, so that $\frac{2}{3}$ of A's share may be equal to $\frac{3}{5}$ of B's.

SOLUTION.—$\frac{1}{3}$ of A's share is $\frac{1}{2}$ of $\frac{3}{5} = \frac{3}{10}$ of B's, and A's share is 3 times $\frac{3}{10} = \frac{9}{10}$ of B's; then, $\frac{10}{10} + \frac{9}{10} = \frac{19}{10}$ of B's share, or 38 ct. $\frac{1}{10}$ of B's share is $\frac{1}{19}$ of 38 ct. = 2 ct., and B's share is 10 times 2 ct. = 20 ct. A's share is $\frac{9}{10}$ of 20 ct. = 18 ct.

10. In a field containing 55 sheep and cows, $\frac{1}{2}$ of the cows $= \frac{2}{7}$ of the sheep: how many are there of each?

11. The sum of two numbers is 60; and $\frac{1}{3}$ of the less equals $\frac{2}{9}$ of the greater: what are the numbers?

12. One-fourth of Mary's age $= \frac{1}{3}$ of Sarah's, and the sum of their ages is 14 years: what is the age of each?

13. Divide the number 51 into two such parts, that $\frac{2}{3}$ of the first will equal $\frac{3}{4}$ of the second.

14. In an orchard of 65 apple and peach-trees, $\frac{2}{3}$ of the apple-trees $= \frac{4}{7}$ of the peach-trees: how many are there of each?

15. From C to D is 66 mi.; A left C at the same time B left D; when they met, $\frac{2}{3}$ of the distance A had traveled $= \frac{5}{9}$ of the distance B had traveled: how much farther did B travel than A?

16. In an orchard of apple, plum, and cherry-trees, 69 in all, the plum-trees $= \frac{1}{3}$ of the apple-trees, and the cherry-trees $= \frac{1}{2}$ of the apple-trees $+ \frac{1}{4}$ of the plum-trees: how many trees are there of each kind?

17. The age of Jane is $\frac{7}{8}$ of the age of Sarah, and $\frac{4}{9}$ of both their ages is $\frac{5}{3}$ of the age of Mary, which is 12 years: what are the ages of Jane and Sarah?

18. How many times $\frac{3}{11}$ of 44 is twice that number of which $\frac{4}{5}$ of 30 is $\frac{4}{9}$?

19. John's money is $\frac{3}{5}$ of Charles's; and $\frac{3}{4}$ of John's $+ \$33 =$ Charles's: how much has each?

20. On a farm there are 104 animals,—hogs, sheep, and cows; there are $\frac{2}{3}$ as many sheep as hogs, and $\frac{3}{4}$ as many cows as sheep: how many are there of each?

21. The time past noon is equal to half the time till midnight: what o'clock is it?

SOLUTION.—$\frac{2}{2} + \frac{1}{2} = \frac{3}{2}$; $\frac{3}{2}$ of the time to midnight $= 12$ hr.: then, $\frac{1}{2}$ the time to midnight, or the time past noon, is $\frac{1}{3}$ of 12 hr. $= 4$ hr.

102

22. The time elapsed since noon is $\frac{3}{5}$ of the time to midnight: what is the hour?

23. The time past noon, $+ 3$ hr., is equal to $\frac{1}{2}$ of the time to midnight: what is the hour?

24. What is the hour in the afternoon, when the time past noon is equal to $\frac{1}{5}$ of the time past midnight?

25. What is the hour in the afternoon, when the time past noon is $\frac{1}{4}$ of the time past midnight?

26. What is the hour of the day, when $\frac{1}{2}$ of the time past noon is $\frac{1}{20}$ of the time past midnight?

LESSON 58

1. What number is that to which, if its half be added, the sum will be 15?

SOLUTION.—$\frac{2}{2} + \frac{1}{2} = \frac{3}{2}$; $\frac{3}{2}$ of the number $= 15$: then, $\frac{1}{2}$ of the number is $\frac{1}{3}$ of $15 = 5$, and the number is 2 times $5 = 10$.

2. What number is that to which if its $\frac{2}{3}$ be added, the sum will be 20?

3. If to Mary's age its $\frac{2}{5}$ be added, the sum will be 21 years: what is her age?

4. What number is that which being doubled, and increased by its $\frac{3}{5}$, the sum will be 52?

5. What number is that which being doubled, and diminished by its $\frac{4}{7}$, the remainder will be 40?

6. What number is that which being trebled, and diminished by its $\frac{3}{5}$, the remainder will be 48?

7. If to David's age you add its $\frac{1}{2}$ and its $\frac{2}{3}$, the sum will be 26: what is his age?

8. If to Sarah's age you add its $\frac{1}{3}$, its $\frac{1}{4}$, and 10 years, the sum will be twice her age: how old is she?

9. Thomas spent $\frac{2}{5}$ of his money, and had 30 cents left: how much had he at first?

10. If to a certain number you add its $\frac{1}{2}$, and its $\frac{3}{5} + 27$, the number will be trebled: what is the number?

11. A father is 40 years older than his son; the son's age is $\frac{3}{11}$ of the father's age: what is the age of each?

12. If to Susan's age you add its $\frac{4}{5} + 18$ years, the sum will be 3 times her age: how old is she?

13. A piece of flannel, having lost $\frac{2}{9}$ of its length by shrinkage, measured 28 yd.: what was its length?

14. The distance from A to B is $\frac{1}{2}$ the distance from C to D, and $\frac{2}{3}$ of the distance from A to B, $+ 20$ mi., $=$ the distance from C to D: what is the distance from A to B, and from C to D?

15. My age plus its $\frac{1}{3}$ and its $\frac{1}{5} = \frac{2}{3}$ of my father's age. My father's age is 69 years; what is my age?

LESSON 59

1. If A can do a piece of work in 2 days, what part of it can he do in 1 day?

2. A can drink a keg of cider in 10 days: what part of it can he drink in 1 day?

3. B can do a piece of work in $\frac{1}{2}$ a day: how many times the work can he do in 1 day?

4. C can mow a certain lot in $\frac{3}{8}$ of a day: how many such lots can he mow in a day?

5. A can mow a certain field in $2\frac{1}{2}$ days: what part of it can he mow in 1 day?

6. B can dig a trench in $3\frac{1}{2}$ days: what part of it can he dig in 1 day?

7. C can walk from Cincinnati to Dayton in $3\frac{1}{3}$ days: what part of the distance can he walk in 2 days?

8. A can do $\frac{1}{2}$ of a piece of work in 1 day, and B $\frac{1}{4}$ of it: what part of the work can both do in a day?

9. A can do $\frac{1}{2}$, B $\frac{1}{4}$, and C $\frac{1}{5}$ of a piece of work in 1 day: what part of it can they all do in a day?

10. If A can do a piece of work in 2 days, and B in 3 days: in what time can they both together do it?

SOLUTION.—A and B can do $\frac{1}{2} + \frac{1}{3} = \frac{5}{6}$ of the work in 1 day; then, they can do $\frac{1}{6}$ of the work in $\frac{1}{5}$ of a day, and the whole work in $\frac{6}{5} = 1\frac{1}{5}$ days.

11. A can dig a trench in 6 days, and B in 12 days: in what time can they both together do it?

12. C alone can do a piece of work in 5 days, and B in 7 days: in what time can both do it?

13. A can do a piece of work in 2 days, B in 3 days, and C in 6 days: in what time can all three do it?

14. A and B mow a field in 4 days; B can mow it alone in 12 days: in what time can A mow it?

SOLUTION.—A can mow $\frac{1}{4} - \frac{1}{12} = \frac{1}{6}$ of the field in 1 day; then, he can mow the whole field in 6 days.

15. A man and his wife can drink a keg of beer in 12 days; when the man is away, it lasts the woman 30 days: in what time can the man drink it alone?

16. Three men, A, B, and C, can together reap a field of wheat in 4 days; A can reap it alone in 8 days, and B in 12 days: in what time can C reap it?

17. A can do $\frac{1}{2}$ a piece of work in a day, and B $\frac{1}{3}$ of it in a day: how long will it take both to do it?

18. A can dig a cellar alone in $2\frac{1}{2}$ days, and B in $3\frac{1}{3}$ days: in what time can both together dig it?

19. C can reap a field of wheat in 5 days, and D in $3\frac{1}{3}$ days: in what time can both reap it?

LESSON 60

1. What part of 8 is 2? What part is 4? Is 1?

2. How many times does 10 contain 2? 2 is what part of 10?

Ratio is the relation which one quantity bears to another of the same kind.

3. What is the ratio of 12 to 2?

SOLUTION.—The ratio of 12 to 2 is $12 \div 2 = 6$.

4. How many times does 18 contain 9? What is the ratio of 18 to 9?

5. What is the ratio of 36 to 12? 45 to 9? 66 to 11? 52 to 13? 1 to 2? 3 to 4?

6. What is the ratio of $2\frac{1}{2}$ to 5? $6\frac{1}{4}$ to $12\frac{1}{2}$? $\frac{1}{4}$ to $\frac{1}{2}$? Of $\frac{2}{3}$ to $\frac{5}{6}$? $\frac{2}{3}$ to $\frac{4}{5}$? $\frac{1}{2}$ to $\frac{1}{3}$?

7. If the ratio of two numbers is 5, and 6 is the less number, what is the greater?

8. The ratio of 21 to 7 is equal to the ratio of 36 to some number: what is the number?

9. Five less than the ratio of 20 to 2, is $\frac{1}{4}$ of the ratio of 40 to what number?

10. The ratio of 18 to 2, plus 3, is 7 less than the ratio of 38 to what number?

11. The ratio of 27 to 9, increased by 5, is equal to the ratio of 20 to what number?

12. Divide 25 ct. between George and John, so that their shares shall be in the ratio of 3 to 2.

SOLUTION.—George's share is $3 \div 2 = \frac{3}{2}$ of John's; $\frac{2}{2} + \frac{3}{2} = \frac{5}{2}$; $\frac{5}{2}$ of John's share are 25 ct.: then, John's share is 10 ct., and George's 15 ct.

13. Divide the number 48 into two parts that shall be in the ratio of 5 to 7.

14. Divide 20 apples between A and B, so that A may get 2 as often as B gets 3.

15. Divide 28 cents between John and James, so that John may get 3 as often as James gets 4.

16. In an orchard of 96 trees there are 5 apple trees to 3 peach trees: how many of each kind?

17. A school of 35 pupils has 2 boys to 3 girls: how many of each in the school?

18. What number is that which being added to 3 times itself will make 48?

19. Mary has 25 yd. of ribbon; she wishes to divide it into two parts, so that one shall be 4 times the length of the other: what will be the length of each part?

20. Divide 28 into two parts, so that one will be to the other as 3 to 4.

21. A and B hired a pasture for $45: A pastured 4 cows, and B 5 cows: what should each pay?

22. Two men paid $3 for $7\frac{1}{2}$ dozen oysters: the first paid $2, and the second, $1: how many dozen oysters should each have?

23. A and B bought a horse for $40; A paid $25, and B the rest: they sold him for $56: what should each receive?

24. C and D sold a horse for $30 less than it cost; C's share was to D's as 3 to 2: what was each one's loss?

1. Divide the number 22 into two parts that shall be to each other as $2\frac{1}{2}$ to 3.

SOLUTION.—The first part is $2\frac{1}{2} \div 3 = \frac{5}{6}$ of the second; $\frac{5}{6} + \frac{6}{6} = \frac{11}{6}$; $\frac{11}{6}$ of the second part $= 22$: then the second part is 12 and the first 10.

2. Divide 16 apples between Henry and Oliver, so that their shares shall be in the ratio of $1\frac{1}{2}$ to $2\frac{1}{2}$.

3. Divide 14 ct. between A and B, so that B may have $1\frac{1}{3}$ times as many as A.

4. John and James have together 33 marbles; James has $1\frac{3}{4}$ times as many as John: how many has each?

5. Two boys bought a silver watch for \$7: the first paid \$$2\frac{1}{2}$, the second, \$$4\frac{1}{2}$, and they sold it for \$28: what was each one's share?

6. William's age is $1\frac{2}{3}$ times Frank's age; the sum of their ages is 32 yr.: what is the age of each?

7. A basket contains 30 apples: the number of sound ones is $2\frac{1}{3}$ times the number not sound: how many are there of each?

8. Two men built 27 ft. of wall: how much did each build, if one built $\frac{4}{5}$ as much as the other?

9. Divide the number 60 into 3 parts that shall be to each other as 3, 4, and 5.

SOLUTION.—$\frac{3}{3} + \frac{4}{3} + \frac{5}{3} = \frac{12}{3}$; $\frac{12}{3}$ of the first part $= 60$: then, the first part is 15, the second 20, and the third 25.

10. Divide the number 70 into four parts that shall be to each other as 1, 2, 3, and 4.

11. Divide 39 into three parts that shall be to each other as $\frac{1}{2}$, $\frac{1}{3}$, and $\frac{1}{4}$.

12. William had 3 ct., Thomas 4 ct., and John 5 ct.; they bought 36 peaches: what was the share of each?

13. A boat worth $864, of which $\frac{1}{8}$ belonged to A, $\frac{1}{4}$ to B, and the rest to C, was lost: what loss did each sustain, it having been insured for $500?

14. A, B, and C have $42; B has $\frac{1}{2}$ as much as A, and C $\frac{1}{2}$ as much as B: how much has each?

15. Divide 45 ct. among A, B, and C, so that A may get 4 ct. as often as B gets 3 ct. and C 2 ct.

16. On a farm there are 60 animals—horses, cows, and sheep; for each horse there are 3 cows, and for each cow there are 2 sheep: how many animals of each kind?

17. Divide 42 plums among A, B, and C, so that B may get twice, and C 3 times as many as A.

18. Divide 35 cherries among Emma, Agnes, and Sarah, so that Agnes shall have twice as many as Emma, and Sarah twice as many as Agnes.

LESSON 62

1. If 5 men can do a piece of work in 18 da., how many men can do it in 9 da.?

SOLUTION.—In 1 day, 18 times 5 men $=$ 90 men can do the work; then, in 9 days, $\frac{1}{9}$ of 90 men $=$ 10 men can do it.

2. If 8 men can do a piece of work in 15 da., how many men can do it in 12 da.?

3. If 8 men can do a piece of work in 5 da., in what time can 5 men do it.?

4. If 9 pipes fill a cistern in $2\frac{1}{2}$ hr., in what time will 5 such pipes fill it?

5. A man, failing in business, paid 80 ct. on each dol-

lar of his indebtedness: what did I receive, if he owed me $60?

SOLUTION.—80 cts. = $⅘. I received 60 times $⅘ = $48.

6. A grocer, failing, pays only 15 ct. on the dollar: what will a creditor receive to whom he owes $80?

7. A trader, failing, pays 60 ct. on the dollar: what will a creditor receive to whom he owes $80?

8. If a certain quantity of flour afford 8 five-cent loaves, how many ten-cent loaves will it furnish?

SOLUTION.—It will afford 5 times 8, or 40, one-cent loaves; and $\frac{1}{10}$ of 40, or 4, ten-cent loaves.

9. If a certain quantity of flour afford 6 five-cent loaves, how many three-cent loaves will it furnish?

10. If a sack of flour make 20 three-cent loaves, how many four-cent loaves will it make? How many five-cent loaves?

11. If a loaf weigh 8 oz. when flour is $3 a barrel, what should it weigh when flour is $4 a bbl.? $5 a bbl.?

12. A loaf weighs 10 oz. when flour is $6 a bbl.: what should it weigh when flour is $5 a bbl.?

13. If a loaf weigh 7 oz. when flour is $5⅓ a bbl.: what ought it to weigh when flour is $4⅔ a bbl.?

14. If 5 men can do a piece of work in a certain time, how many can do a piece twice as large in ⅕ of the time?

15. If 6 men can do a piece of work in 5 days, in what time can they do it, if they receive the assistance of 3 additional men when the work is half completed?

16. If 7 men can do a piece of work in 4 days, in what time can it be done, if 3 of the men leave when the work is half completed?

17. If the wages of 3 men for 5 days is $30, what will be the wages of 4 men for 7 da.?

SOLUTION.—The wages of 1 man for 5 days is $\frac{1}{3}$ of $30 = $10, and the wages of 1 man for 1 day is $\frac{1}{5}$ of $10 = $2; then, the wages of 1 man for 7 days is 7 times $2 = $14, and the wages of 4 men for 7 days is 4 times $14 = $56.

18. If 6 persons spend $36 in 8 days, how much, at that rate, would 5 persons spend in 12 da.?

19. If 3 men can build 12 rd. of wall in 8 da., how many rd. can 5 men build in 3 da.?

20. If 6 horses eat 36 bu. of oats in 10 days, how many bu. will 5 horses eat in 9 da.?

21. If 5 oxen eat 2 A. of grass in 6 days, in how many days will 12 oxen eat 8 A., the grass growing uniformly?

22. If a family of 8 persons spend $400 in 5 mon., how much would maintain them 8 mon., if 3 more persons were added?

23. If 10 oxen can be kept on 5 A. for 3 mon., how many sheep can be kept on 15 A. for 5 mon., if 7 sheep eat as much as 1 ox?

LESSON 63

1. A and B rent a pasture for $25: A puts in 27 oxen, and B 180 sheep: what should each pay, supposing an ox to eat as much as 10 sheep?

SOLUTION.—180 sheep eat as much as $180 \div 10 = 18$ oxen. B should pay $18 \div 27 = \frac{2}{3}$ as much as A; then, $\frac{3}{3} + \frac{2}{3} = \frac{5}{3}$: $\frac{5}{3}$ of what A should pay are $25: then, A should pay $15, and B $10.

2. A and B rent a pasture for $60: A puts in 14

horses, and B, 15 cows: what should each pay, if 2 horses eat as much as 3 cows?

3. A and B rent a pasture for $72: A puts in 8 horses, B 15 oxen and 120 sheep: what should each pay, if a horse eat as much as 20 sheep, and 2 horses as much as 3 oxen?

4. A and B rent a pasture for $35: A puts in 4 horses 2 wk.; B, 3 horses 4 wk.: what ought each to pay?

SOLUTION.—4 horses in 2 wk. eat the same as 1 horse in 4 times $2 = 8$ wk.; and 3 horses in 4 wk. eat the same as 1 horse in 3 times $4 = 12$ wk.; then, B ought to pay $12 \div 8 = \frac{3}{2}$ as much as A, or $3 when A pays $2; whence, A pays $14, and B $21.

5. C and D join their stocks in trade; C puts in $50 for 4 mon., and D $60 for 5 mon.: they gain $45: what is the share of each?

6. Two masons, A and B, built a wall for $81; A sent 3 men for 4 da., and B 5 men for 3 da.: what ought each to receive?

7. A and B traded in company; A put in $2 as often as B put in $3; A's money was employed 5 mon., and B's 4 mon.: they gained $55: what was each man's share?

8. E and F rented a field for $27; E put in 4 horses for 5 mon., and F 10 cows for 6 mon.: what ought each to pay, if 2 horses eat as much as 3 cows?

9. M and N enter into partnership for one year. M puts in $600, and N, $900; they gain $300: after paying $150 expenses, what is each one's share of the gain?

10. At the beginning of the year, C went into business with a capital of $600: four months after, D formed a partnership with C, and put in $600: the gain for the year was $250: what was each one's share?

11. E and F entered into partnership for a year; E's capital was $1000, and F's three times as much; at the end of 8 months, F drew out $1000; the gain for the year was $770: what was each one's share?

12. The capital of a firm, consisting of A and B, was $2400; the gain for the year was $240, A's share being $20 more than B's: how much capital did each furnish?

13. The capital of a firm, consisting of C and D, was $980; C's capital was used 8 months, and D's 6 months, when the gain was equally divided: how much capital did each invest?

14. In a partnership, A's gain was $70, and B's $80. A's capital was employed 10 months, and B's 8 months: their joint capital was $1700: what was the original investment of each?

15. The gain of a firm, consisting of E and F, was $840: E's stock was to F's as 2 to 3, and E's was in use 10 months, F's 12 months: what was each one's share of the gain?

LESSON 64

Any *per cent* of a number is so many *hundredths* of it; thus, one per cent of a number is $\frac{1}{100}$ of it.

1. What part is 2 per cent?

SOLUTION.—2 per cent is $\frac{2}{100} = \frac{1}{50}$.

2. What part is 4 per cent?   5?   6?   8?
3. What part is 10 per cent?   12?   15?
4. What part is 16 per cent?   20?   24?
5. What part is 25 per cent?   28?   30?
6. What part is 32 per cent?   35?   36?
7. What part is 40 per cent?   45?   48?
8. What part is 50 per cent?   60?   70?
9. What part is 75 per cent?   80?   90?
10. What part is $2\frac{1}{2}$ per cent?

SOLUTION. $2\frac{1}{2} = \frac{5}{2}$. 1 per cent is $\frac{1}{100}$; then, $\frac{1}{2}$ per cent is $\frac{1}{2}$ of $\frac{1}{100} = \frac{1}{200}$, and $\frac{5}{2}$ per cent is 5 times $\frac{1}{200} = \frac{1}{40}$.

11. What part is $3\frac{1}{2}$ per cent? $6\frac{1}{4}$?
12. What part is $6\frac{2}{3}$ per cent? $7\frac{1}{2}$?
13. What part is $8\frac{1}{3}$ per cent? $12\frac{1}{2}$?
14. What part is $13\frac{1}{3}$ per cent? $16\frac{2}{3}$?
15. What part is $17\frac{1}{2}$ per cent? $18\frac{3}{4}$?
16. What part is $23\frac{1}{3}$ per cent? $31\frac{1}{4}$?

17. What part is $37\frac{1}{2}$ per cent? $43\frac{3}{4}$?
18. What part is $56\frac{1}{4}$ per cent? $62\frac{1}{2}$?
19. What part is $66\frac{2}{3}$ per cent?
20. What part is $87\frac{1}{2}$ per cent?

LESSON 65

1. What is 4 per cent of 50?

SOLUTION.—4 per cent is $\frac{1}{25}$: $\frac{1}{25}$ of $50 = 2$.

2. What is 6 per cent of 50? 100?
3. What is 10 per cent of 20? 30?
4. What is $12\frac{1}{2}$ per cent of 24? 48?
5. What is 25 per cent of $32? $80?
6. What is $33\frac{1}{3}$ per cent of 51 bushels?
7. What is 50 per cent of 14 horses?
8. I bought a piece of cloth for $32, and sold it so as to gain $6\frac{1}{4}$ per cent: what did I gain?

SOLUTION.—$6\frac{1}{4}$ per cent is $\frac{1}{16}$: I gained $\frac{1}{16}$ of $32 = $2.

9. A grocer bought a bbl. of sugar for $10, and in selling it gained 10 per cent: how much did he gain?

10. A farmer, having a flock of 40 sheep, lost 5 per cent of them: how many had he left?

11. A flock of 50 sheep increases 10 per cent in one year: how many are then in the flock?

12. A lady, having $20, spent 10 per cent for muslin, and 10 per cent of the remainder for calico: how much did she pay for both?

13. I paid 30 ct. per yd. for cambric: at what price must I sell it, to make 10 per cent?

SOLUTION.—10 per cent is $\frac{1}{10}$. I must gain $\frac{1}{10}$ of 30 ct. $= 3$ ct.; then I must sell it for 30 ct. $+ 3$ ct. $= 33$ ct.

14. To make 12½ per cent profit, what must muslin be sold at that cost 8 ct. per yd.? 16 ct.?

15. To make 8⅓ per cent profit, what must sugar be sold for that cost 6 ct. per lb.? 18 ct.?

16. To make 25 per cent profit, what must delaine be sold for that cost 12 ct. per yd.? 16 ct.? 20 ct.? 35 ct.?

LESSON 66

1. How many per cent is $\frac{1}{2}$?

SOLUTION.—It is $\frac{1}{2}$ of $100 = 50$ per cent

2. How many per cent is $\frac{1}{3}$? $\frac{2}{3}$? $\frac{1}{4}$?
3. How many per cent is $\frac{3}{4}$? $\frac{1}{5}$? $\frac{2}{5}$?
4. How many per cent is $\frac{3}{5}$? $\frac{4}{5}$? $\frac{1}{6}$?
5. How many per cent is $\frac{1}{8}$? $\frac{3}{8}$? $\frac{5}{8}$?
6. How many per cent is $\frac{1}{10}$? $\frac{3}{10}$? $\frac{7}{10}$?
7. How many per cent is $\frac{9}{10}$? $\frac{1}{12}$? $\frac{5}{12}$?
8. How many per cent is $\frac{1}{15}$? $\frac{1}{16}$? $\frac{3}{16}$?
9. How many per cent is $\frac{5}{16}$? $\frac{1}{20}$? $\frac{3}{20}$?
10. How many per cent is $\frac{7}{20}$? $\frac{9}{20}$? $\frac{11}{20}$?
11. How many per cent is $\frac{1}{25}$? $\frac{2}{25}$? $\frac{3}{25}$?
12. How many per cent is $\frac{4}{25}$? $\frac{6}{25}$? $\frac{7}{25}$?
13. How many per cent is $\frac{8}{25}$? $\frac{9}{25}$? $\frac{11}{25}$?
14. How many per cent is $\frac{7}{30}$? $\frac{2}{35}$? $\frac{9}{40}$?
15. How many per cent is $\frac{11}{40}$? $\frac{6}{45}$? $\frac{5}{48}$?
16. How many per cent is $\frac{1}{50}$? $\frac{3}{50}$? $\frac{7}{50}$?
17. How many per cent is $\frac{9}{50}$? $\frac{1}{60}$? $\frac{1}{75}$?
18. How many per cent is $\frac{15}{24}$? $\frac{18}{24}$? $\frac{21}{24}$?
19. How many per cent is $\frac{18}{32}$? $\frac{22}{32}$? $\frac{26}{32}$?
20. How many per cent is $\frac{6}{36}$? $\frac{18}{36}$? $\frac{30}{36}$?
21. How many per cent is $\frac{20}{48}$? $\frac{28}{48}$? $\frac{33}{48}$?
22. How many per cent is $\frac{44}{48}$? $\frac{45}{48}$? $\frac{12}{80}$?

LESSON 67

1. Two is what per cent of 5?

SOLUTION.—2 is $\frac{2}{5}$ of 5: $\frac{2}{5} = \frac{40}{100}$, or 40 per cent.

2. Three is what per cent of 5? Of 12?
3. Four is what per cent of 8? Of 32?
4. Five dollars are what per cent of $20? $30?
5. Eight men are what per cent of 160 men?
6. There are 36 pupils enrolled in a certain school; if 9 are absent, what is the per cent of absence?
7. Out of 60 pupils in a school, 20 study geography: what per cent is that of the whole number?
8. There are 45 pupils enrolled in a certain primary school; on a certain day only 30 of them were present, what was the per cent of attendance?
9. A grocer buys coffee at 25 ct. per pound, and sells it at a profit of 5 ct. per pound: what is his gain per cent?
10. A merchant bought cloth at $5 per yard, and sold it at $7 per yard: what per cent did he gain?

SOLUTION.—He gained $7 — $5 = $2: $2 are $\frac{2}{5}$ of the cost; $\frac{2}{5}$ are 40 per cent.

11. James bought a melon for 4 ct., and sold it for 5 ct.: what per cent did he gain?
12. An orange was bought for 5 ct., and sold for 4 ct.: what was the per cent of loss?
13. Thomas bought a watch for $4, and sold it for $6: what per cent did he gain?
14. Henry bought a horse for $15, and sold it for $24: what per cent did he gain?

117

15. A keg of wine holding 5 gal., lost 6 qt. by leakage: what was the loss per cent?

16. By selling citrons at 6 ct. each, John cleared $\frac{1}{5}$ of the first cost: what per cent would he have cleared by selling them at 8 ct. each?

17. A merchant bought cloth at the rate of 6 yd. for $3, and sold it at the rate of 5 yd. for $4: what per cent did he gain?

18. Henry sold melons at 8 ct. each, and lost $\frac{1}{5}$ of the first cost: what per cent would he have lost by selling them at 3 for 25 ct.: what per cent would he have gained by selling them at 2 for 25 ct.?

19. James bought a lot of lemons, at the rate of 2 for 3 ct.; but, finding them damaged, he sold them at the rate of 3 for 2 ct.: what per cent did he lose?

LESSON 68

1. Sold a watch for $12, and gained 20 per cent: what was the cost?

SOLUTION.—20 per cent is $\frac{1}{5}$; $\frac{5}{5} + \frac{1}{5} = \frac{6}{5}$; $\frac{6}{5}$ of the cost are $12; then, the cost is $10.

2. I sold a piece of cloth for $26, and gained 30 per cent: what did the cloth cost me?

3. If there is a gain of 40 per cent when muslin is sold at 14 ct. a yd., what is the cost price?

4. By selling a horse for $81, there was a gain of $12\frac{1}{2}$ per cent: what did the horse cost?

5. Sold a horse for $63, and lost 10 per cent: what was the cost?

6. Thomas sold a watch for $21, and gained 75 per cent: what did he pay for it?

7. James sold 10 oranges for 40 ct., and gained $33\frac{1}{3}$ per cent: how much did each orange cost?

8. Sold a watch for $10, by which I gained 25 per cent: what would I have gained by selling it for $12?

9. By selling muslin at 7 ct. per yd., there is a loss of $12\frac{1}{2}$ per cent: what will be the loss per cent by selling it at 6 ct. per yd.?

10. By selling my horse for $35, there was a loss of $16\frac{2}{3}$ per cent: what would have been the gain per cent by selling him for $63?

11. I bought a watch for $18, which was 20 per cent more than its value: I sold it at 10 per cent less than its value: what sum did I lose?

12. A sold B a watch for $60, and gained 20 per cent: afterward B sold it and lost 20 per cent on what it cost him: how much did B lose more than A gained?

13. A watch-maker sold two watches for $30 each: on one he gained 25 per cent, and on the other he lost 25 per cent: how much did he lose by the sale?

14. By selling 4 apples for 3 ct., a dealer gains 50 per cent: what per cent will he gain by selling them at the rate of 5 for 4 ct.?

15. Sold 5 lemons for 4 ct., and lost 20 per cent: what per cent did I lose by selling 6 for 5 ct.?

16. Two-thirds of 10 per cent of 60 are $\frac{1}{2}$ of what per cent of 40?

17. One-half of $\frac{3}{5}$ of 50 per cent of 120 is 10 less than 20 per cent of what?

18. One-fourth of $\frac{2}{3}$ of 60 per cent of 10 is 5 less than 50 per cent of what?

19. Three-fourths of $\frac{2}{5}$ of 75 per cent of 15 are $1\frac{3}{5}$ more than 50 per cent of what?

20. One and one-half times $\frac{2}{3}$ of 25 per cent of 4 are 25 per cent of $\frac{1}{2}$ of what number?

LESSON 69

Allowances made to purchasers by wholesale dealers are called *per cents off*.

10 per cent off means 10 per cent, or $\frac{1}{10}$, from the retail, or list price.

$\frac{1}{8}$ off means $\frac{1}{8}$, or $12\frac{1}{2}$ per cent, from the list price.

20/5 (read 20 and 5) means 20 per cent off, and 5 per cent taken from the remainder.

$\frac{1}{8}$ and 5 means $12\frac{1}{2}$ per cent off, and 5 per cent taken from the remainder.

1. The price of a book was $3, but the book-seller allowed 20 per cent off: what was paid for the book?

2. The amount of a bill of goods was $125, but the dealer allowed $\frac{1}{5}$ off: what was paid for the goods?

3. A bill of goods amounted to $840, and the dealer gave $\frac{1}{6}$ off: what was paid for the goods?

4. A lot of books amounted to $500: the book-seller allowed 20/5 off: what was paid for the books?

5. A bill of goods amounted to $1200, and the dealer allowed $\frac{1}{6}$ and 5 off: what was paid for the goods?

6. Paid $4.80 for a book, the book-seller having allowed me 20 per cent off: what was the retail price?

7. Paid $720 for a bill of goods, the dealer having allowed $\frac{1}{3}$ off: what was the retail price?

8. Paid $133 for goods, the dealer having allowed 20/5: what was the list price?

9. Paid $399 for goods, the dealer having allowed $\frac{1}{8}$ and 5 per cent for cash, and sold them at the list or retail price: what did I get for the goods.

10. The retail price of a bill of goods was $70; the dealer allowed 20/5 on $50, and 10/5 on the remainder of the amount: what was paid for the goods?

LESSON 70

Commission is the sum allowed to agents for buying, selling, or transacting other business.

1. An agent sold a house for $4000, charging $2\frac{1}{2}$ per cent commission: what was his commission?

2. An agent sells goods to the amount of $560, at 5 per cent commission: what is the commission?

3. A commission merchant sells 1000 bu. of corn, for 50 ct. a bu., and charges $2\frac{1}{2}$ per cent for selling: what is his commission?

4. An agent sells 5 village lots, for $300 each, charging 5 per cent: what is his commission, and how much does the owner receive?

5. A farmer sends 800 bu. of wheat to a commission merchant, who sells it at $1.25 a bu., and charges 2 per cent commission: how much does the farmer receive for his wheat?

6. A collector received $100 for collecting bills, at 5 per cent commission: how much did he collect?

7. A merchant allowed a collector 10 per cent for collecting bills: the commission was $60: how much was collected?

8. A commission merchant sold grain for $1000, charging 5 per cent, and invested the remainder in shares, at $50 a share, without extra charge: how many shares did he buy?

LESSON 71

A *Policy* is the written agreement of an Insurance Company to pay a certain sum of money in case of loss by fire, water, accident, or other hazard.

The *Premium* is the sum paid for insurance.

1. What is paid for an insurance policy of $2000, at ½ per cent premium?

2. A house worth $3000 is insured for ½ its value, at 2 per cent premium : what is the insurance?

3. What does it cost to insure property worth $2400, for ⅔ its value, at 1 per cent, the policy costing $1.50?

4. A man insured his house for $2500, and his furniture for $1500, at a premium of ¾ per cent: what did he pay?

5. A man's house was worth $1800, and his furniture, $1200: he insured both at ⅔ their value, paying 1 per cent premium on the house, ½ per cent premium on the furniture, and $1 for the policy: how much did he pay?

6. A man's house was worth $2600, and his furniture, $1500: he insured the house at ½ its value, and the furniture at ⅔: he paid 2 per cent premium on the house, 1 per cent on the furniture, and $1.50 for the policy: how much did he pay?

LESSON 72

Interest is money paid for the use of money.

The *Principal* is the sum of money which is loaned.

The *Amount* is the principal and interest added together.

1. What is the interest of $2 for 3 yr., at 5 per cent?

SOLUTION.—The interest for 3 yr. is 3 times $5 = 15$ per cent; 15 per cent is $\frac{3}{20}$; $\frac{3}{20}$ of $2 = 30$ ct.

2. Find the interest of $5 for 2 yr., at 6 per cent.
3. Find the interest of $8 for 5 yr., at 5 per cent.
4. Find the interest of $20 for 3 yr., at 8 per cent.
5. Find the interest of $25 for 6 yr., at 4 per cent.

6. Find the interest of $40 for 4 yr., at 5 per cent.
7. Find the interest of $50 for 3 yr., at 6 per cent.
8. Find the interest of $60 for 2 yr., at 7 per cent.
9. Find the interest of $75 for 3 yr., at 4 per cent.
10. Find the interest of $80 for 5 yr., at 9 per cent.

LESSON 73

1. Find the interest of $50 for 6 mo., at 6 per cent.

SOLUTION.—6 mo. are $\frac{1}{2}$ yr.; the interest for $\frac{1}{2}$ yr. is $\frac{1}{2}$ of 6 per cent = 3 per cent; 3 per cent is $\frac{3}{100}$; $\frac{3}{100}$ of $50 = $1 and 50 ct.

2. Find the interest of $60 for 4 mo., at 5 per cent.
3. Find the interest of $80 for 7 mo., at 6 per cent.
4. Find the interest of $40 for 9 mo., at 8 per cent.
5. Find the interest of $75 for 8 mo., at 9 per cent.

What is the interest

6. Of $120 for 6 mo. 15 da., at 6 per cent?

SOLUTION.—6 mo. 15 da. are $\frac{13}{24}$ yr ; the interest for $\frac{13}{24}$ yr. is $\frac{13}{24}$ of 6 per cent = $\frac{13}{4}$ per cent; $\frac{13}{4}$ per cent is $\frac{13}{400}$; $\frac{13}{400}$ of $120 = $3.90.

7. Of $180 for 10 mo. 10 da., at 4 per cent?
8. Of $45 for 11 mo. 23 da., at 8 per cent?

SOLUTION.—The interest of $45 for 1 year is $3.60; for 1 month, $\frac{1}{12}$ of $3.60 = 30 ct.; and for 1 day, $\frac{1}{30}$ of 30 ct. = 1 ct. The interest for 11 months is, therefore, $3.30; for 23 days, 23 ct.; and the total interest is $3.53.

9. Of $200 for 4 mo. 24 da., at 6 per cent?
10. Of $480 for 9 mo. 18 da., at 5 per cent?
11. Of $360 for 5 mo. 19 da., at 5 per cent?
12. Of $144 for 8 mo. 25 da., at 4 per cent?
13. Of $40 for 1 yr. 4 mo., at 6 per cent?

14. Of $60 for 2 yr. 3 mo., at 5 per cent?
15. Of $75 for 1 yr. 3 mo. 6 da., at 4 per cent?

What is the amount

16. Of $25 for 3 yr., at 4 per cent?
17. Of $40 for 2 yr., at 5 per cent?
18. Of $55 for 3 yr., at 8 per cent?
19. Of $30 for 1 yr., 4 mo., at 7 per cent?
20. Of $50 for 2 yr. 3 mo. 6 da., at 6 per cent?
21. Of $90 for 1 yr. 3 mo. 6 da., at 8 per cent?

LESSON 74

1. The interest of a certain principal for 2 yr., at 6 per cent, is $3: what is the principal?

SOLUTION.—The interest is 12 per cent $= \frac{3}{25}$; then, $\frac{3}{25}$ of the principal are $3; whence the principal is $25.

2. The interest of a certain principal for 3 yr., at 4 per cent, is $6: what is the principal?
3. What principal at interest for 4 yr., at 5 per cent, will produce $12 interest?
4. What principal at interest for 5 yr., at 8 per cent, will produce $30 interest?
5. What principal at interest for 4 yr., at $7\frac{1}{2}$ per cent, will produce $42 interest?
6. What principal at interest for 2 yr. 6 mo., at 6 per cent., will produce $36 interest?
7. What principal at interest for 3 yr. 4 mo., at 6 per cent, will produce $70 interest?
8. A father wishes to place such a sum at interest, at 5 per cent., as will produce for his son an annual income of $200: what sum must he invest?

LESSON 75

1. What principal on interest for 2 yr., at 5 per cent, will amount to $55?

SOLUTION.—The interest is 10 per cent $= \frac{1}{10}$; then, $\frac{10}{10} + \frac{1}{10} = \frac{11}{10}$; $\frac{11}{10}$ of the principal are $55; whence the principal is $50.

What principal on interest,

2. At 6 per cent, for 3 yr., will amount to $236?
3. At 5 per cent, for 4 yr., will amount to $600?
4. At 10 per cent, for 5 yr., will amount to $375?
5. At 6 per cent, for 5 yr., will amount to $390?
6. The amount due on a note which has been on interest 3 yr. 4 mo., at 6 per cent, is $30: what is the face of the note?
7. The amount of two-fifths of A's money on interest for 2 yr. 6 mo., at 8 per cent, is $60: what is his whole principal?

LESSON 76

1. In what time, at 6 per cent, will $50 give $10 interest?

SOLUTION.—The interest for 1 yr. is $3; then, the time will be as many years as $3 are contained times in $10, which are $3\frac{1}{3} = 3$ yr. 4 mo.

In what time,

2. At 5 per cent, will $40 give $8 interest?
3. At 8 per cent, will $75 give $15 interest?
4. At 10 per cent, will $60 give $16 interest?
5. At 5 per cent, will $140 give $24 interest?
6. At 6 per cent, will $25 give $10 interest?

7. In what time, at 4 per cent, will any given principal double itself?

Solution.—Any principal will double itself in as many years as 4 per cent is contained times in 100 per cent, which are 25.

8. In what time will any given principal double itself, at 2 per cent? At 3 per cent? At 5 per cent? At 6 per cent? At 7 per cent? At 8? At 10? At 12?

9. In what time will any given principal treble itself, at 5 per cent?

10. In what time will any given principal treble itself, at 8 per cent? At 10 per cent?

LESSON 77

1. At what per cent will $200, in 2 yr., give $24 interest?

Solution.—The interest for 1 yr. is $\frac{1}{2}$ of $24 = $12; this is $\frac{12}{200} = \frac{3}{50}$ of the principal; $\frac{3}{50}$ are 6 per cent.

At what per cent,

2. Will $50 in 5 yr., give $20 interest?
3. Will $75 in 3 yr., give $11\frac{1}{4}$ interest?
4. Will $300 in 3 yr., give $63 interest?
5. Will $300 in 2 yr. 3 mo., give $54 interest?
6. Will $240 in 3 yr. 4 mo., give $56 interest?
7. Will $200 in 4 yr., amount to $240?
8. Will $150 in 3 yr. 8 mo., amount to $183?
9. Will any given principal double itself in 20 yr.?

Solution.—Any principal will double itself at $\frac{1}{20}$ of 100 = 5 per cent.

10. At what per cent will any given principal double itself in 12 yr.? In 10 yr.? 8 yr.? 5 yr.? 4 yr.? 2 yr.?

Discount corresponds to interest, but is paid in advance; *present worth* corresponds to principal; and the *sum given*, to amount.

1. What is the present worth and discount, at 5 per cent, of a note for $72, due 4 yr. hence?

SOLUTION.—The discount is 20 per cent $= \frac{1}{5}$; $\frac{5}{5} + \frac{1}{5} = \frac{6}{5}$; then, $\frac{6}{5}$ of the present worth $= 72; whence the present worth is $60, and the discount $12.

2. What is the present worth and discount, at 6 per cent, of a note for $520, due 5 yr. hence?

3. What is the present worth and discount, at 4 per cent, of a note for $30, due 5 yr. hence?

4. What is the present worth and discount, at 10 per cent, of a note for $750, due 5 yr. hence?

5. What is the discount, at 5 per cent, of a note for $345, due 3 yr. hence?

6. What is the discount, at 6 per cent, of a note for $496, due 4 yr. hence?

7. What is the discount, at 5 per cent, of a note for $24, due 4 yr. hence?

8. What is the present worth, at 6 per cent, of a note for $65, due 5 yr. hence?

9. What is the present worth, at 5 per cent, of a note for $55, due 5 yr. hence?

10. What is the present worth, at 6 per cent, of a note for $77, due 6 yr. 8 mo. hence?

11. What is the discount, at 7 per cent, of a note for $1000, due in 3 yr. 6 mo.?

12. What is the discount, at 8 per cent, of a note for $900, due in 2 yr. 9 mo.?

1. At 6 per cent, for 4 yr. 2 mo., what part of the principal is equal to the interest?

2. At 5 per cent, for 5 yr., what part of the amount is equal to the interest?

3. When the interest for 2 yr. $= \frac{1}{5}$ of the principal, what is the rate per cent?

4. When the interest for 2 yr. 6 mo. $= \frac{1}{4}$ of the principal, what is the rate per cent?

5. When the interest, at 10 per cent. $= \frac{3}{5}$ of the principal, what is the time?

6. When 3 times the yearly interest $= \frac{9}{25}$ of the principal, what is the rate per cent?

7. When $\frac{1}{5}$ of the interest for 2 yr. $= \frac{4}{25}$ of the principal, what is the rate per cent?

8. When $\frac{5}{8}$ of the interest for 3 yr. $= \frac{9}{80}$ of the principal, what is the rate per cent?

9. The interest for 8 mo. is $\frac{1}{25}$ of the principal: what is the interest of $200 for 1 yr. 4 mo.?

10. If the interest for 1 yr. 4 mo., is $\frac{3}{25}$ of the principal, what is the interest of $100 for 1 yr. 8 mo. 12 da.?

11. In what time will any principal, at 5 per cent, give the same interest as in 4 yr., at 10 per cent?

12. The interest of A's and B's money for $3\frac{1}{3}$ yr., at 5 per cent, is $40, and A's money is twice that of B's: what sum has each?

13. Twice A's money $= 3$ times B's; and the interest, at 7 per cent for $1\frac{2}{5}$ yr., of what they both have, is $49: how much money has each?

14. One half of A's money $= \frac{2}{3}$ of B's; and the interest of $\frac{3}{4}$ of A's and $\frac{1}{2}$ of B's money, at 4 per cent, for 2 yr. 3 mo., is $18: how much has each?

PROBLEMS.

LESSON 80

1. If 12 peaches are worth 84 apples, and 8 apples are worth 24 plums, how many plums shall I give for 5 peaches?

2. Divide 32 peaches among Mary, James, and Lucy, giving Mary 2 more than Lucy, and Lucy 3 more than James.

3. Five times a certain number is 16 more than 3 times the same number: what is the number?

4. A has $\frac{1}{2}$ as much money as B; B has $\frac{1}{3}$ as much as C; C has $15 more than A: how much has each?

5. If $\frac{3}{4}$ of James's money be increased by $6, the sum will equal what Thomas has; both together have $34: how much has each?

6. A farmer sold $\frac{3}{8}$ of his sheep, but soon afterward purchased $\frac{4}{9}$ as many as he had left; he then had 65 sheep: how many sheep had he at first?

7. If 3 men can perform a piece of work in 4 days, working 10 hours a day, in how many days can 8 men perform the same job, working 6 hours a day?

8. Thomas bought a number of apples, at 2 for 3 ct., and as many more at 2 for 5 ct.; he sold all at the rate of 3 for 7 ct.: how much per dozen did he gain?

9. A, B, and C rent a pasture for $92; A puts in 4 horses for 2 mo.; B, 9 cows for 3 mo.; and C, 20 sheep

for 5 mo.: what should each pay, if 2 horses eat as much as 3 cows, or as much as 10 sheep?

10. A father who had as many sons as daughters, divided $20 among them, giving to each daughter $2, and to each son $3: how many children had he?

11. A gentleman meeting some beggars, found that if he gave each of them 3 ct. he would have 12 ct. left, but if he gave each of them 5 ct. he would not have money enough by 8 ct.: how many beggars were there?

SOLUTION.—To give each beggar 5 ct. took 5 — 3 = 2 ct. more than to give him 3 ct.; to give all the beggars 5 ct. each took 12 + 8 = 20 ct. more than to give them 3 ct. each; then, there were as many beggars as 2 ct. are contained times in 20 ct., which are 10.

12. A father wishes to distribute some peaches among his children; if he give each of them 2 peaches he will have 9 left, but if he give each 4 peaches he will have 3 left: how many children has he?

13. A hare is 10 leaps before a hound, and takes 4 leaps while the hound takes 3; but 2 of the hound's leaps equal 3 of the hare's: how many leaps must the hound take to catch the hare?

SOLUTION.—One of the hound's leaps = $\frac{3}{2}$ of the hare's, and 3 of them = $4\frac{1}{2}$ leaps of the hare; then, in taking 3 leaps, the hound gains on the hare $4\frac{1}{2} - 4 = \frac{1}{2}$ a leap. Since the hound gains $\frac{1}{2}$ a leap in taking 3 leaps, he gains 1 leap in taking 2 times 3 = 6 leaps, and he gains 10 leaps in taking 10 times 6 = 60 leaps.

14. Henry is 7 steps ahead of John, and takes 6 steps while John takes 5; but 4 of John's steps equal 5 of Henry's: how many steps must John take to overtake Henry?

15. If 1 ox is worth 8 sheep, and 3 oxen are worth 2 horses, what is the value of 1 horse, if a sheep is worth $5?

16. A and B had 24 ct.; B said to A, "Give me 2 ct. and I shall have as much money as you have now": how many cents had each?

17. The age of A is $\frac{1}{2}$ the age of B; twice the age of A is $\frac{1}{3}$ the age of C; C is 20 yr. older than B: what is the age of each?

18. If $\frac{2}{3}$ of A's money equals $\frac{4}{5}$ of B's, and $\frac{3}{4}$ of their difference is $15: how much money has each?

19. If 10 gal. of water per hour run into a vessel containing 15 gal., and 17 gal. run out in 2 hr.: how long will the vessel be in filling?

20. Charles bought a number of eggs at 2 ct. each, and twice as many at 3 ct. each; he sold them at the rate of 3 for 10 ct.: what per cent did he gain?

21. Mary wishes to divide some cherries among her playmates; she finds if she give each of them 5 she will have 21 left, but if she give each 8 she will have none left: what is the number of her playmates?

22. Henry is 30 steps before John, but John takes 7 steps while Henry takes 5: supposing the length of their steps to be equal, how many steps must John take to overtake Henry?

23. My chain cost $\frac{2}{7}$ as much as my watch; 3 times the price of my chain and twice the price of my watch are $100: what did each cost?

24. A can do a piece of work in $4\frac{1}{2}$ days; A and B together in $2\frac{4}{7}$ days: in what time can B do it alone?

25. I bought a number of pears at 2 for 1 ct., and as many more at 4 for 1 ct.; by selling 5 for 3 ct. I gained 18 ct.: how many pears did I buy?

26. A note for $50, bearing interest at 6 per cent, and due in 3 years, was disposed of by the holder for $50, 2 years before it was due: what rate of interest did the buyer receive for his money?

27. A lady wished to buy a certain number of yards of silk for a dress: if she paid $1 a yard she would have $5 left, but if she paid 1\frac{1}{2}$ a yard, it would take all her money: how many yards did she want?

28. If $5 be taken from $\frac{2}{5}$ of A's money, the remainder will equal B's; both together have $51: how much has each?

29. If $\frac{2}{3}$ of the gain be $\frac{4}{15}$ of the selling price, for how much will 3$\frac{3}{4}$ yards of cloth be sold, that cost $4 a yard?

30. A hare is 100 leaps before a hound, and takes 5 leaps while the hound takes 3; but 3 leaps of the hound equal 10 leaps of the hare: how many leaps must the hound take to catch the hare?

31. Thomas's age is 3 times that of James, and the difference of their ages is 10 years: how old is each?

32. John started from C the same time that George started from D; when they met, $\frac{3}{7}$ of the distance John had traveled was $\frac{4}{5}$ of the distance George had traveled; from C to D is 86 miles: how far had each traveled?

33. I sell a certain kind of cloth for 24 cents a yard, and make 20%; if I could buy it for 25 per cent less, and should sell it at 30 cents a yard, how much greater would be my profit?

34. If I sell a lot of eggs at 6 ct. a dozen, I will lose 12 ct., but if I sell them at 10 ct. a dozen, I will gain 18 ct.: what did they cost a dozen?

35. The age of A is twice the age of B, and $\frac{3}{5}$ of B's age + 44 years equals 2$\frac{1}{2}$ times the age of A: what is the age of each?

36. Three towns, A, B, and C, are situated on the same road; the distance from A to B is 24 miles, and $\frac{7}{8}$ of the distance from A to B equals $\frac{3}{7}$ of the distance from B to C: how far is it from A to C?

37. A, B, and C can do a piece of work in 4 days, A and B in 8 days, B and C in 6 days: in what time can each do it alone?

38. A provision dealer bought a number of ducks, at the rate of 6 for $1; and twice as many chickens, at the rate of 8 for $1; by selling them at the rate of 2 chickens and 1 duck for $\frac{1}{2}$, he gained $2\frac{1}{2}$: how many of each did he buy?

39. To buy a certain number of oranges, at 8 ct. each, requires 6 cents more than all the money James has; but if he buy the same number of lemons, at 3 ct. each, he will have 29 ct. left: how much money has he?

40. A rides 10 miles in $1\frac{1}{4}$ hours, and B, 8 miles in $1\frac{3}{5}$ hours: how far will B travel while A is traveling 18 miles?

41. If A had $\frac{1}{2}$ as many dollars more, and $2\frac{1}{2}$ besides, he would have $40: how many has he?

42. A person having three sons, A, B, and C, willed $\frac{3}{7}$ of his estate to A, $\frac{1}{3}$ to B, and the remainder to C; the difference of the legacies of A and C was $160: what amount did each receive?

43. A man and his wife consume a sack of meal in 15 days; after living together 6 days, the woman alone consumed the remainder in 24 days: how long would a sack last either of them alone?

44. If sugar, worth $3\frac{1}{2}$ cents a pound, be mixed in equal quantities with sugar worth $6\frac{1}{2}$ cents a pound, how many pounds of the mixture will be worth $1?

45. The age of A is 5 times the age of B, and the age of B is twice the age of C. A is 45 years older than C: what is the age of each?

46. The age of Mary is $\frac{2}{5}$ of the age of Ella, and the sum of their ages is 6 years less than twice the age of Ella: what is the age of each?

47. A and B together can do a piece of work in 16 days; they work 4 days, when A leaves, and B finishes the work in 36 days more: in how many days can each do it?

48. A man bought 84 eggs, which he intended to sell as follows: 3 dozen, at 1 ct. apiece; 2 dozen, at 4 eggs for 3 ct.; and the rest at 4 eggs for 5 ct.: but, having mixed them, how must he sell them per dozen to get the intended price?

49. A man agreed to pay a laborer $2 for every day he worked; the laborer, for every day he was idle, was to forfeit $1; at the expiration of 20 days he received $25: how many days was he idle?

SOLUTION.—If the laborer had worked every day he would have received 20 times $2 = $40; then, he lost by being idle $40 — $25 = $15. Every day he was idle he lost $2 + $1 = $3; then, he was idle as many days as $3 are contained times in $15, which are 5.

50. James was hired for 30 days; for every day he worked he was to receive 30 cents, and for every day he was idle he was to pay 20 cents for his board; at the end of the time he received $5: how many days did he work?

51. There are two pieces of muslin, each containing the same number of yards; to buy the first, at 12½ cents a yard, requires 40 cents more than to buy the second, at 10 cents a yard: how many yards in each?

52. Noah is 35 steps ahead of Moses, and takes 7 steps while Moses takes 5; but 4 of Moses's steps equal 7 of Noah's: how many steps must Moses take to overtake Noah?

53. If 1 man does as much work as 2 women, and 1 woman as much as 3 boys: how many men would it take to do in 1 day what 12 boys are a week in doing?

54. A farmer's sheep are in three fields; the second contains 4 times as many as the first; the third contains 3 times as many as the second, and 70 more than both the first and second: how many sheep are there in each field?

55. A laborer engaged to work 24 days, for $2 a day and his board; he agreed to pay 50 cents a day for his board when he did not work; at the end of the time he received $38: how many days did he work?

56. Three persons, A, B, and C, are to share a certain sum of money, of which A's part is $12; this is $\frac{2}{7}$ of the sum of the shares of B and C; $\frac{3}{8}$ of C's share is equal to $\frac{3}{10}$ of the sum of the shares of A and B: what is the share of each?

57. For how much should a package of sugar weighing $6\frac{6}{7}$ lb. be sold, to gain $16\frac{2}{3}$ per cent, when sugar costs 8 cents a pound?

58. Two men formed a partnership for 1 year; the first put in $100, and the second, $200: how much must the first put in at the end of 6 months, to entitle him to $\frac{1}{2}$ the profit?

59. If I sell my sugar at 9 cents a pound I will lose $1, but if I sell it at 12 cents a pound, I will gain 50 cents: how many pounds have I?

60. B is pursuing A, who is some distance in advance; B goes 4 steps while A goes 5, but 3 of A's steps equal 2 of B's; B goes 36 steps before overtaking A: how many steps is A in advance of B?

61. John bought 5 oranges and James 4 oranges; they were then joined by Thomas, and each one ate an equal part of the oranges; when Thomas left, he gave them 9 cents: how should this be divided?

KEY TO
RAY'S INTELLECTUAL
ARITHMETIC

答 案

SOLUTIONS

MORE DIFFICULT EXAMPLES

IN

RAY'S NEW INTELLECTUAL ARITHMETIC.

LESSON I.

18. All together have the sum of 5 dollars, 3 dollars, and 1 dollar, which is 9 dollars.

25. As many as the sum of 4, 4, and 2, which is 10.

LESSON II.

25. I have the sum of 10 cents, 5 cents, 3 cents, and 3 cents, which is 21 cents.

LESSON V.

37. William's age is the sum of 8 years and 5 years, which is 13 years; and the sum of all their ages is 13 years, plus 5 years, plus 8 years, which is 26 years.

139

LESSON VII.

24. I received in money as many dollars as the difference between 17 dollars and 6 dollars, which is 11 dollars.

LESSON VIII.

19. I spent the sum of 20 cents and 10 cents, which is 30 cents; I had left the difference between 65· cents and 30 cents, which is 35 cents.

LESSON IX.

8. Both had the sum of 18 marbles and 18 marbles, which is 36 marbles; if when they quit one had 25 marbles, the other had the difference between 36 marbles and 25 marbles, which is 11 marbles.

14. He is worth the sum of 20 dollars and 10 dollars, which is 30 dollars. He owes the sum of 5 dollars, 6 dollars, and 10 dollars, which is 21 dollars. Should he pay his debts, he would be worth the difference between 30 dollars and 21 dollars, which is 9 dollars.

LESSON XI.

4. The sum of 19 and 10 is 29; the difference between 17 and 10 is 7; if I take 7, the difference, from 29, the sum, 22 will be left.

21. There are as many peach-trees in the orchard as the sum of 15 peach-trees, 9 peach-trees, and 10 peach-trees, which is 34 peach-trees. There are as many apple-trees as the sum of 5 apple-trees, 11 apple-trees, and 10 apple-trees, which is 26 apple-trees. Then there are as many more peach-trees than apple-trees as the difference between 34 trees and 26 trees, which is 8 trees.

LESSON XII.

22. If 1 yard of muslin cost 11 cents, 3 yards will cost 3 times 11 cents, which is 33 cents.

LESSON XIV.

11. If a man travel 7 miles in 1 hour, in 8 hours he will travel 8 times 7 miles, which is 56 miles.

17. In one hour they would be as far apart as the sum of 2 miles and 4 miles, which is 6 miles; in 3 hours they would be 3 times 6 miles apart, which is 18 miles.

LESSON XVI.

22. Each one would receive one sixth of 36 dollars, which is 6 dollars.

23. Since there are 4 quarts in 1 gallon, in 36 quarts there are as many gallons as 4 quarts are contained times in 36 quarts, which are 9.

LESSON XVIII.

24. One man will earn in 3 days one ninth of $108, which is $12. In one day he would earn one third of $12, which is $4.

25. In 1 day the former travels one third of 15 miles, which is 5 miles. In 1 day the latter travels one half of 20 miles, which is 10 miles; and if the latter travels 10 miles in 1 day, and the former, 5 miles, the latter travels as much farther in 1 day than the former as the difference between 10 miles and 5 miles, which is 5 miles.

LESSON XIX.

7. The sum of 1, 2, and 3 is 6, and 6 is contained in 60 ten times. If I have as many marbles as 3 times the number of times 6 is contained in 60, I have 3 times 10 marbles, which is 30 marbles.

8. Six hats will cost 6 times $5, which is $30; 4 yards of cloth will cost 4 times $3, which is $12. Both will cost the sum of $30 and $12, which is $42; and if he gave in exchange flour at $6 a barrel, it took as many barrels as $6 are contained times in $42, which are 7.

9. If a man gain 6 miles in 5 hours, it will take as many times 5 hours to gain 24 miles as 6 miles are contained times in 24 miles, which are 4; and 4 times 5 hours are 20 hours.

34. It will take 1 man 3 times 10 days, which is 30 days. It will take as many men to do it in 5 days as 5 days are contained times in 30 days, which are 6.

LESSON XXII.

2. One third of an apple is worth $\frac{1}{3}$ of three cents, which is 1 cent.

5. One fourth of a melon is worth $\frac{1}{4}$ of 8 cents, which is 2 cents; and if $\frac{1}{4}$ of a melon is worth 2 cents, $\frac{3}{4}$ of a melon are worth 3 times 2 cents, which is 6 cents.

23. One calf cost $\frac{1}{12}$ of $120, which is $10; and if 1 calf cost $10, he sold the 7 calves for 7 times $10, which is $70.

LESSON XXIII.

9. For $1 you can buy $\frac{1}{8}$ of a bushel, and for $5 you can buy 5 times $\frac{1}{8}$ of a bushel, which is $\frac{5}{8}$ of a bushel.

16. One fifth of 30 is 6; then $\frac{3}{5}$ of 30 are 3 times 6, which is 18; and 18 is $\frac{18}{23}$ of 23.

LESSON XXIV.

7. One sixth of a gallon will cost $\frac{1}{6}$ of 35 cents, which is 7 cents; and if $\frac{1}{6}$ of a gallon cost 7 cents, $\frac{6}{6}$, or 1 gallon, will cost 6 times 7 cents, which is 42 cents.

17. One fourth of 8 cents is 2 cents, and $\frac{3}{4}$ are 3 times 2 cents, which is 6 cents; and if 6 cents are $\frac{2}{3}$ of mine, $\frac{1}{3}$ of mine is $\frac{1}{2}$ of 6 cents, which is 3 cents; and if 3 cents are $\frac{1}{3}$, then $\frac{3}{3}$ will be 3 times 3 cents, which is 9 cents.

LESSON XXV.

4. One yard will cost $\frac{1}{3}$ of 5 dollars, which is $1\frac{2}{3}$ dollars.

LESSON XXVI.

4. Since there are $\frac{4}{4}$ in 1, in 3 there are 3 times $\frac{4}{4}$, which is $\frac{12}{4}$; and $\frac{12}{4} + \frac{1}{4} = \frac{13}{4}$. Other answers, $\frac{19}{4}$, $\frac{21}{4}$, $\frac{27}{4}$.

LESSON XXVII.

13. To reduce a fraction to its lowest terms, divide both terms by their greatest common divisor. Of 27 and 36, the G. C. D. is 9; 9 in 27 is contained 3 times, and 9 in 36 is contained 4 times.

Therefore, $\frac{27}{36}$ changed to its lowest terms $= \frac{3}{4}$.

LESSON XXVIII.

10. Since there are $\frac{8}{8}$ in 1, in $\frac{1}{4}$ there is $\frac{1}{4}$ of $\frac{8}{8}$, which is $\frac{2}{8}$; and if $\frac{2}{8} = \frac{1}{4}$, then $\frac{3}{4}$ will be 3 times $\frac{2}{8}$, which is $\frac{6}{8}$.

LESSON XXIX.

4. The common denominator is 15. $1 = \frac{15}{15}$; $\frac{1}{3} = \frac{5}{15}$, and $\frac{2}{3} = \frac{10}{15}$; $\frac{1}{5} = \frac{3}{15}$, and $\frac{2}{5} = \frac{6}{15}$.

LESSON XXX.

2. Three fourths $= \frac{6}{8}$, and $\frac{1}{2} = \frac{4}{8}$. He gave for both $\$\frac{6}{8} + \$\frac{4}{8} = \$\frac{10}{8} = \$1\frac{1}{4}$.

LESSON XXXI.

3. One half of the first $= \frac{3}{6}$ of a melon; $\frac{2}{3}$ of the second $= \frac{4}{6}$ of a melon. $\frac{4}{6} - \frac{3}{6} = \frac{1}{6}$.

LESSON XXXII.

14. Find how much is in both air and water: as much as the sum of $\frac{1}{2}$ and $\frac{1}{3}$. $\frac{1}{2} = \frac{3}{6}$, and $\frac{1}{3} = \frac{2}{6}$; their sum is $\frac{5}{6}$. Since there are $\frac{6}{6}$ in the pole, there would be as much in the earth as the difference between $\frac{6}{6}$ and $\frac{5}{6}$, which is $\frac{1}{6}$.

LESSON XXXIII.

2. To 5 horses he would give 5 times $\frac{1}{2}$ peck, which is $\frac{5}{2}$ pecks; and $\frac{5}{2}$ pecks $= 2\frac{1}{2}$ pecks.

LESSON XXXIV.

8. One pound of cheese will sell for $\frac{1}{4}$ of 30 cents, which is $7\frac{1}{2}$ cents. Then 3 pounds will sell for 3 times $7\frac{1}{2}$ cents, which is $22\frac{1}{2}$ cents.

28. One seventh of 18 is $2\frac{4}{7}$; then $\frac{2}{7} = 2$ times $2\frac{4}{7}$ feet, which is $5\frac{1}{7}$ feet; and $\frac{5}{7} = 5$ times $2\frac{4}{7}$ feet, which is $12\frac{6}{7}$ feet.

29. One ninth of $15 is $1\frac{2}{3}$; then $\frac{2}{9} = 2$ times $1\frac{2}{3}$, which is $3\frac{1}{3}$; $\frac{1}{3}$ of $15 is $5; $5 + $3\frac{1}{3} = $8\frac{1}{3}$, $15 - $8\frac{1}{3} = $6\frac{2}{3}$.

31. $\frac{5}{5} - \frac{2}{5} = \frac{3}{5}$. $18 = \frac{3}{5}$ of the number, then $\frac{1}{5}$ would be $\frac{1}{3}$ of $18, which is $6; and $\frac{2}{5}$ would be 2 times $6, which is $12.

32. $45 = \frac{7}{7} + \frac{2}{7}$, which is $\frac{9}{7}$ of the cost. $\frac{1}{7}$ is $\frac{1}{9}$ of $45 = $5; and $\frac{7}{7}$ would be 7 times $5 = $35.

LESSON XXXVI.

22. Five and three sevenths pounds of sugar cost $5\frac{3}{7}$ times 7 cents, which is 38 cents. It would take as many pounds of raisins to pay for it as 6 cents are contained times in 38 cents, which are $6\frac{1}{3}$.

LESSON XXXVIII.

9. One pound will cost $\frac{1}{4}$ of $\$\frac{5}{4} = \$\frac{5}{16}$; then 7 pounds will cost 7 times $\$\frac{5}{16} = \$\frac{35}{16} = \$2\frac{3}{16}$.

LESSON XXXIX.

16. The sum of $\frac{1}{5}$ and $\frac{2}{5} = \frac{3}{5}$; $\frac{5}{5} - \frac{3}{5} = \frac{2}{5}$; then 14 ft. $= \frac{2}{5}$ of the pole; $\frac{1}{5} = 7$ ft.; $\frac{5}{5} = 35$ ft.

23. $\$12 = \frac{4}{3}$ of the cost; $\frac{1}{3}$ of the cost is $\frac{1}{4}$ of $\$12 = \$3$; $\frac{3}{3} = \$9$. One yard cost $\frac{1}{5}$ of $\$9 = \$1\frac{4}{5}$.

28. One eighth of the cost was $\frac{1}{5}$ of $\$50$, which is $\$10$; then $\frac{8}{8}$ are 8 times $\$10$, which is $\$80$. It would take as many yards as $\$4$ are contained times in $\$80$, which are 20.

LESSON XL.

11. One third of the number is $\frac{1}{8}$ of 56, which is 7; then $\frac{3}{3}$ are 3 times 7, which is 21; 21 is 3 times 7.

LESSON XLI.

9. One fourth of a bu. of wheat is worth $\frac{1}{8}$ of a bu. of rye; then $\frac{4}{4}$ of a bu. of wheat are worth $\frac{4}{8}$ of a bu. of rye; and $\frac{1}{5}$ of a bu. of wheat is worth $\frac{1}{5}$ of $\frac{4}{8}$ of a bu. of rye, which is $\frac{4}{15}$ of a bu. of rye; and $\frac{4}{5}$ of a bu. of wheat are worth 4 times $\frac{4}{15}$ of a bu. of rye, which is $\frac{16}{15}$, or $1\frac{1}{15}$ bu. of rye.

LESSON XLIII

22. As many bu. of rye as $\frac{3}{4}$ are contained times in $4\frac{1}{2}$. $4\frac{1}{2} = \frac{18}{4}$; $\frac{18}{4} \div \frac{3}{4} = 6$.

LESSON XLIV.

11. $3\frac{1}{10} = \$\frac{31}{10}$; $7\frac{3}{4} = \frac{31}{4}$; $\frac{1}{4}$ of a doz. cost $\frac{1}{31}$ of $\$\frac{31}{10}$, which is $\$\frac{1}{10}$; then 1 pair cost $\frac{1}{3}$ of $\$\frac{1}{10}$, or $\$\frac{1}{30}$. He gained the difference between $\$\frac{1}{10}$ and $\$\frac{1}{30}$, which is $\$\frac{1}{15}$.

12. $2\frac{1}{2} = \frac{5}{2}$. $\frac{1}{2}$ doz. cost $\frac{1}{5}$ of $15, which is $3; then each one cost $\frac{1}{6}$ of $3, which is $\frac{1}{2}$. He gained on each one the difference between $\$\frac{3}{5}$ and $\$\frac{1}{2}$, which is $\$\frac{1}{10}$.

On $\frac{1}{2}$ doz. he gained $\$\frac{6}{10}$; and on $\frac{5}{2}$ doz. $\$\frac{30}{10}$, or $3.

LESSON XLV.

22. A walks 5 miles 7 times in walking 35 miles; B walks 3 miles 7 times in the same time. Therefore, B walks 7 times 3 miles, which is 21 miles.

25. One horse will eat $\frac{1}{6}$ of 12 bu. in a week, which is 2 bu. a week; then 10 horses will eat 10 times 2 bu. in a week, which is 20 bushels.

26. Five horses will eat in 1 week $\frac{1}{2}$ of 16 bu., which is 8 bu; to eat 56 bu., it will take them as many weeks as 8 is contained times in 56, which are 7.

28. It will take 6 times 12 horses, which is 72 horses, to eat it in 1 day; and to eat it in 9 days it will take $\frac{1}{9}$ of 72 horses, which is 8 horses.

LESSON XLVI.

6. Nine times $9 = 81$. $81 \div 12 = 6\frac{9}{12}$, or $6\frac{3}{4}$.

8. $\frac{48}{120} = \frac{2}{5}$. $\frac{54}{189} = \frac{2}{7}$. $\frac{240}{288} = \frac{5}{6}$.

9. One ninth $= \frac{16}{144}$, $\frac{3}{9} = \frac{48}{144}$; $\frac{1}{16} = \frac{9}{144}$, $\frac{4}{16} = \frac{36}{144}$; $\frac{1}{72} = \frac{2}{144}$, $\frac{17}{72} = \frac{34}{144}$.

12. If he traveled $\frac{1}{4}$, or $\frac{3}{12}$, the first day, and $\frac{1}{3}$, or $\frac{4}{12}$, the second day, then the third day he must have traveled $\frac{12}{12}$ less $\frac{7}{12}$, which is $\frac{5}{12}$; $\frac{5}{12}$ of 84 miles $= 35$ miles.

21. $99 = \frac{8}{8} + \frac{3}{8}$, or $\frac{11}{8}$, of the cost; then $\frac{1}{8} = \$9$, and $\frac{8}{8}$, the cost, $= \$72$.

22. One eighth of $96 = \$12$, or $\frac{1}{5}$ of the cost; then the cost was 5 times $12 = \$60$. It took as many barrels of flour to pay for the horse as $6 are contained times in $60, which are 10.

23. Eighty-four is $\frac{7}{6}$ of 72, and 72 is 8 times 9.

25. Eight ninths of $81 = 72$, and $72 = \frac{9}{8}$ of 64.

26. Four sevenths of 35 are 20, and 20 is $\frac{5}{6}$ of 24. Three eighths of 16 are 6, and 24 is 4 times 6.

27. $17\frac{1}{2} = \$\frac{35}{2}$. $4\frac{3}{8}$ yd. $= \frac{35}{8}$ yd. $\frac{1}{8}$ of a yd. would cost $\frac{1}{35}$ of $\$\frac{35}{2}$, which is $\$\frac{1}{2}$; then $\frac{8}{8}$ of a yd. would cost $\$\frac{8}{2}$, or $4.

33. In one week he would earn $\frac{1}{8}$ of $72, which is $9; in one day he would earn $\frac{1}{6}$ of $9, which is $1\frac{1}{2}$.

37. One half of 20 years $= 10$ years, or $\frac{1}{5}$ of the father's age; then 5 times 10 years $= 50$ years, the father's age. $\frac{1}{10}$ of 50 years $= 5$ years, or the age of the youngest son.

38. $21 = \frac{7}{5}$ of the cost. $\frac{1}{5} = \frac{1}{7}$ of $21, which is $3. $\frac{5}{5} = \$15$, or the cost. At $1 a bushel, it would take 15 bushels of corn to pay for it; at $\$\frac{1}{3}$, it would take 3 times 15 bushels, which is 45 bushels.

39. Three yards $= \frac{15}{5}$ yards. $\frac{15}{5}$ are 5 times $\frac{3}{5}$, and will cost 5 times $\$\frac{2}{3}$, which is $\$3\frac{1}{3}$.

41. One half of $12 = 6$. $6 + 2 = 8$. 8 is $\frac{1}{3}$ of 24.

44. Three fourths of $24 = 18$. $18 - 6 = 12$. 12 is $\frac{2}{3}$ of 18. 18 is 6 more than $\frac{2}{3}$ of itself.

50. Two fifths of 30 yards $= 12$ yards. He sold one yard for $\frac{1}{12}$ of $48, which is $4.

60. Three fifths of $20 are $12. Fourteen is $\frac{7}{9}$ of 18, and 2 times 18 are 36. Twelve is $\frac{1}{3}$ of 36.

79. Two fifths of 10 yards are 4 yards, and they cost $\frac{2}{5}$ of $90, which is $36. $40 - $36 = $4, the gain on 4 yards, and on 1 yard the gain is $1.

80. B gains in one day 23 miles less 18 miles, which are 5 miles. It will take as many days to gain 40 miles as 5 miles are contained times in 40 miles, which are 8.

81. The hound gains in one second 10 feet less 7 feet $= 3$ ft., or 1 yd.; then to gain 90 yards it will take 90 seconds, or $1\frac{1}{2}$ min. The hound runs 90 times 10 feet, which are 900 ft. $= 300$ yd. The hare runs 90 times 7 ft. $= 630$ feet, or 210 yd.

85. In one hour the cistern would lose 9 gallons less 6 gallons, which are 3 gallons; and it would take as many hours to empty the cistern as 3 gallons are contained times in 36 gallons, which are 12.

89. Such part of the journey as $2\frac{1}{4}$ days are of $3\frac{3}{8}$ days. $3\frac{3}{8} = \frac{27}{8}$. $2\frac{1}{4} = \frac{18}{8}$. $\frac{18}{8} = \frac{18}{27}$, or $\frac{2}{3}$, of $\frac{27}{8}$. He can therefore perform $\frac{2}{3}$ of the journey in $2\frac{1}{4}$ days.

90. In one day A can do $\frac{1}{2}$, B $\frac{1}{4}$, and C $\frac{1}{6}$; then all do the sum of $\frac{1}{2}$, $\frac{1}{4}$, and $\frac{1}{6}$, which is $\frac{11}{12}$, in one day. To do $\frac{12}{12}$, it will take as many days as $\frac{11}{12}$ are contained times in $\frac{12}{12}$, which are $1\frac{1}{11}$.

91. Twenty yards at $4 per yard $= \$80$. 15 yards at $3 per yard $= \$45$. $\$80 + \$45 = \$125$, or what I paid for 35 yards. I received for $\frac{6}{7}$, or 30 yards, $3 per yard $= \$90$, and for $\frac{1}{7}$, or 5 yards, $4 per yard $= \$20$. For all I received $\$90 + \$20 = \$110$. My loss on 35 yards was $\$125 - \$110 = \$15$, or $\$\frac{15}{35} = \$\frac{3}{7}$ per yard.

93. Three fourths of 6 miles are $4\frac{1}{2}$ miles. 6 miles less $4\frac{1}{2}$ miles $= 1\frac{1}{2}$ miles, the distance B gains in one hour. To gain 36 miles, it will take as many hours as $1\frac{1}{2}$ miles are contained times in 36 miles, which are 24.

LESSON LIII.

1. Five bu. will cost 5 times 60 cents, which is $3; 3 pk. will cost $\frac{3}{4}$ of 60 cents, which is 45 cents; then 5 bu. and 3 pk. will cost $3.45.

2. Four gal. 2 qt. 1 pt. $= 37$ pt.; at 5 cents a pint, the milk will cost 37 times 5 cents, which is $1.85.

4. One rod contains 198 in.; 2 yd. 2 ft. 3 in. $= 99$ in., or $\frac{1}{2}$ a rod; then $5\frac{1}{2}$ rods will cost $5\frac{1}{2}$ times $12, which is $66.

5. Twenty-six min. and 40 sec. $= \frac{4}{9}$ of an hour; 9 hours $+ \frac{4}{9}$ hours $= 9\frac{4}{9}$ hours. If it traveled 9 miles an hour, the distance is $9\frac{4}{9}$ times 9 miles $= 85$ miles.

8. Three tenths da. $= \frac{3}{10}$ of 24 hr., which is $7\frac{1}{5}$ hr.; $7\frac{1}{5}$ hr. $+ \frac{2}{5}$ hr. $= 7\frac{3}{5}$ hours.

9. One third rd. $= 5\frac{1}{2}$ ft., or $5\frac{2}{4}$ ft.; $\frac{1}{2}$ yd. $= 1\frac{1}{2}$ ft., or $1\frac{2}{4}$; then $5\frac{2}{4}$ ft. $+ 1\frac{2}{4} + \frac{3}{4}$ ft. $= 7\frac{3}{4}$ ft.

11. One bu. 3 pk. $= 7$ pk; 1 pk. is worth $\frac{1}{7}$ of 70 cents, which is 10 cents; 2 bu. 1 pk. $= 9$ pk.; and 4 qt. $= \frac{1}{2}$ pk.; then $9\frac{1}{2}$ pk. are worth $9\frac{1}{2}$ times 10 cents, which is 95 cents.

13. One third of a T. cost $\frac{1}{2}$ of $8, which is $4; 1 T. cost $12; 1 cwt. cost $\frac{1}{20}$ of $12, which is 60 ct.; 3 cwt. 75 lb. $= 3\frac{3}{4}$ cwt.; then $3\frac{3}{4}$ cwt. cost $3\frac{3}{4}$ times 60 ct., which is $2.25.

14. In 2 hr. 24 min. there are 144 min.; the rate per min. is $\frac{1}{144}$ of 60 miles $= \frac{60}{144}$ mi., or $\frac{5}{12}$ mi.; the rate per hr. is 60 times $\frac{5}{12}$ mi., which is $\frac{300}{12}$ mi. $= 25$ mi.

15. In 3 yd. 1 ft. 6 in. there are $3\frac{1}{2}$ yd.; in 1 rd. 5 yd. there are $10\frac{1}{2}$ yd.; the wheel would make as many revolutions in going $10\frac{1}{2}$ yd. as $3\frac{1}{2}$ yd. are·contained times in $10\frac{1}{2}$ yd., which are 3.

17. I bought as many pounds as 40 ct. are contained times in 235 ct., which are $5\frac{7}{8}$; $\frac{7}{8}$ lb. = 14 oz. I bought 5 lb. 14 oz.

20. In 150 bu. are 6 T.; 6 T. will cost 6 times $3.75, which is $22.50; 1 bu. will cost $\frac{1}{25}$ of $3.75, which is 15 ct.

21. The distance around the lot is 50 ft. + 100 ft. $\times$ 2 = 300 ft.; 300 ft. = 100 yd.; 100 yd. = $18\frac{2}{11}$ rd. If 1 rd. cost $5, then $18\frac{2}{11}$ rd. cost $18\frac{2}{11}$ times $5, which is $90\frac{10}{11}$.

LESSON LIV.

15. The entire cost was $90 plus $3 $\times$ 6 = $108; the sum received for him was $42 + $99 = $141; all gained $141 − $108 = $33; each man received $\frac{1}{3}$ of $33, which is $11.

LESSON LV.

12. In 6 da. of 8 hr. each there are 48 hr.; in 7 da. of 9 hr. each there are 63 hr.; $9\frac{3}{5} = \frac{48}{5}$. In 1 hr. he would earn $\frac{1}{48}$ of $\frac{48}{5}$, which is $\frac{1}{5}$; in 63 hr., $\frac{63}{5} = $12\frac{3}{5}$.

15. In $3\frac{1}{2}$ are $\frac{7}{2}$; $2\frac{1}{3} = \frac{7}{3}$. $\frac{1}{3}$ of the number is $\frac{1}{7}$ of $\frac{7}{2} = \frac{1}{2}$; then $\frac{3}{3} = \frac{3}{2}$, or $1\frac{1}{2}$. $1\frac{1}{2} \times 2\frac{1}{2} = \frac{3}{2} \times \frac{5}{2} = \frac{15}{4} = 3\frac{3}{4}$.

18. Two thirds of $\frac{6}{5} = \frac{4}{5}$. If $\frac{4}{5}$ are $\frac{2}{7}$, then $\frac{1}{7}$ is $\frac{1}{2}$ of $\frac{4}{5}$, which is $\frac{2}{5}$; and $\frac{7}{7}$ would be 7 times $\frac{2}{5}$, which is $\frac{14}{5} = 2\frac{4}{5}$.

152

22. Two thirds of $\frac{12}{5}$ are $\frac{8}{5}$. If $\frac{8}{5}$ are $\frac{1}{2}$, then $\frac{2}{2}$ are $\frac{16}{5}$; and 2 is contained in $\frac{16}{5}$, $\frac{8}{5}$ or $1\frac{3}{5}$ times.

25. Four fifths of 10 marbles are 8 marbles. If 8 is $\frac{8}{11}$, then $\frac{1}{11}$ is 1, and $\frac{11}{11}$ are 11.

26. Three fifths of 60 plums are 36 plums; $\frac{3}{4}$ of 36 are 27; $\frac{4}{9}$ of 27 are 12, or what she gave away. She had left $36 - 12 = 24$.

27. Five sevenths of the distance is 35 mi.; then $\frac{1}{7}$ is 7 mi., and $\frac{2}{7}$ are 14 mi.; $\frac{3}{7}$ of 14 mi. $= 6$ mi.; 14 mi. $- 6$ mi. $= 8$ mi.

30. Seven sevenths less $\frac{2}{7} = \frac{5}{7}$; $\frac{2}{5}$ of $\frac{5}{7} = \frac{2}{7}$; $\frac{5}{7} - \frac{2}{7} = \frac{3}{7}$, the part she had left. $\frac{3}{7} = 6$, $\frac{1}{7} = 2$, $\frac{7}{7} = 14$.

31. Two thirds of 12 ct. are 8 ct If 8 is $\frac{1}{2}$, then $\frac{2}{2}$ are 16; if 16 ct. are $\frac{4}{5}$ of William's money, then William has 20 ct.

32. If $\frac{1}{2}$ of B's money equals $\frac{2}{7}$ of A's, then all of B's money $= \frac{4}{7}$ of A's; $\frac{7}{7} - \frac{4}{7} = \frac{3}{7}$, the difference between A's and B's money; $\frac{3}{7} = 12$ ct., $\frac{1}{7} = 4$ ct., $\frac{7}{7} = 28$ ct., A's money; 28 ct. $- 12$ ct. $= 16$ ct., B's.

33. One third $= \frac{4}{12}$, $\frac{1}{4} = \frac{3}{12}$; $\frac{4}{12} + \frac{3}{12} + \frac{1}{12} = \frac{8}{12} = \frac{2}{3}$; then $32 = \frac{1}{3}$; $\frac{3}{3} = 96$, the number of trees in the orchard. $\frac{1}{3}$ of $96 = 32$; $\frac{1}{4}$ of $96 = 24$; $\frac{1}{12}$ of $96 = 8$.

34. If $\frac{2}{9}$ are pear-trees, $\frac{7}{9}$ must be apple-trees. The excess of apple-trees is therefore $\frac{5}{9}$ of the whole; 25 is then $\frac{5}{9}$ of the whole; $\frac{2}{9}$, or the pear-trees, $= 10$, and $\frac{7}{9}$, or the apple-trees, $= 35$.

3. If the second is three times the first, then the whole number is four times the first. Therefore, the first is $\frac{1}{4}$ of $16 = 4$, and the second $4 \times 3 = 12$.

5. The whole number will be six times the first part; then the first part $= \frac{1}{6}$, the second $\frac{2}{6}$, the third $\frac{3}{6}$, or 4, 8, and 12, respectively.

10. The difference of the two numbers is $6 + 2 = 8$; the sum of 8, the difference, and 4, one of the numbers, $= 12$, the other number.

11. The sum of 19 and 6 is 25; $25 - 10 = 15$, the difference between the numbers; then $19 - 15 = 4$, the smaller number.

12. The sum of the numbers is $10 + 8 = 18$; $18 - 5 = 13$, the other number.

18. They had at first 32 ct. $- 8$ ct. $= 24$ ct.; each had $\frac{1}{2}$ of 24 ct. $= 12$ ct. If Thomas found 8 more, he had 12 ct. $+ 8$ ct. $= 20$ ct.

19. They bought 4 peaches $+ 6$ peaches $+ 20$ peaches $= 30$ peaches; each one bought $\frac{1}{2}$ of 30 peaches, which is 15 peaches. Thomas had left $15 - 4 = 11$; William had left $15 - 6 = 9$.

20. Both bought 24 cherries $+ 7$ cherries $+ 5$ cherries $= 36$ cherries. Since Mary bought twice as many as Sarah, both bought three times as many as Sarah; there-

fore Sarah bought $\frac{1}{3}$ of 36 cherries $= 12$ cherries, and Mary bought 2 times 12 cherries $= 24$ cherries; $24 - 7 = 17$, the number of cherries Mary had left; $12 - 5 = 7$, the number Sarah had left.

21. Three times the number is $50 - 5 = 45$; $\frac{1}{3}$ of 45 is 15, the number.

22. Three fourths of the number would be $31 - 10 = 21$; $\frac{1}{4}$ would be $\frac{1}{3}$ of $21 = 7$; $\frac{4}{4}$, or the number, would be 28.

23. Four fifths of the number would be $21 + 7 = 28$; then $\frac{1}{5}$ is $\frac{1}{4}$ of $28 = 7$, and $\frac{5}{5} = 35$.

25. Since Sarah has 3 cents less than Mary, she has only 5 cents more than Jane. Three times Jane's money is 43 ct. $- 8$ ct. $- 5$ ct. $= 30$ ct.; then Jane's money is $\frac{1}{3}$ of 30 ct. $= 10$ ct.; Mary's is 10 ct. $+ 8$ ct. $= 18$ ct.; Sarah's is 10 ct. $+ 5$ ct. $= 15$ ct.

26. Three times Frank's age $= 42$ yr. $+ 3$ yr., which is 45 yr.; then Frank's age is $\frac{1}{3}$ of 45 yr. $= 15$ yr. Mary's age is 2 times 15 yr. less 3 yr. $= 27$ yr.

27. The ring cost $5 and the watch $12 more than the chain; then $62 - $12 - $5 = 45, which is 3 times the cost of the chain; $\frac{1}{3}$ of $45 = $15, the cost of the chain; $15 + $5 = 20, cost of the ring; and $15 + $12 = $27, cost of the watch.

28. One half of $\frac{4}{7}$ is $\frac{2}{7}$. If $30 + 6$, or 36, is $\frac{2}{7}$, then $\frac{1}{7}$ is 18, and $\frac{7}{7}$ are 7 times $18 = 126$.

29. James has one part; John has two parts + $3; Frank has three parts + $3 + $7; $55 — $3 — $3 — $7 = $42, which is 6 times James's money. $\frac{1}{6}$ of $42 is $7, James's money; 2 times $7, + $3 = $17, John's money; and 3 times $7, + $3, + $7 = $31, Frank's.

30. Thomas has 1 part; Joseph has 3 parts less $2; Paul has 8 parts less $4 less $20; then $20 + $4 + $2 + $22 equal $48, which is 12 times Thomas's money. $\frac{1}{12}$ of $48 is $4, Thomas's money; 3 times $4, — $2 = $10; Joseph's money; 8 times $4, — $24 = $8, Paul's money.

31. The harness cost 1 part; the horse, 1 part + $50; the buggy, 2 parts + $50 + $25; then $225 — $50 — $50 — $25 = $100, which is 4 times the cost of the harness. $\frac{1}{4}$ of $100 is $25, cost of harness; $25 + $50 = $75, cost of horse; 2 times $25 + $75 = $125, cost of buggy.

LESSON LVII.

2. Both have to pay $\frac{3}{7} + \frac{7}{7} = \frac{10}{7}$; $\frac{1}{7}$ is $\frac{1}{10}$ of $60 = $6. John pays 3 times $6 = $18; Thomas pays 7 times $6 = $42.

3. Four fourths + $\frac{3}{4} = \frac{7}{4}$; $\frac{1}{4}$ is $\frac{1}{7}$ of 56 mi. = 8 mi.; $\frac{4}{4}$ are 32 mi., and $\frac{3}{4}$ are 24 mi., the distance traveled each day, respectively.

4. Since the first, plus $\frac{5}{7}$ of the first, less 8 (that is $\frac{12}{7}$ of the first less 8), = 100, then $\frac{12}{7}$ of the first = 108; $\frac{1}{7}$ is $\frac{1}{12}$ of 108 = 9; $\frac{7}{7}$ = 63, the first; $\frac{5}{7}$ = 45, and 45 less 8 = 37, the second.

5. Four fourths $+ \frac{2}{4} + \frac{3}{4} = \frac{9}{4}$, or 45; $\frac{1}{4}$ is $\frac{1}{9}$ of $45 = 5$. $\frac{4}{4} = 20$, the first part; $\frac{2}{4} = 10$, the second part; $\frac{3}{4} = 15$, the third part.

10. If $\frac{1}{2}$ of the cows $= \frac{2}{7}$ of the sheep, then all of the cows $= \frac{4}{7}$ of the sheep, and $1 + \frac{4}{7} = \frac{11}{7}$ of the sheep; $\frac{1}{7}$ of the sheep is $\frac{1}{11}$ of $55 = 5$; $\frac{7}{7} = 35$, the number of sheep; $\frac{4}{7} = 20$, the number of cows.

11. If $\frac{1}{3}$ of the less $= \frac{2}{9}$ of the greater, $\frac{3}{3}$, or the whole of the less, $= 3$ times $\frac{2}{9}$, which is $\frac{6}{9} = \frac{2}{3}$; then $\frac{3}{3} + \frac{2}{3} = 60$; $\frac{1}{3}$ is $\frac{1}{5}$ of $60 = 12$; $\frac{3}{3} = 36$, the greater number; $\frac{2}{3} = 24$, the smaller number.

12. If $\frac{1}{4}$ of Mary's age $= \frac{1}{3}$ of Sarah's, $\frac{4}{4}$ of Mary's age $= \frac{4}{3}$ of Sarah's; $\frac{3}{3} + \frac{4}{3} = \frac{7}{3}$; $\frac{1}{3}$ of Sarah's age is $\frac{1}{7}$ of $14 = 2$; $\frac{3}{3} = 6$, Sarah's age; $\frac{4}{3} = 8$, Mary's age.

13. If $\frac{2}{3}$ of the first $= \frac{3}{4}$ of the second, $\frac{1}{3}$ is $\frac{1}{2}$ of $\frac{3}{4} = \frac{3}{8}$, and $\frac{3}{3}$, or the whole of the first, $= \frac{9}{8}$ of the second. If the first is $\frac{9}{8}$ of the second, and the second $\frac{8}{8}$, both $= \frac{17}{8}$ of the second. $\frac{1}{8}$ is $\frac{1}{17}$ of $51 = 3$; $\frac{9}{8} = 27$, the first part; $\frac{8}{8} = 24$, the second.

14. If $\frac{2}{3}$ of the apple-trees $= \frac{4}{7}$ of the peach-trees, $\frac{1}{3} = \frac{2}{7}$, and $\frac{3}{3} = \frac{6}{7}$; $\frac{3}{3} = \frac{7}{7}$; then $\frac{7}{7}$ of the peach-trees $+ \frac{6}{7}$ of the peach-trees $= \frac{13}{7}$ of the peach-trees, and $\frac{1}{7}$ is $\frac{1}{13}$ of 65 trees $= 5$ trees. $\frac{7}{7} = 35$, the number of peach-trees; $\frac{6}{7} = 30$, the number of apple-trees.

15. If $\frac{2}{3}$ of A's distance $= \frac{5}{9}$ of B's, then $\frac{1}{3} = \frac{5}{18}$, and $\frac{3}{3} = \frac{15}{18}$, or $\frac{5}{6}$; then A travels $\frac{5}{6}$ as far as B, and both traveled $\frac{5}{6} + \frac{6}{6} = \frac{11}{6}$, or 66 miles. $\frac{1}{6}$ is $\frac{1}{11}$ of 66 mi. $= 6$ mi.; $\frac{6}{6} = 36$ mi., B's distance; $\frac{5}{6} = 30$ mi., A's distance; and 36 mi. $- 30$ mi. $= 6$ mi., the number of miles B traveled more than A.

16. Let $\frac{12}{12} =$ the apple-trees; $\frac{4}{12} =$ the plum-trees; $\frac{1}{2}$ of $\frac{12}{12} + \frac{1}{4}$ of $\frac{4}{12} = \frac{7}{12}$, the cherry-trees; then $\frac{12}{12} + \frac{4}{12} + \frac{7}{12} = \frac{23}{12}$, or 69 trees. $\frac{1}{12}$ is $\frac{1}{23}$ of $69 = 3$; $\frac{12}{12} = 36$, the number of apple-trees; $\frac{4}{12} = 12$, the plum-trees; and $\frac{7}{12} = 21$, the cherry-trees.

17. Five thirds of 12 yr. are 20 yr. If 20 yr. are $\frac{4}{9}$ of both Jane's and Sarah's age, $\frac{1}{9}$ is 5 yr., and $\frac{9}{9}$ are 45 yr. If Jane's age is $\frac{7}{8}$ of Sarah's, then $\frac{8}{8} + \frac{7}{8} = \frac{15}{8}$, and $\frac{15}{8} = $ 45 yr.; $\frac{1}{8} = 3$ yr., and $\frac{8}{8} = 24$ yr., Sarah's age; $\frac{7}{8} = 21$ yr., Jane's age.

18. Three elevenths of 44 are 12; $\frac{4}{5}$ of 30 is 24; 24 is $\frac{4}{9}$ of 54; twice 54 are 108; 12 is contained in 108 nine times.

19. John's money is $\frac{3}{5}$, and Charles's $\frac{5}{5}$, or $\frac{20}{20}$; $\frac{3}{4}$ of $\frac{3}{5}$ $= \frac{9}{20}$, and $\frac{9}{20} + \$33 = \frac{20}{20}$, Charles's money; then $\frac{11}{20} = $ \$33. $\frac{1}{20} = \$3$, and $\frac{20}{20} = \$60$, Charles's money; $\frac{3}{5}$ of \$60 $= \$36$, John's money.

20. Let $\frac{12}{12} =$ the hogs; then $\frac{8}{12} =$ the sheep, and $\frac{6}{12}$ the cows; $\frac{12}{12} + \frac{8}{12} + \frac{6}{12} = \frac{26}{12}$, and $\frac{26}{12} = 104$; $\frac{1}{12} = 4$. $\frac{12}{12} = 48$, the hogs; $\frac{8}{12} = 32$, the sheep; and $\frac{6}{12} = 24$, the cows.

22. From noon to midnight is 12 hr. If the time elapsed since noon is $\frac{3}{5}$ of the time to midnight, then it is still $\frac{5}{5}$ to midnight; $\frac{3}{5} + \frac{5}{5} = \frac{8}{5}$, and $\frac{8}{5} = 12$ hr; $\frac{1}{5}$ is $\frac{1}{8}$ of 12 hr. $= 1\frac{1}{2}$ hr.; $\frac{3}{5} = 4\frac{1}{2}$ hr. Therefore it is half-past four o'clock, P. M.

23. Since once the time past noon $+ 3$ hr. is $\frac{1}{2}$ the time to midnight, twice the time past noon $+ 6$ hr. $=$ the whole time to midnight; but the time past noon $+$

the time to midnight is 12 hr.; hence the time past noon, with twice the time past noon + 6 hr. = 12 hr.; hence 3 times the time past noon is 6 hr., and the time past noon is $\frac{1}{3}$ of 6 hr. = 2 hr.

24. Let $\frac{5}{5}$ = the whole time; the time past noon is $\frac{1}{5}$; from midnight to noon is $\frac{4}{5}$; then $\frac{4}{5}$ = 12 hr; $\frac{1}{5}$ = 3 hr. It is 3 o'clock in the afternoon.

25. Let $\frac{4}{4}$ = the whole time; from midnight to noon is $\frac{3}{4}$; the time past noon = $\frac{1}{4}$; $\frac{3}{4}$ = 12 hr.; $\frac{1}{4}$ = 4 hr. It is 4 o'clock in the afternoon.

26. If $\frac{1}{2}$ the time past noon = $\frac{1}{20}$ of the time past midnight, the whole time past noon = $\frac{1}{10}$ the time past midnight; $\frac{10}{10}$ = the whole time; $\frac{1}{10}$ = the time past noon; $\frac{9}{10}$ = the time from midnight to noon, or 12 hr.; $\frac{1}{10}$ = $1\frac{1}{3}$ hr. It is 20 min. past one o'clock P. M.

LESSON LVIII.

2. One $+ \frac{2}{3} = \frac{5}{3}$; $\frac{1}{3}$ is $\frac{1}{5}$ of 20 = 4; $\frac{3}{3}$ = 12, the number.

4. Twice the number is $\frac{10}{5}$, and $\frac{10}{5} + \frac{3}{5} = \frac{13}{5}$. If $\frac{13}{5}$ = 52, then $\frac{1}{5}$ is $\frac{1}{13}$ of 52 = 4, and $\frac{5}{5}$ = 20, the number.

5. Twice the number is $\frac{14}{7}$, and $\frac{14}{7}$ less $\frac{4}{7}$ = $\frac{10}{7}$. If $\frac{10}{7}$ = 40, then $\frac{1}{7}$ is $\frac{1}{10}$ of 40, which is 4, and $\frac{7}{7}$ = 28.

6. Let $\frac{5}{5}$ = the number; 3 times $\frac{5}{5}$ less $\frac{3}{5}$ = $\frac{12}{5}$. If $\frac{12}{5}$ = 48, then $\frac{1}{5}$ is $\frac{1}{12}$ of 48 = 4, and $\frac{5}{5}$ = 20.

7. Let $\frac{6}{6}$ = his age; then $\frac{6}{6} + \frac{3}{6} + \frac{4}{6} = \frac{13}{6}$. If 26 = $\frac{13}{6}$, then $\frac{1}{6}$ = 2, and $\frac{6}{6}$ = 12.

8. Her age $= \frac{12}{12}$, and $\frac{12}{12} + \frac{4}{12} + \frac{3}{12} = \frac{19}{12}$; twice her age is $\frac{24}{12}$, and $\frac{24}{12} - \frac{19}{12} = \frac{5}{12}$; ten years $= \frac{5}{12}$, and $\frac{1}{12} = 2$ years; then $\frac{12}{12}$, her age, is 24 years.

9. Five fifths less $\frac{2}{5} = \frac{3}{5}$; $\frac{3}{5}$ are 30 cents, then $\frac{5}{5}$ are 50 cents.

10. Let $\frac{10}{10} =$ the number; $\frac{10}{10} + \frac{5}{10} + \frac{6}{10} = \frac{21}{10}$; three times the number is $\frac{30}{10}$; $\frac{30}{10} - \frac{21}{10} = \frac{9}{10}$; $27 = \frac{9}{10}$; $\frac{1}{10} = 3$; $\frac{10}{10} = 30$.

11. Let $\frac{11}{11} =$ the father's age; $\frac{11}{11} - \frac{3}{11} = \frac{8}{11}$; $\frac{8}{11} = 40$ yr.; $\frac{1}{11} = 5$ yr.; $\frac{11}{11} = 55$ yr.

12. Let $\frac{5}{5} =$ her age; $\frac{5}{5} + \frac{4}{5} = \frac{9}{5}$; three times her age is $\frac{15}{5}$; $\frac{15}{5} - \frac{9}{5} = \frac{6}{5}$; 18 yr. $= \frac{6}{5}$; $\frac{1}{5} = 3$ yr.; $\frac{5}{5} = 15$ yr.

13. Let $\frac{9}{9} =$ the whole length; then $\frac{9}{9} - \frac{2}{9} = \frac{7}{9}$; $\frac{7}{9} = 28$ yd.; $\frac{1}{9} = 4$ yd.; $\frac{9}{9} = 36$ yd.

14. Let $\frac{3}{6} =$ the distance from A to B, and $\frac{6}{6}$ the distance from C to D; $\frac{2}{3}$ of $\frac{3}{6}$ are $\frac{6}{18} = \frac{2}{6}$. $\frac{2}{6} + 20 = \frac{6}{6}$; then $20 = \frac{4}{6}$; $\frac{1}{6} = 5$; $\frac{6}{6} = 30$, the distance from C to D; $\frac{3}{6} = 15$, the distance from A to B.

15. Let $\frac{15}{15} =$ my age; $\frac{15}{15} + \frac{5}{15} + \frac{3}{15} = \frac{23}{15}$; $\frac{2}{3}$ of 69 years $= 46$ years; $\frac{23}{15} = 46$ years; $\frac{1}{15} = 2$ years; $\frac{15}{15} = 30$ years.

LESSON LIX.

4. As many lots as $\frac{3}{8}$ are contained times in $\frac{6}{8}$, which are $2\frac{2}{3}$.

5. In $2\frac{1}{2}$ days are $\frac{5}{2}$ days; in $\frac{1}{2}$ day he would do $\frac{1}{5}$ of the work; in 1 day he would do $\frac{2}{5}$ of the work.

7. In $3\frac{1}{3}$ days are $\frac{10}{3}$ days. In $\frac{1}{3}$ of a day he would walk $\frac{1}{10}$; in 1 day, $\frac{3}{10}$; in 2 days, $\frac{6}{10} = \frac{3}{5}$.

8. Both do $\frac{1}{2} + \frac{1}{4}$, which are $\frac{3}{4}$.

9. All do the sum of $\frac{1}{2}$, $\frac{1}{4}$ and $\frac{1}{5}$, which is $\frac{19}{20}$.

11. A digs $\frac{1}{6}$ in 1 day; B digs $\frac{1}{12}$ in 1 day; both dig $\frac{3}{12} = \frac{1}{4}$ in 1 day. If they dig $\frac{1}{4}$ in 1 day, it will take 4 days to dig the whole trench.

12. C does $\frac{1}{5}$ in 1 day; B does $\frac{1}{7}$ in 1 day; both do $\frac{12}{35}$ in 1 day. It will take as many days to do it all as $\frac{12}{35}$ are contained times in $\frac{35}{35}$, which are $2\frac{11}{12}$

13. A can do $\frac{1}{2}$ in 1 day, B $\frac{1}{3}$, and C $\frac{1}{6}$; all do in 1 day the sum of $\frac{1}{2}$, $\frac{1}{3}$, and $\frac{1}{6}$, which is $\frac{6}{6}$. Therefore, all three do it in 1 day.

15. Both drink $\frac{1}{12}$ in 1 day; the woman drinks $\frac{1}{30}$ in 1 day; the man drinks $\frac{1}{12} - \frac{1}{30} = \frac{1}{20}$ in 1 day. If he drink $\frac{1}{20}$ in 1 day, he would drink it all in 20 days.

16. All do $\frac{1}{4}$ in 1 day; A and B do $\frac{1}{8} + \frac{1}{12} = \frac{5}{24}$ in 1 day; C does in 1 day $\frac{1}{4} - \frac{5}{24} = \frac{1}{24}$. Therefore, C can reap it all in 24 days.

17. Both do in 1 day $\frac{1}{2} + \frac{1}{3} = \frac{5}{6}$. If they do $\frac{5}{6}$ in 1 day, they would do it all in $1\frac{1}{5}$ days.

18. A digs $\frac{2}{5}$ in 1 day, and B digs $\frac{3}{10}$ in 1 day; both dig $\frac{2}{5} + \frac{3}{10} = \frac{7}{10}$ in 1 day. Therefore, if they dig $\frac{7}{10}$ in 1 day, they would dig it all in $1\frac{3}{7}$ days.

19. C reaps $\frac{1}{5}$ in 1 day; D reaps $\frac{3}{10}$ in 1 day; both reap in 1 day $\frac{1}{5} + \frac{3}{10} = \frac{5}{10} = \frac{1}{2}$. If they reap $\frac{1}{2}$ in 1 day, they would reap the whole in 2 days.

LESSON LX.

8. The ratio of 21 to 7 is 3; $36 \div 3 = 12$, the number.

9. The ratio of 20 to 2 is 10; $10 - 5 = 5$, 5 is $\frac{1}{4}$ of 20, and 20 is the ratio of 40 to 2.

10. The ratio of 18 to 2 is $9, + 3 = 12, + 7 = 19$; and 19 is the ratio of 38 to 2.

11. The ratio of 27 to 9 is $3, + 5 = 8$; and 8 is the ratio of 20 to $2\frac{1}{2}$.

13. Five $+ 7 = 12$; $\frac{5}{12}$ of $48 = 20$, the first part; $\frac{7}{12}$ of $48 = 28$, the second part.

18. Once the number $+ 3$ times the number $= 4$ times the number, or 48; and $\frac{1}{4}$ of 48 is 12, the number.

19. One $+ 4 = 5$; the first is $\frac{1}{5}$ of 25 yd. $= 5$ yd.; the second is $\frac{4}{5} = 20$ yd.

22. The first has $\frac{2}{3}$ of $7\frac{1}{2}$ doz. $= 5$ doz.; the second has $\frac{1}{3}$ of $7\frac{1}{2}$ doz. $= 2\frac{1}{2}$ doz.

23. A paid $\frac{25}{40} = \frac{5}{8}$ of the cost, and B paid $\frac{15}{40} = \frac{3}{8}$ of the cost. A should receive $\frac{5}{8}$ of $56 = 35, and B should receive $\frac{3}{8}$ of $56 = 21.

24. Three $+ 2 = 5$. C's loss was $\frac{3}{5}$ of $30 = 18; D's loss was $\frac{2}{5}$ of $30 = 12.

3. Three thirds $+ \frac{4}{3} = \frac{7}{3}$. A has $\frac{3}{7}$ of 14 ct. $= 6$ ct.; B has $\frac{4}{7}$ of 14 ct. $= 8$ ct.

5. In $2\frac{1}{2}$ are $\frac{5}{2}$, and $4\frac{1}{2} = \frac{9}{2}$; $\frac{5}{2} + \frac{9}{2} = \frac{14}{2}$. The first would receive $\frac{5}{14}$ of $28 = \$10$; the second would receive $\frac{9}{14}$ of $28 = \$18$.

6. Three thirds $+ \frac{5}{3} = \frac{8}{3}$. William's age is $\frac{5}{8}$ of 32 yr. $= 20$ yr.; Frank's age is $\frac{3}{8}$ of 32 yr. $= 12$ yr.

7. Three thirds $+ \frac{7}{3} = \frac{10}{3}$. $\frac{7}{10}$ of 30 apples $= 21$ apples, the number of sound ones; $\frac{3}{10}$ of 30 apples $= 9$ apples, the number not sound.

8. Four fifths $+ \frac{1}{5} = \frac{5}{5}$. One built $\frac{4}{9}$ of 27 ft. $= 12$ ft.; the other, $\frac{5}{9} = 15$ ft.

10. One $+ 2 + 3 + 4 = 10$. The first part is $\frac{1}{10}$ of 70 $= 7$; the second, $\frac{2}{10}$ of 70 $= 14$; the third, $\frac{3}{10}$ of 70 $= 21$; the fourth, $\frac{4}{10}$ of 70 $= 28$.

11. One half $= \frac{6}{12}$; $\frac{1}{3} = \frac{4}{12}$; $\frac{1}{4} = \frac{3}{12}$; and $\frac{6}{12} + \frac{4}{12} + \frac{3}{12} = \frac{13}{12}$. The first is $\frac{6}{13}$ of 39 $= 18$; the second, $\frac{4}{13} = 12$; the third is $\frac{3}{13} = 9$.

12. All had 3 ct. $+ 4$ ct. $+ 5$ ct. $= 12$ ct. William's share, $\frac{3}{12}$ of 36, $= 9$; Thomas's, $\frac{4}{12}$ of 36, $= 12$; John's, $\frac{5}{12}$ of 36, $= 15$.

13. The whole loss was $864 - \$500 = \$364$; $\frac{1}{8}$ of $364 is $45\frac{1}{2}$, A's loss; $\frac{1}{4}$ of $364 is $91, B's loss; $\frac{5}{8}$ of $364 are $227\frac{1}{2}$, C's loss.

14. A has $\frac{4}{4}$, B $\frac{2}{4}$, and C $\frac{1}{4}$; all have $\frac{4}{4} + \frac{2}{4} + \frac{1}{4} = \frac{7}{4}$. A has $\frac{4}{4}$ of $42 = \$24$; B has $\frac{2}{4}$ of $\$24 = \$12$; and C has $\frac{1}{4}$ of $\$24 = \$6$.

15. Four $+ 3 + 2 = 9$. A has $\frac{4}{9}$, B $\frac{3}{9}$, and C $\frac{2}{9}$, or 20, 15, and 10, respectively.

16. One $+ 3 + 6 = 10$. $\frac{1}{10}$ of $60 = 6$, the horses; $\frac{3}{10}$ of $60 = 18$, the cows; $\frac{6}{10}$ of $60 = 36$, the sheep.

17. One $+ 2 + 3 = 6$. A has $\frac{1}{6}$ of $42 = 7$; B, $\frac{2}{6} = 14$; C, $\frac{3}{6} = 21$.

18. One $+ 2 + 4 = 7$. Emma has $\frac{1}{7}$ of $35 = 5$; Agnes has $\frac{2}{7}$ of $35 = 10$; Sarah has $\frac{4}{7}, = 20$.

LESSON LXII.

2. It will take 15 times 8 men $= 120$ men to do the work in 1 day; to do it in 12 days it will take $\frac{1}{12}$ of 120 men $= 10$ men.

4. One will fill it in 9 times $2\frac{1}{2}$ hr. $= 22\frac{1}{2}$ hr.; then 5 pipes will fill it in $\frac{1}{5}$ of $22\frac{1}{2}$ hr. $= 4\frac{1}{2}$ hr

6. Fifteen ct. $= \$\frac{3}{20}$; 80 times $\$\frac{3}{20} = \$\frac{240}{20} = \$12$.

7. Sixty ct. $= \$\frac{3}{5}$; 80 times $\$\frac{3}{5} = \$\frac{240}{5} = \$48$.

10. It will make 3 times $20 = 60$ one cent loaves. $\frac{1}{4}$ of $60 = 15$ four cent loaves; $\frac{1}{5}$ of $60 = 12$ five cent loaves.

11. A loaf will weigh 3 times 8 oz. $= 24$ oz., when flour is $1 a barrel; it will weigh $\frac{1}{4}$ of 24 oz. $= 6$ oz., when flour is $4 a barrel.

12. Six times 10 oz. $= 60$ oz.; $\frac{1}{5}$ of 60 oz. $= 12$ oz.

13. In $5\frac{1}{3}$ are $\$1\frac{6}{3}$; $\frac{16}{3}$ times 7 oz. $= \frac{112}{3}$ oz.; $\$4\frac{2}{3} = \$1\frac{4}{3}$. When flour is worth $\$4\frac{2}{3}$ a barrel, a loaf will weigh as many oz. as $\frac{14}{3}$ are contained times in $\frac{112}{3} = 8$.

14. It will take 5 times 5 men $= 25$ men to do the same work in $\frac{1}{5}$ of the time; to do twice as much will take 2 times 25 men $= 50$ men.

15. Six men will do $\frac{1}{2}$ of it in $\frac{1}{2}$ of 5 days $= 2\frac{1}{2}$ days; one man will do the other $\frac{1}{2}$ in 6 times $2\frac{1}{2}$ days $= 15$ days. $6 + 3 = 9$; 9 men will do it in $\frac{1}{9}$ of 15 days $= 1\frac{2}{3}$ days. Therefore, the whole time is $2\frac{1}{2}$ days $+ 1\frac{2}{3}$ days $= 4\frac{1}{6}$ days.

16. Seven men will do $\frac{1}{2}$ of the work in 2 days; one man will do the other half in 7 times 2 days $= 14$ days. $7 - 3 = 4$; 4 men will do it in $\frac{1}{4}$ of 14 days $= 3\frac{1}{2}$ days. Therefore, it will take 2 days $+ 3\frac{1}{2}$ days $= 5\frac{1}{2}$ days to do the whole work.

18. One man would spend $\frac{1}{6}$ of $\$36 = \$6$ in 8 days; in 1 day he would spend $\frac{1}{8}$ of $\$6 = \$\frac{6}{8}$. 5 persons would spend 5 times $\$\frac{6}{8} = \$\frac{30}{8}$ in 1 day; in 12 days, 12 times $\$\frac{30}{8} = \$\frac{360}{8} = \$45$.

19. One third of 12 rd. is 4 rd; $\frac{1}{8}$ of 4 rd. is $\frac{4}{8}$ rd. $= \frac{1}{2}$ rd; 5 times $\frac{1}{2}$ rd. $= \frac{5}{2}$ rd.; 3 times $\frac{5}{2}$ rd. $= \frac{15}{2}$ rd. $= 7\frac{1}{2}$ rd.

20. One sixth of 36 bu. $= 6$ bu.; $\frac{1}{10}$ of 6 bu. $= \frac{3}{5}$ bu.; 5 times $\frac{3}{5}$ bu. $= \frac{15}{5}$ bu.; 9 times $\frac{15}{5}$ bu. $= \frac{135}{5}$ bu. $= 27$ bu.

21. One ox will eat 2 A. in 5 times 6 days = 30 days; one ox will eat 8 A. in 4 times 30 days = 120 days; 12 oxen will eat 8 A. in $\frac{1}{12}$ of 120 days = 10 days.

22. One person would spend $\frac{1}{8}$ of $400 = $50 in 5 months; in 1 month he would spend $\frac{1}{5}$ of $50 = $10; in 8 mo. 1 person would spend 8 times $10 = $80, and 11 persons would spend 11 times $80 = $880.

23. One ox can be kept on $\frac{1}{10}$ of 5 A. = $\frac{1}{2}$ A. for 3 mo.; one ox can be kept 1 mo. on $\frac{1}{3}$ of $\frac{1}{2}$ A. = $\frac{1}{6}$ A.; for 5 mo. on 5 time $\frac{1}{6}$ A. = $\frac{5}{6}$ A. 15 A. = $\frac{90}{6}$ A., and $\frac{90}{6}$ A. will keep as many oxen as $\frac{5}{6}$ are contained times in $\frac{90}{6}$ = 18. If 7 sheep eat as much as an ox, it will keep 18 times 7 sheep = 126 sheep.

LESSON LXIII.

2. One horse eats as much as $1\frac{1}{2}$ cows, and 14 horses eat as much as 21 cows; 15 cows + 21 cows = 36 cows. A pays $\frac{21}{36} = \frac{7}{12}$ of $60 = $35; B pays $\frac{15}{36} = \frac{5}{12}$ of $60 = $25.

3. B's 120 sheep = 6 horses; his 15 oxen = 10 horses; then B has the same as 6 horses + 10 horses = 16 horses. Both have 16 horses + 8 horses = 24 horses. A pays $\frac{8}{24}$, or $\frac{1}{3}$, of $72 = $24; B pays $\frac{2}{3}$ of $72 = $48.

5. C's $50 for 4 mo. = $200 for 1 mo.; D's $60 for 5 mo. = $300 for 1 mo.; $200 + $300 = $500. C has $\frac{2}{5}$ of $45 = $18; D has $\frac{3}{5}$ of $45 = $27.

6. Three men for 4 days = 12 men 1 day; 5 men 3 days = 15 men 1 day; 12 men + 15 men = 27 men. A receives $\frac{4}{9}$ of $81 = $36; B receives $\frac{5}{9}$ of $81 = $45.

7. A's $2 for 5 mo. $= 10 for 1 mo.; B's $3 for 4 mo. $=$ $12 for 1 mo.; $10 $+ $12 = 22. A receives $\frac{5}{11}$ of $55 $= 25; B, $\frac{6}{11} = 30.

8. E's 4 horses $= 6$ cows; 6 cows for 5 mo. $= 30$ cows 1 mo.; F's 10 cows for 6 mo. $= 60$ cows 1 mo.; 30 cows $+ 60$ cows $= 90$ cows. E pays $\frac{1}{3}$ of $27 = 9; F pays $\frac{2}{3}$ of $27 = 18.

9. The net gain is $300 $-$ $150 = 150; $600 $+ $900 $= 1500. M has $\frac{2}{5}$ of $150 = 60; N has $\frac{3}{5}$ of $150 = 90.

10. C's capital $= 600 for 12 mo., or $7200 for 1 mo.; D's $= 600 for 8 mo., or $4800 for 1 mo.; $7200 $+ $4800 $= 12000. C has $\frac{72}{120} = \frac{3}{5}$ of $250 = 150; D has $\frac{48}{120} = \frac{2}{5}$ of $250 = 100.

11. E had $1000 for 12 mo. $= 12000 for 1 mo.; F had $3000 for 12 mo. $= 36000 for 1 mo., less $1000 for 4 mo. $= 4000 for 1 mo., and $36000 $-$ $4000 = 32000; $32000 $+ $12000 = 44000. E has $\frac{3}{11}$ of $770 = 210; F has $\frac{8}{11}$ of $770 = 560.

12. $240 $-$ $20 = 220; B's share is $\frac{1}{2}$ of $220 = 110; A's share is $110 $+ $20 = 130. B has $\frac{110}{240} = \frac{11}{24}$ of the gain, and also $\frac{11}{24}$ of the capital, $2400, = 1100; A has $\frac{13}{24}$ of the gain, and also $\frac{13}{24}$ of $2400, = 1300.

13. Since D's time was only $\frac{3}{4}$ of C's, he must have had $\frac{1}{4}$ more capital than C; then $\frac{4}{4} = $ D's capital, and $\frac{3}{4} = $ C's capital; $\frac{4}{4} + \frac{3}{4} = \frac{7}{4}$, and $\frac{7}{4} = 980. $\frac{1}{4} = \frac{1}{7}$ of $980 = 140; $\frac{4}{4} = 560, D's capital; $\frac{3}{4} = 420, C's capital.

14. A's gain per mo. was $\frac{1}{10}$ of $70 = \$7$; B's gain per mo. was $\frac{1}{8}$ of $80 = \$10$. Both gained $\$7 + \$10 = \$17$ per mo. If A has $\frac{7}{17}$ of the gain, his capital is $\frac{7}{17}$ of $1700 = \$700$; B's capital is $\frac{10}{17}$ of $1700 = \$1000$.

15. The ratio of their stock was as 2 to 3, and of the time as 10 to 12; $2 \times 10 = 20$; $3 \times 12 = 36$; $20 + 36 = 56$. E's gain was $\frac{5}{14}$ of $840 = \$300$; F's gain was $\frac{9}{14}$ of $840 = \$540$.

LESSON LXVII.

8. $\frac{30}{45} = \frac{2}{3} = 66\frac{2}{3}$ per cent.

9. He gains $\frac{5}{25} = \frac{1}{5}$, and $\frac{1}{5} = 20$ per cent.

14. He gains $24 - \$15 = \$9$; $\$9 = \frac{3}{5}$ of the cost, or 60 per cent.

15. In 5 gal. are 20 qt. He lost $\frac{6}{20} = \frac{3}{10} = 30$ per cent.

16. Six cents $= \frac{6}{5}$ of the cost; $\frac{5}{5} = 5$ cents, the cost; 8 ct. $-$ 5 ct. $= 3$ ct.; $\frac{3}{5} = 60$ per cent.

17. He paid $\frac{1}{6}$ of $3 = 50$ cents for 1 yd.; he sold 1 yd. for $\frac{1}{5}$ of $4 = 80$ ct.; 80 ct. $-$ 50 ct. $= 30$ ct.; $\frac{30}{50} = \frac{3}{5}$ $= 60$ per cent.

18. Eight ct. $= \frac{4}{5}$ of the cost; $\frac{5}{5} = 10$ ct., the cost. $\frac{1}{3}$ of 25 ct. $= 8\frac{1}{3}$ ct.; $10 - 8\frac{1}{3} = 1\frac{2}{3} = \frac{1\frac{2}{3}}{10} = \frac{5}{30} = \frac{1}{6} = 16\frac{2}{3}$ per cent loss. $\frac{1}{2}$ of 25 ct. $= 12\frac{1}{2} - 10 = 2\frac{1}{2}$; $\frac{2\frac{1}{2}}{10} = \frac{5}{20} = \frac{1}{4}$; $\frac{1}{4} = 25$ per cent gain.

19. One lemon cost $\frac{1}{2}$ of 3 ct. $= 1\frac{1}{2}$ ct. He sold 1 lemon for $\frac{1}{3}$ of 2 ct. $= \frac{2}{3}$ ct. $1\frac{1}{2} = \frac{9}{6}$; $\frac{2}{3} = \frac{4}{6}$; $\frac{9}{6} - \frac{4}{6} = \frac{5}{6}$; $\frac{5}{6}$ are $\frac{5}{9}$ of $\frac{9}{6}$, and $\frac{5}{9} = 55\frac{5}{9}$ per cent.

2. \$26 = 130 per cent of the cost, or $\frac{13}{10}$; $\frac{1}{10} = \frac{1}{13}$ of \$26 = \$2; $\frac{10}{10} = 20, the cost.

3. Fourteen cents = $\frac{14}{10}$ of the cost; $\frac{1}{10}$ is $\frac{1}{14}$ of 14 ct. = 1 ct.; $\frac{10}{10} = 10$ ct., the cost.

4. \$81 = $\frac{9}{8}$ of the cost; $\frac{1}{8} = 9; $\frac{8}{8} = 72.

5. \$63 = $\frac{9}{10}$ of the cost; $\frac{1}{10} = 7; $\frac{10}{10} = 70.

6. \$21 = $\frac{7}{4}$ of the cost; $\frac{1}{4} = 3; $\frac{4}{4} = 12.

7. Forty ct. = $\frac{4}{3}$ of the cost; $\frac{1}{3} = 10$ ct.; $\frac{3}{3} = 30$ ct. Each orange cost $\frac{1}{10}$ of 30 ct. = 3 ct.

8. \$10 = $\frac{5}{4}$ of the cost; $\frac{1}{4} = 2; $\frac{4}{4} = 8, the cost; \$12 — \$8 = \$4. He would gain $\frac{4}{8} = 50$ per cent.

9. Seven ct. = $\frac{7}{8}$ of the cost; $\frac{1}{8} = 1$ ct.; $\frac{8}{8} = 8$ ct., the cost. 8 ct. — 6 ct. = 2 ct.; and 2 ct. are $\frac{1}{4}$ of the cost = 25 per cent loss.

10. \$35 = $\frac{5}{6}$ of the cost; $\frac{1}{6} = 7; $\frac{6}{6} = 42, the cost. \$63 — \$42 = 21; \$21 is $\frac{1}{2}$ of the cost = 50 per cent gain.

11. \$18 = $\frac{6}{5}$ of its value; $\frac{5}{5} = 15, its value; 10 per cent of \$15 is $\frac{1}{10}$ of \$15 = \$1.50; \$18 — \$15 = \$3. He lost \$3 + \$$1\frac{1}{2}$ = \$$4\frac{1}{2}$.

12. \$60 = $\frac{6}{5}$ of the cost; $\frac{5}{5} = 50, the cost. A gained \$60 — \$50 = \$10; B lost 20 per cent, or $\frac{1}{5}$ of \$60 = \$12. B lost \$12 — \$10 = \$2 more than A gained.

13. $30 = $\frac{5}{4}$ of the cost of the first; $\frac{4}{4}$ = $24, the cost. The gain was $30 — $24 = $6. $30 = $\frac{3}{4}$ of the cost of the second; $\frac{4}{4}$ = $40, the cost. The loss on the watch was $40 — $30 = $10; loss by sale $10 — $6 = $4.

14. One apple sold for $\frac{1}{4}$ of 3 ct. = $\frac{3}{4}$ ct.; $\frac{3}{4}$ ct. = 150%, or $\frac{3}{2}$% of the cost. $\frac{1}{2} = \frac{1}{4}$ ct.; $\frac{2}{2} = \frac{2}{4}$ ct. = $\frac{1}{2}$ ct., the cost. 5 apples for 4 ct. = $\frac{4}{5}$ ct. for 1 apple. Gain $\frac{4}{5} - \frac{1}{2} = \frac{3}{10}$, and $\frac{3}{10} = \frac{3}{5}$ of $\frac{5}{10}$, or 30 per cent.

15. One lemon sold for $\frac{4}{5}$ ct.; $\frac{4}{5}$ ct. = $\frac{4}{5}$ per cent of the cost; 1 ct. = the cost; 6 for 5 ct. = $\frac{5}{6}$ ct. for 1; 1 ct. — $\frac{5}{6}$ ct. = $\frac{1}{6}$ ct.; $\frac{1}{6}$ of 1 ct. = $16\frac{2}{3}$ per cent.

16. Ten per cent of 60 = 6; $\frac{2}{3}$ of 6 = 4; 4 is $\frac{1}{2}$ of 8; 8 = $\frac{1}{5}$, or 20 per cent, of 40.

17. Fifty per cent of 120 = 60; $\frac{3}{5}$ of 60 = 36; $\frac{1}{2}$ of 36 = 18; 18 is 10 less than 28, and 28 is 20 per cent, or $\frac{1}{5}$, of 140.

18. Sixty per cent of 10 is 6; $\frac{2}{3}$ of 6 = 4; $\frac{1}{4}$ of 4 = 1. 1 is 5 less than 6, and 6 is 50 per cent, or $\frac{1}{2}$, of 12.

19. Seventy-five per cent of 15 = $\frac{45}{4}$; $\frac{2}{5}$ of $\frac{45}{4}$ = $\frac{18}{4}$; $\frac{3}{4}$ of $\frac{18}{4} = \frac{27}{8}$; $\frac{27}{8}$ are $1\frac{3}{5}$ more than $\frac{71}{40}$, and $\frac{71}{40}$ are 50 per cent, or $\frac{1}{2}$, of $\frac{142}{40} = 3\frac{11}{20}$.

20. Twenty-five per cent of 4 is 1; $\frac{2}{3}$ of 1 = $\frac{2}{3}$; $\frac{3}{2}$ times $\frac{2}{3} = \frac{3}{3} = 1$; 1 is 25 per cent, or $\frac{1}{4}$, of 4; and 4 is $\frac{1}{2}$ of 8.

LESSON LXIX.

1. One fifth of $3 is 60 ct.; $3 — 60 ct. = $2.40.

2. One fifth of $125 = $25; $125 — $25 = $100.

3. One sixth of $840 = $140; $840 — $140 = $700.

4. Twenty% = $\frac{1}{5}$; $\frac{1}{5}$ of $500 = $100; $500 — $100 = $400. 5% = $\frac{1}{20}$; $\frac{1}{20}$ of $400 = $20; $400 — $20 = $380.

5. One sixth of $1200 = $200; $1200 — $200 = $1000. 5% = $\frac{1}{20}$; $\frac{1}{20}$ of $1000 = $50; $1000 — $50 = $950.

6. $4.80 = $\frac{4}{5}$ of the retail price; $\frac{1}{5}$ = $1.20; $\frac{5}{5}$ = $6.

7. $720 = $\frac{2}{3}$ of the retail price; $\frac{1}{3}$ = $360; $\frac{3}{3}$ = $1080.

8. One hundred per cent less 5 per cent = 95%, or $\frac{19}{20}$; $\frac{19}{20}$ = $133; $\frac{1}{20}$ = $7; $\frac{20}{20}$ = $140. $140 is $\frac{4}{5}$ of the list price; $\frac{1}{5}$ = $35; $\frac{5}{5}$ = $175.

9. $399 = $\frac{19}{20}$ of the remainder after $\frac{1}{8}$ per cent discount; $\frac{1}{20}$ = $21; $\frac{20}{20}$ = $420. $420 = $\frac{7}{8}$ of the list price; $\frac{1}{8}$ = $60; $\frac{8}{8}$ = $480.

10. $50 less $\frac{1}{5}$ = $40; $40 less $\frac{1}{20}$ = $38; $20 less $\frac{1}{10}$ = $13; $18 less $\frac{1}{20}$ = $17.10; $38 + $17.10 = $55.10.

LESSON LXX.

1. His commission was 2½ per cent, or $\frac{1}{40}$, of $4000, = $100.

2. One twentieth of $560 = $28.

3. The corn cost 1000 times 50 ct. = $500; $\frac{1}{40}$ of $500 = $12.50.

4. Five times $300 = $1500; $\frac{1}{20}$ of $1500 = $75. The owner receives $1500 — $75 = $1425

5. The wheat sells for 800 times $1.25 = $1000; $\frac{1}{50}$ of $1000 = $20, the commission; $1000 − $20 = $980.

6. $100 = $\frac{1}{20}$ of $2000.

7. $60 = $\frac{1}{10}$; $\frac{10}{10}$ = $600.

8. The commission was $\frac{1}{20}$ of $1000 = $50; $1000 − $50 = $950. He bought as many shares as $50 are contained times in $950 = 19.

LESSON LXXI.

1. One per cent of $2000 = $20; $\frac{1}{2}\%$ = $\frac{1}{2}$ of $20 = $10.

2. One half of $3000 = $1500; $\frac{1}{50}$ of $1500 = $30.

3. Two thirds of $2400 = $1600; 1% of $1600 is $16, and $16 + $1.50 = $17.50.

4. $2500 + $1500 = $4000; 1% of $4000 is $40; $\frac{3}{4}\%$ is $\frac{3}{4}$ of $40 = $30.

5. Two thirds of $1800 are $1200; $\frac{1}{100}$ of $1200 is $12; $\frac{2}{3}$ of $1200 are $800; 1% of $800 is $\frac{1}{100}$ of $800 = $8; $\frac{1}{2}\%$ is $\frac{1}{2}$ of $8 = $4; and $12 + $4 + $1 = $17.

6. One half of $2600 = $1300; $\frac{1}{50}$ of $1300 = $26; $\frac{2}{3}$ of $1500 are $1000; $\frac{1}{100}$ of $1000 is $10; and $26 + $10 + $1.50 = $37.50.

LESSON LXXII.

4. The interest on $1 for 1 year is 8 ct.; for 3 yr. 3 times 8 ct = 24 ct.; for $20 it is 20 times 24 ct. = $4.80.

5. The interest on $1 for 6 yr. at 4% is 24 ct.; and for $25 it is 25 times 24 ct. = $6.

6. The interest for $1 is 20 ct.; for $40 it is $8.

7. $9.   (8.) $8.40.

9. $9.   (10.) $36.

LESSON LXXIII.

2. Four mo. = ⅓ of a year. The interest on $1 for 4 mo. is ⅓ of 5 ct. = 1⅔ ct.; on $60 it is 60 times 1⅔ ct. = $1.

3. The interest on $1 for 7 mo. at 6% is 3½ ct.; on $80 it is $2.80.

4. On $1 it is ¾ of 8 ct. = 6 ct.; on $40 it is $2.40.

5. Two thirds of 9 ct. = 6 ct.; 75 times 6 ct. = $4.50.

7. The interest for 1 year is 180 times 4 ct. = $7.20; for 1 mo. $\frac{1}{12}$ of $7.20 = $0.60; for 10 mo. 10 times 60 ct. = $6; for 10 days ⅓ of 60 ct. = 20 ct.; for 10 mo. 10 da., $6.20.

9. One year's interest = $12; 1 mo. interest = $1; for 4 mo. $4; for 24 days ⅘ of $1 = 80 ct.; for 4 mo. 24 da., $4.80.

10. The int. for 1 yr. is $24; for 1 mo. $2; for 9 mo. $18; for $18 ⅗ of $2 = $1.20; for 9 mo. 18 da. it is $19.20.

11. $8.45.

12. The int. for 1 yr. is $5.76; for 1 mo. 48 ct.; for 8 mo. $3.84; for 25 da. $\frac{5}{6}$ of 48 ct. = 40 ct.; for 8 mo. 25 da., $3.84 + $0.40 = $4.24.

13. $3.20.   (14.) $6.75.   (15.) $3.80.

16. The int. for 1 year is $1; for 3 yr. $3. The amount is $25 + $3 = $28.

17. $44.   (18.) $68.20.   (19.) $32.80.

20. $56.80.   (21.) $99.12.

LESSON LXXIV.

2. The int. for $1 for 3 yr. at 4% is 12 ct. It will take as many dollars to acquire $6 int. as 12 ct. are contained times in 600 ct., which are 50. *Ans.* $50.

3. $60.   (4.) $75.   (5.) $140.

6. $240.   (7.) $350.

8. As many dollars as 5 ct. are contained times in $200, which are 4000. *Ans.* $4000.

LESSON LXXV.

2. The amount of $1 for 3 yr. at 6% is $1.18. It will take as many dollars to amount to $236 as $1.18 is contained times in $236, which are 200.

3. $500.   (4.) $250.

5. $300.   (6.) $25.

7. The amount of $1 for 2 yr. 6 mo. at 8% is $1.20. It will take as many dollars to amount to $60 as $1.20 is contained times in $60, which are 50. If $50 = $\frac{2}{5}$ of the principal, $\frac{5}{5}$, or the whole, = $125.

LESSON LXXVI.

2. The int. on $40 for 1 yr. at 5% is $2. To gain $8, it will take 4 yr.

3. 2 yr. 6 mo.   (4.) 2 yr. 8 mo.

5. $3\frac{3}{7}$ years.   (6.) $6\frac{2}{3}$ yr. = 6 yr. 8 mo.

9. Any principal to treble itself must gain 200%. At 5% it will take as many years as 5 is contained times in 200 = 40.

LESSON LXXVII.

2. At 1 per cent the int. on $50 for 5 yr. is $2.50. To amount to $20, the rate will be as many times 1% as $2.50 are contained times in $20, which are 8. *Ans.* 8 per cent.

3. Int. at 1% = $2.25; $11.25 ÷ $2.25 = 5. *Ans.* 5%.

4. 7%.

5. Int. at 1% = $6.75; $54.00 ÷ $6.75 = 8. *Ans.* 8%.

6. Int. at 1% = $8; $56 ÷ $8 = 7. *Ans.* 7%.

7. $240 less $200 = $40, the interest; int. at 1% = $8; $40 ÷ $8 = 5. *Ans.* 5%.

8. \$183 less \$150 = \$33, the int. ; int. at 1% = \$5.50 ; \$33 ÷ \$5.50 = 6. *Ans. 6%.*

LESSON LXXVIII.

2. The amount of \$1, for the given time and rate, is \$1.30 = $\frac{13}{10}$. \$520 = $\frac{13}{10}$; $\frac{1}{10}$ = \$40; $\frac{3}{10}$ = \$120, the discount; $\frac{10}{10}$ = \$400, the present worth.

3. \$30 = $\frac{6}{5}$; $\frac{5}{5}$ = \$25, present worth; \$30 — \$25 = \$5, discount.

4. Present worth, \$500; discount, \$250.

5. \$345 = $\frac{23}{20}$; $\frac{1}{20}$ = \$15; $\frac{20}{20}$ = \$300. \$345 — \$300 = \$45, discount.

6. \$96.　　(7.) \$4.　　(8.) \$50.　　(9.) \$44.

10. Int. for 6 yr. 8 mo. = 40 ct. ; amt. of \$1 = \$1.40 = $\frac{7}{5}$. \$77 = $\frac{7}{5}$; $\frac{1}{5}$ = \$11; $\frac{5}{5}$ = \$55, present worth.

11. Amt. of \$1 for 3 yr. 6 mo. at 7% is \$1.24$\frac{1}{2}$ = $\frac{1245}{1000}$ = $\frac{249}{200}$; $\frac{1}{200}$ is $\frac{1}{249}$ of \$1000 = \$4$\frac{4}{249}$; $\frac{200}{200}$ = \$803$\frac{53}{249}$; \$1000 — \$803$\frac{53}{249}$ = \$196$\frac{196}{249}$, discount.

12. Amt. of \$1 is \$1.22 = $\frac{61}{50}$; \$900 = $\frac{61}{50}$; $\frac{1}{50}$ is $\frac{1}{61}$ of \$900 = \$14$\frac{46}{61}$; $\frac{50}{50}$ = \$737$\frac{43}{61}$; \$900 — \$737$\frac{43}{61}$ = \$162$\frac{18}{61}$.

LESSON LXXIX.

1. For 4 yr. 2 mo. 25% ; $\frac{25}{100}$ = $\frac{1}{4}$.

2. For 5 yr. 25% int. ; 100% + 25% = 125%, amt. ; $\frac{25}{125}$ = $\frac{1}{5}$.

3. For 1 yr. $\frac{1}{2}$ of $\frac{1}{5}=\frac{1}{10}$; $\frac{1}{10}$ of 100% is 10%.

4. Two yr. 6 mo. $= 30$ mo.; $\frac{1}{30}$ of $\frac{1}{4}=\frac{1}{120}$ for 1 mo.; 12 times $\frac{1}{120}=\frac{1}{10}$; $\frac{1}{10}$ of $100\% = 10\%$.

5. The int. at $10\% = \frac{1}{10}$ of the principal in 1 yr.; to equal $\frac{3}{5}$, or $\frac{6}{10}$, it will take 6 yr.

6. The yearly interest is $\frac{1}{3}$ of $\frac{9}{25}=\frac{3}{25}$; $\frac{3}{25}=\frac{12}{100}=12\%$.

7. The interest for 2 yr. is 5 times $\frac{4}{25}=\frac{20}{25}=\frac{4}{5}$; for 1 yr. $\frac{1}{2}$ of $\frac{4}{5}=\frac{2}{5}$; $\frac{2}{5}=\frac{40}{100}=40\%$.

8. Five eighths of the interest for 1 yr. $= \frac{3}{80}$ of the principal. If $\frac{3}{80}$ are $\frac{5}{8}$, then $\frac{1}{8}$ is $\frac{1}{5}$ of $\frac{3}{80}=\frac{3}{400}$, and $\frac{8}{8}=\frac{24}{400}=\frac{6}{100}=6\%$.

9. The int. for 4 mo. is $\frac{1}{50}$ of the principal; for 12 mo. 3 times $\frac{1}{50}=\frac{3}{50}=\frac{6}{100}=6\%$. Int. for $1 for 1 yr. 4 mo. $= 8$ ct.; for $200 it is 200 times 8 ct. $= $16

10. One yr. 4 mo. $= 16$ mo., or 4 times 4 mo.; $\frac{1}{4}$ of $\frac{3}{25}=\frac{3}{100}$; $\frac{3}{4}=\frac{9}{100}=9\%$. The interest of $100 for 1 yr. 8 mo. 12 da., at 9%, is $15.30.

11. In 2 times 4 yr. $= 8$ yr.

12. In $3\frac{1}{3}$ are $\frac{10}{3}$; $\frac{1}{3}$ is $\frac{1}{10}$ of $40 = $4; $\frac{3}{3} = $12; $12, the int. for 1 yr. $= 5\%$, or $\frac{1}{20}$ of the principal; the principal $= \frac{20}{20}$, or $240. A has 2 parts; B, 1 part; both, 3 parts. A has $\frac{2}{3}$ of $240 = $160; B has $\frac{1}{3} = $80.

13. In $1\frac{2}{5}$ are $\frac{7}{5}$; $\frac{1}{5} = \frac{1}{7}$ of $49 = $7; $\frac{5}{5} = $35. $35 $= \frac{7}{100}$ of the principal; $\frac{1}{100} = $5; $\frac{100}{100} = $500. If twice A's money $= 3$ times B's, then once A's money $= 1\frac{1}{2}$ times B's; B's, $\frac{2}{2}$; A's, $\frac{3}{2}$; both, $\frac{5}{2}$; $\frac{2}{2} = $200, B's money; $\frac{3}{2} = $300, A's money.

14. Two yr. 3 mo. $= 27$ mo. The int. for 1 mo. is $\frac{1}{27}$ of $18 = \$\frac{18}{27} = \$\frac{2}{3}$; for 1 yr. 12 times $\$\frac{2}{3} = \$8$. $8 is 4 per cent, or $\frac{4}{100}$, of $\frac{3}{4}$ of A's and $\frac{1}{2}$ of B's; $\frac{1}{100}$ is $2; $\frac{100}{100}$ is is $200. $\frac{3}{4}$ of A's $+ \frac{1}{2}$ of B's $= \$200$; but $\frac{1}{2}$ of A's $= \frac{2}{3}$ of B's, or $\frac{1}{4}$ of A's $= \frac{1}{3}$ of B's, and B's $= \frac{3}{4}$ of A's. Then, $\frac{6}{4}$ of B's $= \$200$, and B's money $= \$133.33\frac{1}{3}$. Since B's $= \frac{3}{4}$ of A's $= \$133.33\frac{1}{3}$, $\frac{1}{4}$ of A's $= \$44.44\frac{4}{9}$, and $\frac{4}{4}$ or A's money $= \$177.77\frac{7}{9}$.

LESSON LXXX.

1. One apple is worth $\frac{1}{8}$ of 24 plums $= 3$ plums; and 84 apples are worth 84 times 3 plums $= 252$ plums. One peach is worth $\frac{1}{12}$ of 252 plums $= 21$ plums; and 5 peaches are worth 105 plums.

2. Mary has 5 more than James, and Lucy 3 more than James. $5 + 3 = 8$, and $32 - 8 = 24$; $\frac{1}{3}$ of $24 = 8$, James's share; $8 + 3 = 11$, Lucy's; $8 + 5 = 13$, Mary's.

3. Sixteen is twice the number; the number is 8.

.4. C has $\frac{6}{6}$; B has $\frac{2}{6}$; A has $\frac{1}{6}$; C has $\frac{5}{6}$ more than A; $\frac{5}{6} = \$15$; $\frac{1}{6} = \$3$, A's; $\frac{6}{6} = \$18$, C's; $\frac{2}{6} = \$6$, B's.

5. Four fourths $=$ James's money; $\frac{4}{4} + \frac{3}{4} = \frac{7}{4}$; $34 - $6 = \$28$; $28 = \frac{7}{4}$; $\frac{1}{4} = \$4$; $\frac{4}{4} = \$16$, James's money; $\frac{3}{4} + \$6 = \$18$, Thomas's money.

6. Eight eighths less $\frac{3}{8} = \frac{5}{8}$; $\frac{1}{9}$ of $\frac{5}{8} = \frac{5}{72}$; $\frac{4}{9} = \frac{20}{72}$; $\frac{5}{8} = \frac{45}{72}$; and $\frac{45}{72} + \frac{20}{72} = \frac{65}{72}$; $\frac{1}{72} = \frac{1}{65}$ of 65 sheep $= 1$ sheep; $\frac{72}{72} = 72$ sheep.

7. One man will do the work in 12 da. of 10 hr., or in 120 da. of 1 hr. each; 8 men will do it in 15 da. of 1 hr., or in $2\frac{1}{2}$ da. of 6 hr.

8. At 2 for 3 ct., 1 dozen cost 6 times 3 ct. $=$ 18 ct.; at 2 for 5 ct., 1 doz. cost 6 times 5 ct. $=$ 30 ct., and 2 doz. cost 18 ct. $+$ 30 ct. $=$ 48 ct. At 3 for 7 ct., 1 doz. sold for 4 times 7 ct. $=$ 28 ct.; 2 doz. cost 56 ct.; and 56 ct. $-$ 48 ct. $=$ 8 ct., the gain on 2 doz.; 4 ct., gain on 1 doz.

9. Four horses, 2 mo. $=$ 8 horses 1 mo.; 9 cows, 3 mo. $=$ 27 cows, 1 mo.; 20 sheep, 5 mo. $=$ 100 sheep, 1 mo. If 10 sheep $=$ 2 horses, 5 sheep $=$ 1 horse, and 100 sheep $=$ 20 horses; 1 cow $= \frac{2}{3}$ of a horse, and 27 cows $=$ 18 horses. Then A has the same as 8 horses; B, 18; and C, 20; and all have 46. A pays $\frac{8}{46}$ of \$92 $=$ \$16; B, $\frac{18}{46}$ $=$ \$36; C, $\frac{20}{46} =$ \$40.

10. He gave to each pair \$5; and \$5 in \$20 are contained 4 times. He had 4 sons and 4 daughters.

12. Nine less 3 $=$ 6; 4 $-$ 2 $=$ 2; 6 $\div$ 2 $=$ 3, number of children.

14. One of John's steps $= 1\frac{1}{4}$ of Henry's; 5 of John's $= 6\frac{1}{4}$ of Henry's. He gains in taking 5 steps, $6\frac{1}{4}$ steps $-$ 6 steps $= \frac{1}{4}$ step. He will take 4 times 5 steps $=$ 20 steps to gain 1 step, and 7 times 20 steps $=$ 140 steps to gain 7.

15. If 1 ox is worth 8 sheep, 3 oxen are worth 24 sheep, or 2 horses are worth 24 sheep; and 24 sheep are worth 24 times \$5 $=$ \$120; 1 horse is worth $\frac{1}{2}$ of \$120 $=$ \$60.

16. Two ct. $+$ 24 ct. $=$ 26 ct., and $\frac{1}{2}$ of 26 ct. $=$ 13 ct., A's money; 13 ct. $-$ 2 ct. $=$ 11 ct., B's money.

17. Let $\frac{6}{6} =$ C's; $\frac{2}{6} =$ B's; $\frac{1}{6} =$ A's; then $\frac{6}{6} - \frac{2}{6} = \frac{4}{6}$, and $\frac{4}{6} = 20$ yr. $\frac{1}{6} = 5$ yr., A's age; $\frac{2}{6} = 10$ yr., B's age; $\frac{6}{6} = 30$ yr., C's age.

18. If \$15 is $\frac{3}{4}$ of their difference, then \$20 $=$ the whole of the difference. If $\frac{2}{3}$ of A's $= \frac{4}{5}$ of B's, $\frac{2}{3}$ of A's $= \frac{6}{5}$ of B's; $\frac{3}{3} = \frac{5}{5}$, and $\frac{6}{5} - \frac{5}{5} = \frac{1}{5}$, their difference; and $\frac{1}{5} =$ \$20; $\frac{5}{5} = 100$, B's; $\frac{6}{5} =$ \$120, A's.

19. One half of 17 is $8\frac{1}{2}$; and 10 less $8\frac{1}{2} = 1\frac{1}{2}$; and $1\frac{1}{2}$ in 15 is contained 10 times.

20. If 1 egg cost 2 ct., and 2 cost 6 ct., 3 cost 8 ct., and the average cost is $2\frac{2}{3}$ ct. 1 egg sells for $\frac{1}{3}$ of 10 ct. $= 3\frac{1}{3}$ ct. The gain on 1 is $3\frac{1}{3} - 2\frac{2}{3} = \frac{2}{3}$; $\frac{2}{3}$ is $\frac{1}{4}$ of $2\frac{2}{3}$, or 25 per cent.

21. Eight less $5 = 3$; $21 \div 3 = 7$, number of playmates.

22. John gains 2 steps every time he takes 7; to gain 30 steps he must take 7 steps as many times as 2 is contained in 30, or 15 times; 15 times 7 steps $= 105$ steps.

23. Let $\frac{7}{7} =$ the watch, and $\frac{2}{7} =$ the chain; three times $\frac{2}{7}$ plus 2 times $\frac{7}{7} = \frac{20}{7}$, and $\frac{20}{7} =$ \$100; $\frac{1}{7} =$ \$5; $\frac{2}{7} =$ \$10, price of the chain; $\frac{7}{7} =$ \$35, price of the watch.

24. In $4\frac{1}{2}$ are $\frac{9}{2}$; $2\frac{4}{7} = \frac{18}{7}$; A does $\frac{2}{9}$ in 1 day; both do $\frac{7}{18}$ in 1 day; $\frac{7}{18}$ less $\frac{2}{9} = \frac{3}{18} = \frac{1}{6}$, what B does in 1 day. If B does $\frac{1}{6}$ in 1 day, he would do it all in 6 days.

25. He gave $\frac{1}{2}$ ct. each for the first lot, and $\frac{1}{4}$ ct. each for the second lot; for two he gave $\frac{1}{2}$ ct. $+ \frac{1}{4}$ ct. $= \frac{3}{4}$ ct.; average price, $\frac{3}{8}$ ct. He sold them for $\frac{3}{5}$ ct. each; gain on each, $\frac{3}{5} - \frac{3}{8} = \frac{9}{40}$. If he gained $\frac{9}{40}$ ct. on one, to gain 18 ct. it took as many pears as $\frac{9}{40}$ ct. is contained times in 18 ct. $= 80$.

26. He discounts the interest on \$50 for 1 yr., which is \$3; \$3 is $\frac{3}{50}$, or 6%, of the principal.

27. She wished to buy as many yards as $\frac{1}{2}$ is contained times in $5 = 10$.

28. A's money $= \frac{5}{5}$; B's money $= \frac{2}{5} - \$5$; $\frac{5}{5} + \frac{2}{5} - \$5 = \$51$; $\frac{7}{5} = \$56$; $\frac{1}{5} = \$8$; $\frac{5}{5} = \$40$, A's money; $\$51 - \$40 = \$11$, B's.

29. One third of the gain $= \frac{2}{15}$ of the selling price, and $\frac{3}{3} = \frac{6}{15}$, or $\frac{2}{5}$; $3\frac{3}{4}$ times $\$4 = \$15$, the cost. If the gain is $\frac{2}{5}$ of the selling price, then $\frac{5}{5} - \frac{2}{5} = \frac{3}{5}$, or the cost; $\frac{3}{5} = \$15$; $\frac{5}{5} = \$25$, the selling price.

30. The hound gains 5 of the hare's leaps every time the hare takes 3; to gain 100, he must take 3 leaps as many times as 5 is contained in $100 = 20$, and 20 times $3 = 60$.

31. Thomas's age $= 3$ parts; James's $= 1$ part; 3 parts $- 1$ part $= 10$, the difference. If $10 = 2$ parts, then 5 yr. $=$ James's age, and 15 yr. $=$ Thomas's.

32. If $\frac{3}{7} = \frac{4}{5}$, then $\frac{7}{7} = \frac{28}{15}$; and $\frac{28}{15} + \frac{15}{15} = \frac{43}{15}$ of George's distance; $\frac{43}{15} = 86$ miles; $\frac{1}{15} = 2$ miles; $\frac{15}{15} = 30$ miles, George's distance; $\frac{28}{15} = 56$ miles, John's distance.

34. The difference between selling the lot at 6 ct. a doz. and 10 ct. a doz. is 12 ct. $+ 18$ ct. $= 30$ ct. The difference on 1 doz. is 10 ct. $- 6$ ct. $= 4$ ct. There were as many doz. as 4 ct. are contained times in 30 ct. $= 7\frac{1}{2}$ doz. The cost of the lot was $6 \times 7\frac{1}{2} + 12 = 57$ ct.; and the cost of 1 doz. was 57 ct. $\div 7\frac{1}{2} = 7\frac{3}{5}$ ct.

35. Let $\frac{10}{10}$ = A's age, and $\frac{5}{10}$ = B's; $\frac{3}{5}$ of $\frac{5}{10}$ are $\frac{3}{10}$, and $\frac{3}{10} + 44 = 2\frac{1}{2}$ times $\frac{10}{10} = \frac{25}{10}$. If $\frac{3}{10} + 44 = \frac{25}{10}$, then $\frac{22}{10} = 44$, and $\frac{1}{10} = 2$, and $\frac{10}{10} = 20$ yr., A's age; $\frac{5}{10} = 10$ yr., B's age.

36. Seven eighths of 24 miles = 21 miles. If 21 mi. are $\frac{3}{7}$, then $\frac{1}{7}$ is 7 mi., and $\frac{7}{7}$ are 49 mi., the distance from B to C; 49 mi. + 24 mi. = 73 mi., distance from A to C.

37. A, B, and C together can do $\frac{1}{4}$ in 1 da.; A and B together can do $\frac{1}{8}$ in 1 da.; B and C together can do $\frac{1}{6}$ in 1 da.; C can do in 1 da. $\frac{1}{4} - \frac{1}{8} = \frac{1}{8}$, and the whole in 8 da.; A can do in 1 da. $\frac{1}{4} - \frac{1}{6} = \frac{1}{12}$, and the whole in 12 da.; B can do in 1 da. $\frac{1}{6} - \frac{1}{8} = \frac{1}{24}$, and the whole in 24 da.

38. One duck cost $\$\frac{1}{6}$; 1 chicken, $\$\frac{1}{8}$, and 2 chickens, $\$\frac{2}{8}$; $\frac{1}{6} + \frac{2}{8} = \frac{10}{24}$; $\frac{1}{3}$ of $\frac{10}{24} = \frac{10}{72} = \frac{5}{36}$, the average cost. One third of $\frac{1}{2} = \frac{1}{6}$, the average selling price; $\frac{1}{6} = \frac{6}{36}$ $- \frac{5}{36} = \frac{1}{36}$, the average gain; the whole gain was $\$2\frac{1}{2}$ $= \$\frac{5}{2}$; $\frac{5}{2} = \frac{90}{36}$; $\frac{90}{36} \div \frac{1}{36} = 90$, the whole number; $\frac{2}{3}$ of $90 = 60$, the chickens; $\frac{1}{3}$ of $90 = 30$, the ducks.

39. Eight ct. — 3 ct. = 5 ct.; 6 ct. + 29 ct. = 35 ct.; 35 ct. = $\frac{5}{8}$ of cost of oranges; $\frac{1}{8} = 7$ ct., and $\frac{8}{8} = 56$ ct.; 56 ct. — 6 ct. = 50 ct., James's money.

40. A rides $\frac{1}{5}$ of 10 miles in $\frac{1}{4}$ of an hour, and 8 miles in 1 hour; A will travel 18 miles in $18 \div 8 = 2\frac{1}{4}$ hr. B travels $\frac{1}{8}$ of a mile in $\frac{1}{5}$ hr., and 5 miles an hour; B will travel $2\frac{1}{4}$ times 5 mi. $= 11\frac{1}{4}$ mi., while A travels 18 mi.

41. Three halves + $\$2\frac{1}{2} = \$40$; then $\frac{3}{2} = \$37\frac{1}{2}$; $\frac{1}{2} = \$12\frac{1}{2}$; $\frac{2}{2} = \$25$, his money.

42. C received $\frac{21}{21} - \frac{6}{21} - \frac{7}{21} = \frac{8}{21}$; $\frac{8}{21} - \frac{6}{21} = \frac{2}{21}$; $\frac{2}{21}$
$= \$160$; $\frac{1}{21} = \$80$; $\frac{6}{21} = \$480$, A's legacy; $\frac{7}{21} = \$560$, B's legacy; $\frac{8}{21} = \$640$, C's legacy.

43. Both consume $\frac{6}{15}$ in 6 days, and $\frac{15}{15}$ less $\frac{6}{15} = \frac{9}{15}$ $= \frac{3}{5}$ remaining. The woman consumes $\frac{1}{24}$ of $\frac{3}{5}$ in one day $= \frac{3}{120} = \frac{1}{40}$, and all in 40 days. Both consume $\frac{1}{15}$ in one day; $\frac{1}{15} - \frac{1}{40} = \frac{5}{120} = \frac{1}{24}$, what the man consumes in one day. It would last him alone 24 days.

44. Three and one half ct. $+ 6\frac{1}{2}$ ct. $= 10$ ct., the price of 2 pounds of the mixture; $100 \div 10 = 10$; 10 times 2 pounds $= 20$, the number of pounds.

45. Let $\frac{1}{10} = $ C's age; $\frac{2}{10} = $ B's; and $\frac{10}{10} = $ C's. $\frac{10}{10} -$ $\frac{1}{10} = \frac{9}{10}$; $\frac{9}{10} = 45$ yr.; $\frac{1}{10} = \frac{1}{9}$ of 45 yr. $= 5$ yr., C's age; $\frac{2}{10} = 10$ yr., B's age; $\frac{10}{10} = 50$ yr. $= $ A's age.

46. Three fifths $= $ Mary's age, and $\frac{5}{5} = $ Ella's; their sum is $\frac{8}{5}$; twice Ella's is $\frac{10}{5}$; $\frac{10}{5} - \frac{8}{5} = \frac{2}{5}$, and $\frac{2}{5} = 6$ yr.; $\frac{1}{5}$ $= 3$ yr.; $\frac{5}{5} = 15$ yr., Ella's age; $\frac{3}{5} = 9$ yr., Mary's age.

47. Both do $\frac{4}{16}$ in 4 days; and $\frac{16}{16} - \frac{4}{16} = \frac{3}{4}$, that B finishes in 36 days. In one day he does $\frac{1}{36}$ of $\frac{3}{4} = \frac{3}{144}$ $= \frac{1}{48}$, and he does all in 48 days; $\frac{1}{16} - \frac{1}{48} = \frac{1}{24}$, what A does in 1 day, and he would do all in 24 days.

48. Three doz. at 1 ct. each $= 36$ ct.; 2 doz. at 4 eggs for 3 ct. $= 18$ ct.; 2 doz., the remainder, at 4 eggs for 5 ct. $= 30$ ct.; 36 ct. $+ 18$ ct. $+ 30$ ct. $= 84$ ct.; $84 = 7$ doz.; $\frac{1}{7}$ of 84 ct. $= 12$ ct. a doz.

50. If he had worked 30 days, he would have received 30 times 30 ct. $= \$9$. Each day he is idle he gives 20 ct. for board and forfeits 30 ct. for not working $= 50$ ct. $\$9 - \$5 = \$4$; $\$4.00 \div 50$ ct. $= 8$, number of days idle; 30 days $- 8$ days $= 22$, number of days he worked.

51. The difference per yard is $2\frac{1}{2}$ ct.; $40 \div 2\frac{1}{2} = 16$, the number of yards.

52. If 4 of Moses's steps $= 7$ of Noah's, then one of Moses's $= 1\frac{3}{4}$ of Noah's, and 5 of Moses's $= 8\frac{3}{4}$ of Noah's; Moses gains $8\frac{3}{4} - 7 = 1\frac{3}{4}$ of Noah's steps every time he takes 5 steps; to gain 35 he must take 5 steps as many times as $1\frac{3}{4}$ are contained in 35. $35 = \frac{140}{4}$; $1\frac{3}{4} = \frac{7}{4}$; $\frac{140}{4} \div \frac{7}{4} = 20$; 20 times 5 steps $= 100$ steps.

53. One man will do as much work as 6 boys; 2 men as much as 12 boys; then 2 men would do in a week as much as 12 boys, and to do it in 1 day it would take 6 times 2 men $= 12$ men.

54. Let $\frac{1}{12} =$ the number in the first field; $\frac{4}{12}$, in the second; and $\frac{12}{12}$, in the third; then $\frac{12}{12} - \frac{1}{12} - \frac{4}{12} = \frac{7}{12}$, and $\frac{7}{12} = 70$; $\frac{1}{12} = 10$, the number in the first field; $\frac{4}{12} = 40$, the number in the second; $\frac{12}{12} = 120$, the number in the third.

55. For 24 days he would have received $\$48$. He loses $\$2$ each day he is idle, and pays 50 ct. for board $= \$2\frac{1}{2}$; $\$48 - \$38 = \$10$; $\$10 \div \$2\frac{1}{2} = 4$, number of days idle; $24 - 4 = 20$, number of days he worked.

56. Since $\$12 = \frac{2}{7}$ of B's and C's, $\frac{7}{7} = \$42$; and $\$42 + \$12 = \$54$, what all had. If $\frac{3}{8}$ of C's $= \frac{3}{10}$ of A's and B's,

then $\frac{1}{8} = \frac{1}{10}$, and the whole of C's $= \frac{8}{10}$ of A's and B's; hence, $\frac{18}{10}$ of A's and B's $= \$54$; $\frac{1}{10} = \$3$, and $\frac{10}{10} = \$30$; $\$30 - \$12 = \$18$, B's share; $\$54 - \$30 = \$24$, C's share.

57. Six and six sevenths pounds cost $6\frac{6}{7}$ times 8 ct. $= 54\frac{6}{7}$ ct.; $\frac{1}{6}$ of $54\frac{6}{7}$ ct. $= 9\frac{1}{7}$ ct.; $54\frac{6}{7}$ ct. $+ 9\frac{1}{7}$ ct. $= 64$ ct.

58. The first has $\$1200$ for 1 mo.; the second has $\$2400$ for 1 mo., or $\$1200$ more than the first; the first must put in for the remaining 6 mo. $\frac{1}{6}$ of $\$1200 = \$200$.

59. The difference between selling at 9 ct. and 12 ct. is $\$1.50$ on the whole; on one pound the difference is 3 ct.; there are as many pounds as $\$1.50 \div 3 = 50$.

60. One of B's steps $= 1\frac{1}{2}$ of A's, and 4 of B's $= 6$ of A's; B gains $6 - 5 = 1$ step every time he takes 4 steps; B takes 4 steps 9 times in taking 36 steps. If he gains 1 step every time he takes 4, then A is 9 steps in advance of B.

61. Both had 9 oranges; each ate $\frac{1}{3}$ of $9 = 3$. Thomas ate 2 of John's oranges, and should give him $\frac{2}{3}$ of 9 ct. $= 6$ ct.; he ate one of James's, and should give him $\frac{1}{3}$ of 9 ct. $= 3$ ct.